Nanoscience and Nanotechnology

Nanoscience and Nanotechnology

Editor

B.K. Parthasarathy

ISHA

ISHA BOOKS

Delhi-110009

Nanoscience and Nanotechnology

ISBN: 81-8205-429-X

Published in 2007 in India by
ISHA Books
B-63, 1st Floor, New Gupta Colony,
Near DDA Market,
Delhi-110009
Phone: 9212142040
ishabooks@hotmail.com

Laser Type Setting by: Rudra Computer Graphics, Delhi
Printed at: Salasar Imaging System, Delhi

Preface

The industrial revolution was perhaps the biggest turning point in human history-from millenniums and centuries of archaic, simple and unscientific methods of living, humanity had, within the space of a mere few decades, transformed itself into a technologically superior race of beings, well on the path of ushering in a new era of scientific, machine controlled existence. Indeed, since its advent, humanity completely usurped the ways of living of its forefathers, and brought about a new dawn in civilisation. Whether the repercussions were good or bad, are entirely debatable, but assuredly, it has made the pace of human life faster and easier. Today, we live in an era where it is difficult to imagine life without the marvels of science, and as a species, are entirely dependent upon technology. Nanotechnology, one of the most fascinating and promising sciences to emerge in latter half of the 20th century, is one of those rare opportunities that have presented itself before humanity — placing itself in our hands to usher in an entirely new age of Industrial Revolution, one where miniaturisation and scaling down of technology would be the buzzword.

Nanotechnology is that science whose basic principle is the control of matter at the nanoscale, or at the size of 1 to 100 micrometers, or 1 nanometer, and the fabrication of devices along the same scale. It is a highly multidisciplinary field, cutting across fields as varied as device physics, colloidal science and electrical engineering. U. S. scientists have already etched from silicon workable motors which are less in diamter than a human hair, and nanoparticles and materials find applications in bulk materials such as suntan lotions, besides in fields such as medicine, engineering, life sciences, etc. Adhering to the adage "small is beautiful", this science holds the potential to transform other sciences within the nano-scale, and exerts great influence in the scientific community. today. This is one branch of science which looks forward to not just becoming an offshoot of science, but the whole of science itself, downsised to nano.

This book has been brought out to acquaint the readers with the hype and the rigmarole behind nanoscience and nanotechnology. The emphasis of the book is on presenting forth a thorough introductory manual on the subject, detailing its history, the science and the practice, the techniques, the trends and developments, and the future of this science. The multifold implications of nanoscience and nanotechnology have been discussed most comprehensively, as this science holds the key to understanding the future of humanity in terms of scientific developments. The critical insights presented forth in the book are highly informative, and it is hoped that the book serves well for all those interested in understanding nanotechnology and nanoscience in all its machinations, and manifestations.

Editor

Contents

1

Nanotechnology Opportunities

Nanotechnology as disruptive technology can lead to next generation (enhanced or new) applications, but also has the characteristics to create and facilitate next generation (initially unknown) markets. This gives additional dimensions and challenges to innovation processes concerning development and commercialisation of nanotechnology in an international market arena, especially for small nanotechnology firms.

Scanning the environment for business opportunity related signals concerning market, technological, regulatory and other developments is essential in the innovation development process. Although small technology firms in comparison with large firms are more responsive to commercialise disruptive technologies, small high-tech enterprises compared with large companies are inclined to the nature to have less (continuous) attention on business opportunities and strategies. The question is in what way it is possible to support small nanotechnology firms in signal scanning and processing in order to recognise business opportunities in a dynamic international market?

Manipulating atoms arrangements is the basis of nanotechnology and ideas in this field were first communicated by physicist Feynman. Nanotechnology is according to Roco concerned with 'development and utilisation of structures and devices with organisational features at the intermediate scale between individual molecules and about 100 nanometres where novel properties occur as compared to bulk materials' (100 nanometres is 1/10.000 millimetre). These nanoscale structures and devices may have unique chemical, electrical, magnetic, optical or biological properties. It is a field at the junction of chemistry, physics, biology, computer science and engineering. Nanotechnology embeds nanoscience insight in order to fabricate new materials, structures or devices which exploits nanoscale properties.

The nature of nanotechnology is strongly multidisciplinary and Hullmann and Meyer show this via the range of scientific disciplines nanotechnology publications and nanotechnology patents covers. Some discipline examples for instance are material science, polymer science, electrical and electronic engineering, optics, biophysics, organic chemistry, or cell biology. They conclude that patent data suggests that the core activities of nanotechnology focus on electronics, instrumentation, and chemicals/pharmaceuticals.

Besides this conclusion based on patent data, Bhat sees the following industries likely to be immediately affected by nanotechnology: aerospace, automotive, biotechnology, ceramics, chemicals, computing, defence, electronics, metals, materials, paper, plastics, renewable/sustainable energy, textiles and tele-communications.

Nanotechnology as a cluster of new technologies undergoes typical patterns of scientific, technological and economic developments. First, nanoscience has lead to a strong scientificpush and resulted in a dramatic increase of scientific publications and patents on nanotechnology. Additionally, the technology-pull has emerged in order to use and transform nanoscience knowledge into technologies.

Table 1. Examples of nanotechnology-based applications

Industry	*Nanotechnology-based applications on the market*
Automotive	Automobile General Motors GMC Safari nanocomposite step from Southern Clay. Advantages: stiff and light car parts.
	Antireflection coating on instruments of Audi cars and DaimlerChrysler trucks based on nanolayers on glass. Advantages: better antireflection.
Building materials	Duravit sinks and toilets using nanocoatings from Nanogate. Advantages: improved anti-stick properties.
Consumer electronics and instruments	Kodak EasyShare LS633 using nano-enhanced OLEDs.
	Advantages: brighter and less energy consuming displays.
	Germicidal nanocoating in Audio Service hearing aids from Germany's Institute of New Materials. Advantages: better non-stick properties of coating.
Cosmetics and body care	Nucelle sunscreen using titanium dioxide nanoparticles from Nanophase. Advantages: better absorption of UV-light.
	L'Oreal nanocapsules in cosmetics. Advantages: better skin moisturising properties.
Fashion	Maui Jim sunglasses with nanocoatings from Nanofilm. Advantages: better anti-reflection properties.
	Eddie Bauer khaki pants using molecular textile coatings from Nano-Tex. Advantages: for instance anti-wrinkle properties.
Medical equipment	Evidots (quantum dots) for medical imaging from Evident Technologies. Advantages: fluorescent biomarker with narrow, predictable emission band of light.
Sports	Babolat tennis rackets using nanotubes. Advantage: lighter but stronger rackets.
	Nanowax Derax ski wax from Nanogate. Advantages: hard and fast-gliding surface.

Lately, a premature market-pull era has been initiated which stimulates the use of nanotechnology in applications in order to create innovations. In this phase companies are actually producing and selling nanotechnology-based applications.

Everyday life examples of nanotechnology-based applications on the market are given in the Table 1. On the other hand Mazzola points out that many nanotechnology applications are still at concept level, requiring much more basic research before they can be incorporated into viable applications. Related to the typical sigmoidal curve of innovation diffusion, nanotechnology is just about in the so-called 'take-off' phase. Although industries and applications are or will be (further) influenced by nanotechnology, Bhat argues that the mentioned multidisciplinary nature of nanotechnology makes it very difficult to pin down and prophesy the future impact in any specific sector appropriately.

This is a major reason why nanotechnology is mostly seen as a disruptive technology. Kostoff et al. and Walsh suggest some literature related to the usage of terms such as disruptive technology and discontinuous innovation in different contexts. According to Brower and Christensen a technology is considered disruptive when its utilisation generates products with different performance attributes that may not have been valued by existing customers. In case of nanotechnology this means that it has the ability to introduce enhanced or new nanotechnology-enabled products, services or processes for existing or new markets.

Disruptive technology—like nanotechnology — promises considerable opportunities for early and strong entry into existing and new markets, however they also involve a high risk of failure. Besides the disruptive character of nanotechnology, the dynamic international market puts pressure on small nanotechnology firms' proposit ions. It could be stated that last decades markets became more international and dynamic. Important drivers for this globalisation process are greater participation in, and integration of, world trade, liberal government policies, changing corporate strategies, creation of global capital markets, capacities of information and communication technologies, increasing market homogeneity and global creation, use and sale of technology.

A relatively faster obsolescence of modern technologies is related to the last-mentioned driver. All these 'inherent' global drivers influence a global market that could be characterised as high-velocity and hypercompetitive. In this dynamic environment Foster and Kaplan foresee a competitive role for those companies who are able to master the Schumperian concepts of creative destruction. Due to the fact that nanotechnology is an enabler for enhanced or new applications in a variety of industries, it is likely that a substantial part of small nanotechnology firms will be confronted directly or indirectly with the hypercompetitive aspects of the dynamic international business environment.

Survey results of ENA indicate that a substantial part of the mainly European respondents expect that nanotechnology will have an impact in their business within a few years. Besides the fact that the survey report does not further discuss introduced terms such as nanotechnology, impact or business, its indication points out that nanotechnology firms or nanotechnology-focused application firms will be confronted with an even more dynamic business environment within a few years. Next to the mentioned 'inherent' international market dynamics and the nanotechnology diffusion take-off, specific nanotechnology market related influences can be identified: societal discussions on nanotechnology, regulations and governmental funding programmes.

Results of societal discussions on the ethical, legal and social implications of nanotechnology could lead to certain boundary settings on some form of nanotechnology and/or nanotechnology-related production, usage or recycling processes. Therefore market segments within nanotechnology and nanotechnology-based applications markets do have a chance to be influenced by these discussions.

Additionally, new regulations on nanotechnology and/or nanotechnology-based applications will mark business opportunities. Furthermore, the market dynamics are directly and indirectly influenced by (supra)national governmental funding on nanotechnology R&D, diffusion and adoption programmes. Examples are the growing budgets of the U.S. National Nanotechnology Initiative and the EU Sixth Framework for nanotechnology research and development programmes. Concluding, besides the disruptive character of nanotechnology, the increased dynamics of international markets puts intense pressure on the competitive capabilities and actions of small nanotechnology-focused firms. With respect to disruptive technologies like nanotechnology, research organisations are not fully able to introduce flexibility with respect to science-based technology that needs to response to or create markets.

That is why research organisations and large firms form the major two sources of new technology-based firms: the university spin-offs and the corporate spin-offs. Small nanotechnology firms form important links between the science and technology domain of nanotechnology and the market domain. These entrepreneurial firms are more able to take advantage of disruptive technologies and redefine markets, whereas large firms will have serious problems with the introduction of disruptive technologies due to own market cannibalising and organisational inertia as a result of procedures and short-term focused incentives.

Small nanotechnology companies have the entrepreneurial character to operate in a dynamic and uncertain nanotechnology business environment. Scenarios are a tool in the process of strategic thinking of entrepreneurs and managers and reduce three shortcomings of the learning cycle at the strategic level.

The time span between experience, activity and implications is reduced by simulating and communicating specific uncertain situations that can occur in reality in a brief period of time. In this way scenarios stretch the mental models of the people involved, so that the degree of cognitive inertia is reduced. Moreover, scenarios stimulate creativity and are a way to promote the internal communication of ideas, so that the variations in mental models of the people involved can become more balanced. This provides collective insight into the opportunities and threats that accompany particular uncertainties.

Table 2. Two generations of scenarios

Original functions of the first-generation scenarios

- Evaluation and selection of strategies
- Integration of various kinds of future-oriented data
- Exploration of the future and identification of future possibilities

The second-generation scenarios: more recently added functions

- Making managers aware of environmental uncertainties
- Stretching of managers' mental models
- Triggering and accelerating processes of organisational learning

The creation and construction of scenarios is a practical matter and many methods are listed in the literature. The development process of scenarios often involves an iterative process in which entrepreneurs or managers should be involved during the entire process. Mercer indicates that the simpler a scenario and the simpler the process to construct scenarios, the stronger the scenarios are at broadening the mental models of the people involved. Furthermore he notes that convincing entrepreneurs or managers to use the constructed scenarios is the hardest part of the scenario planning process.

In case of small nanotechnology firms and business awareness, it is necessary to construct a method that creates scenarios that can stimulate business opportunity awareness. In the case of nanotechnology it is advisable to construct scenarios that are influenced by a broad range of elements that originate from science, technology, market, political, legal, and ethical domains.

Key factors need to be identified in a variety of segments: developments in nanoscience and nanotechnology, general developments in nanotechnology-influenced industries and markets, specific developments in industries related to alliances, mergers, intellectual property (patent) aspects, (supra)national go· ernment (innovation and subsidy) policies on nanotechnology, legal aspects related to nanotechnology and nanotechnologybased applications, societal discussions on implications of nanotechnology, etc. The two uncertainties with the highest impacts form the basis to construct four scenarios. These four scenarios are based on more-or-less known elements.

Next, with respect to a vision on the unknown elements (or elements that are not in the scope) wild-cards on the basis of the 'what must happen, so that ...' questions are discussed. In order to explain the above-mentioned concept some 'what if ... ' questions and 'what must happen, so that ...' questions that could relate to a fictive small producer of carbon nanotubes are worked out. Carbon nanotubes can be described as graphite sheets rolled to form a tube-like structure with a diameter of a few nanometres and possess relatively advanced properties in fields like strength-to-weight ratio, weight density, heat transmission or current conductivity. These particles are used or will be used in industries like electronics and chips manufacturing, automotive, aerospace or biomedicine. Due to the fact that carbon nanotubes can be used in a variety of applications in several industries, international market dynamics—as mentioned earlier—are present in the context of small manufacturers of carbon nanotubes.

Additionally, up-scaling of production processes and introduction of new production processes could lead to severe disturbances in market penetration strategies due to lower prices, more purified batches or specialised products. Moreover, it is likely that substitutes of carbon nanotubes could have substantial disruptive impact in certain industries.

Opportunities and Challenges

Nanoscience is the study of phenomena and manipulation of materials at atomic, molecular and macromolecular scales, in order to understand and exploit properties that differ significantly from those on a larger scale. Nanotechnologies are the design, characterisation, production and application of structures, devices and systems by controlling shape and size on a nanometer scale. Modern industrial nanotechnology had its origins in the 1930s, in processes used to create silver coatings for photographic film; and chemists have been making polymers, which are large molecules made up of nanoscale subunits, for many decades. Today's nanotechnology, i.e. the planned manipulation of materials and properties on a nanoscale, exploits the interaction of three technological streams:

1. new and improved control of the size and manipulation of nanoscale building blocks
2. new and improved characterisation of materials on a nanoscale (e.g., spatial resolution, chemical sensitivity)
3. new and improved understanding of the relationships between nanostructure and properties and how these can be engineered.

The properties of materials can be different on a nanoscale for two main reasons.

First, nanomaterials have, relatively, a larger surface area than the same mass of material produced in a larger form. This can make materials more chemically reactive (in some cases materials that are inert in their larger form are reactive when produced in their nanoscale form), and affect their strength or electrical properties.

Second, below 50 nm, the laws of classical physics give way to quantum effects, provoking optical, electrical and magnetic behaviours different from those of the same material at a larger scale. These effects can give materials very useful physical properties such as exceptional electrical conduction or resistance, or a high capacity for storing or transferring heat, and can even modify biological properties, with silver for example becoming a bactericide on a nanoscale. These properties, however, can be very difficult to control.

If nanoparticles touch each other, they can fuse, losing both their shape and those special properties-such as the magnetism-that scientists hope to exploit for a new generation of microelectronic devices and sensors. On a nanoscale, chemistry, biology, electronics, physics, materials science, and engineering start to converge and the distinctions as to which property a particular discipline measures no longer apply.

All these disciplines contribute to understanding and exploiting the possibilities offered by nanotechnology, but if the basic science is converging, the potential applications are infinitely varied, encompassing everything from tennis rackets to medicines to entirely new energy systems. This twin dynamic of convergent science and multiplying applications means that nanotechnology's biggest impacts may arise from unexpected combinations of previously separate aspects, just as the internet came about through the convergence of telephony and computing.

Nanomaterials

Carbon Nanotubes

Carbon nanotubes, long thin cylinders of atomic layers of graphite, may be the most significant new material since plastics and are the most significant of today's nanomaterials. They come in a range of different structures, allowing a wide variety of properties. They are generally classified as single-walled (SWNT), consisting of a single cylindrical wall, or multiwalled nanotubes (MWNT), which have cylinders within the cylinders. When the press mentions the amazing properties of nanotubes, it is generally SWNT they are referring to. However, SWNT are more difficult to make than MWNT, and confusion arises about the quantities of nanotubes actually being manufactured. Carbon Nanotechnologies of Houston, one of the world's leading producers, only makes up to 500g per day.

One problem is that economies of scale are practically impossible with today's production technologies—the machines used to manufacture the tubes cannot be scaled up, so producing bigger quantities means using more machines. Another drawback is that it is difficult to make nanotubes interact with other materials. For example, to fully exploit their strength in composite materials, nanotubes need to be "attached" to a polymer. They are chemically modified to facilitate this, but this process reduces the very properties the nanotubes are being used for. In the long-term, the ideal solution would be to use pure nanomaterials, e.g. nanotubes spun into fibers of any desired length, but such a development is unlikely in the next couple of decades unless a radically more efficient production process is developed. The most promising applications of nanotubes may be in electronics and optoelectronics.

Today, the electronics industry is producing the vital components known as MOSFETs with critical dimensions of just under 100 nm, with half that size projected by 2009 and 22 nm by 2016. However, the industry will then encounter technological barriers and fundamental physical limitations to size reduction. At the same time, there are strong financial incentives to continue the process of scaling, which has been central in the effort to increase the performance of computing systems in the past.

A new microchip manufacturing plant costs around $1.5 billion, so extending the technology's life beyond 2010 is important. One approach to overcoming the impending barriers while preserving most of the existing technology, is to use new materials. With carbon nanotubes, it is possible to get higher performance without having to use ultra thin silicon dioxide gate insulating films.

In addition, semiconducting SWNTs, unlike silicon, directly absorb and emit light, thus possibly enabling a future optoelectronics technology. The SWNT devices would still pose manufacturing problems due to quantum effects at the nanoscale, so the most likely advantage in the foreseeable future is that carbon nanotubes will allow a simpler fabrication of devices with superior performance at about the same length as their scaled silicon counterparts. Other proposed uses for nanotubes are:

Chemical and Genetic Probes: A nanotube-tipped atomic force microscope can trace a strand of DNA and identify chemical markers that reveal which of several possible variants of a gene is present in the strand. This is the only method yet invented for imaging the chemistry of a surface, but it is not yet used widely. So far it has been used only on relatively short pieces of DNA.

Mechanical memory (nonvolatile RAM): A screen of nanotubes laid on support blocks has been tested as a binary memory device, with voltages forcing some tubes to contact (the "on" state) and others to separate ("off"). The switching speed of the device was not measured, but the speed limit for a mechanical memory is probably around one megahertz, which is much slower than conventional memory chips.

Field Emission Based Devices: Carbon Nanotubes have been demonstrated to be efficient field emitters and are currently being incorporated in several applications including flat-panel display for television sets or computers or any devices requiring an electron producing cathode such as X-ray sources (e.g. for medical applications).

Nanotweezers: Two nanotubes, attached to electrodes on a glass rod, can be opened and closed by changing voltage. Such tweezers have been used to pick up and move objects that are 500 nm in size. Although the tweezers can pick up objects that are large compared with their width, nanotubes are so sticky that most objects can't be released. And there are simpler ways to move such tiny objects.

Supersensitive Sensors: Semiconducting nanotubes change their electrical resistance dramatically when exposed to alkalis, halogens and other gases at room temperature, raising hopes for better chemical sensors. The sensitivity of these devices is 1,000 times that of standard solid state devices.

Hydrogen and Ion Storage: Nanotubes might store hydrogen in their hollow centres and release it gradually in efficient and inexpensive fuel cells. They can also hold lithium ions, which could lead to longer-lived batteries. So far the best reports indicate 6.5 percent hydrogen uptake, which is not quite dense enough to make fuel cells economical. The work with lithium ions is still preliminary.

Sharper Scanning Microscope: Attached to the tip of a scanning probe microscope, nanotubes can boost the instruments' lateral resolution by a factor of 10 or more, allowing clearer views of proteins and other large molecules. Although commercially available, each tip is still made individually. The nanotube tips don't improve vertical resolution, but they do allow imaging deep pits in nanostructures that were previously hidden.

Superstrong Materials: Embedded into a composite, nanotubes have enormous resilience and tensile strength and could be used to make materials with better safety features, such as cars with panels that absorb significantly more of the force of a collision than traditional materials, or girders that bend rather than rupture in an earthquake. Nanotubes still cost 10 to 1,000 times more than the carbon fibers currently used in composites. And nanotubes are so smooth that they slip out of the matrix, allowing it to fracture easily. There are still many technical obstacles to overcome before carbon nanotubes can be used on an industrial scale, but their enormous potential in a wide variety of applications has made them the "star" of the nanoworld and encouraged many companies to commit the resources needed to ensure that the problems will be solved.

Nanoparticles

Nanoparticles have been used since antiquity by ceramists in China and the West, while 1.5 million tons of carbon black, the most abundant nanoparticulate material, are produced every year. But, as mentioned earlier, nanotechnology is defined as knowingly exploiting the nanoscale nature of materials, thereby excluding these examples. Although metal oxide ceramic, metal, and silicate nanoparticles constitute the most common of the new generation of nanoparticles, there are others too. A substance called chitosan for example, used in hair conditioners and skin creams, has been made in nanoparticle form to improve absorption. Moving to nanoscale changes the physical properties of particles, notably by increasing the ratio of surface area to volume, and the emergence of quantum effects. High surface area is a critical factor in the performance of catalysis and structures such as electrodes, allowing improvement in performance of such technologies as fuel cells and batteries. The large surface area also results in useful interactions between the materials in nanocomposites, leading to special properties such as increased strength and/or increased chemical/heat resistance. The fact that nanoparticles have dimensions below the critical wavelength of light renders them transparent, an effect exploited in packaging, cosmetics and coatings.

Quantum Dots

Just as carbon nanotubes are often described as the new plastics, so quantum dots are defined as the ball bearings of th. nano-age. Quantum dots are like "artificial atoms". They are 1 nm structures made of materials such as silicon, capable of confining a single electron, or a few thousand, whose energy states can be controlled by applying a given voltage. In theory, this could be used to fulfil the alchemist's dream of changing the chemical nature of a material, making lead emulate gold, for example.

One more likely set of possible applications exploits the fact that quantum dots can be made to emit light at different wavelengths, with the smaller the dot the bluer the light. The dots emit over a narrow spectrum making them well suited to imaging, particularly for biological samples.

Currently, biological molecules are imaged using naturally fluorescent molecules, such as organic dyes, with a different dye attached to each kind of molecule in a sample. But the dyes emit light over a broad range of wavelengths, which means that their spectra overlap and only about three different dyes emit light over a broad range of wavelengths, which means that their spectra overlap and only about three different dyes can be used at the same time.

With quantum dots, full-colour imaging is possible because large numbers of dots of different sizes can be excited by a light source with a single wavelength. The wide range of colors that can be produced by quantum dots also means they have great potential in security. They could, for example, be hidden in bank notes or credit cards, producing a unique visible image when exposed to ultraviolet light. It is possible to make light-emitting diodes (LEDs) from quantum dots which could produce white light e.g. for buildings or cars. By controlling the amount of blue in the emission-control the "flavour" or "tone" of the white light can be tuned.

Quantum dots are also possible materials for making ultrafast, all-optical switches and logic gates that work faster than 15 terabits a second. For comparison, the Ethernet generally can handle only 10 megabits per second. Other possible applications are all-optical demultiplexers (for separating various multiplexed signals in an optical fiber), all-optical computing, and encryption, whereby the spin of an electron in a quantum dot represent a quantum bit or qubit of information. Biologists are experimenting with composites of living cells and quantum dots.

These could possibly be used to repair damaged neural pathways or to deliver drugs by activating the dots with light. Once again, significant advances in manufacturing will be needed to realise the potential of quantum dots. For example, the quantum state needed to make a quantum computer is relatively easily to create, but its behaviour is still unpredictable.

Legend has it that the people who profited most from the Klondike gold rush at the end of the 19th century were the sellers of picks and shovels. The same may hold true for nanotechnology, at least in the coming decade before production techniques are improved. According to market researchers Freedonia, the $245 million nanotech tools industry will grow by 30 % annually over the next few years. Microscopes and related tools dominate now, but measurement, fabrication/production and simulation/ modelling tools will grow the fastest. Electronics and life sciences markets will emerge first; industrial, construction, energy generation and other applications will arise later.

Nanotechnology uses two main kinds of microscopy. The first involves a stationary sample in line with a high-speed electron gun. Both the scanning electron microscope (SEM) and transmission electron microscope (TEM) are based on this technique. The second class of microscopy involves a stationary scanner and a moving sample. The two microscopes in this class are the atomic force microscope (AFM) and the scanning tunnelling microscope (STM).

Microscopy plays a paradoxical role in nanotechnology because, although it is the key to understanding materials and processes, on a nanoscale samples can be damaged by the high-energy electrons fired at them. This is not a problem with STM, but a further drawback is that most microscopes require very stringent sample preparation. The SEM, TEM, and STM need well prepared samples that are also electrically conductive. There are ways to get around this, but the fact remains that it can take hours to prepare and mount a sample correctly (and hours to actually synthesise the sample).

There are two approaches to building nanostructures, both having their origins in the semiconductor industry. In the traditional "top-down" approach a larger material such as a silicon wafer is processed by removing matter until only the nanoscale features remain. Unfortunately, these techniques require the use of lithography, which requires a mask that selectively protects portions of the wafer from light. The distance from the mask to the wafer, and the size of the slit define the minimum feature size possible for a given frequency of light, e.g. extreme ultraviolet light yields feature sizes of 90 nm across, but this scale is near the fundamental limit of lithography. Nonetheless lithography can be used for patterning substrates used to produce nanomaterials, e.g. guiding the growth of quantum dots and nanowires.

The "bottom-up" approach starts with constituent materials (often gases or liquids) and uses chemical, electrical, or physical forces to build a nanomaterial atom-by-atom or molecule-by-molecule. The simplest bottom up synthesis route is electroplating to create a material layer-by-layer, atom-by-atom. By inducing an electric field with an applied voltage, charged particles are attracted to the surface of a substrate where bonding will occur.

Most nanostructured metals with high hardness values are created with this approach. Chemical vapour deposition (CVD) uses a mix of volatile gases and takes advantage of thern.odynamic principles to have the source material migrate to the substrate and then bond to the surface. This is the one proven method for creating nanowires and carbon nanotubes, and is a method of choice for creating quantum dots.

Molecular self-assembly promises to be a revolutionary new way of creating materials from the bottom up. One way to achieve self-assembly is to use attractive forces like static electricity, Van der Waals forces, and a variety of other short-range forces to orient constituent molecules in a regular array. This has proven very effective in creating large grids of quantum dots. The bottom up approach promises an unheard-of level of customisability in materials synthesis, but controlling the process is not easy and can only produce simple structures, in time-consuming processes with extremely low yields. It is not yet possible to produce integrated devices from the bottom up, and any overall order aside from repeating grids cannot be done without some sort of top-down influence like lithographic patterning. Nanotechnology synthesis is thus mainly academic, with only a few companies in the world that can claim to be nanotechnology manufacturers. And until understanding of synthesis is complete, it will be impossible to reach a point of mass production.

In the present phase, nanotechnology is incorporated selectively into high-end products, especially in automotive and aerospace applications. Through 2009, commercial breakthroughs unlock markets for nanotechnology innovations. Electronics and IT applications dominate as microprocessors and memory chips built using new nanoscale processes come to market.

From 2010 onwards, nanotechnology becomes commonplace in manufactured goods. Health- care and life sciences applications finally become significant as nano-enabled pharmaceuticals and medical devices emerge from lengthy human trials. Following the dotcom fiasco, potential investors are justifiably wary of treating nanotech (or anything else) as "the next big thing". While the excitement and hype generated by nanotech's apostles may be reminiscent of how internet was going to change the world and make everybody rich, there are two crucial differences that counteract the likelihood of a nanobubble: nanotechnology is extremely difficult and extremely expensive, which is why it is concentrated in wellfunded companies and institutes that can attract and nurture the scarce scientific and technical expertise needed to understand the problems and challenges. Moreover, the long lead times involved in moving from concept to commercialisation make nanotech particularly unsuitable for making money fast.

Medical and life-science applications may prove to be the most lucrative markets for nanotechnologies, with "lab-on-a-chip" devices already being manufactured and animal testing and early clinical trials starting on nanotechniques for drug delivery. However, the long product approval processes typical of the domain may mean that the health benefits to users and economic benefits to companies will take longer to realise than in other domains.

Nanotech's promise comes from the fact that nanoscale devices are a hundred to ten thousand times smaller than human cells and are similar in size to large biological molecules ("biomolecules") such as enzymes and receptors. Haemoglobin, the molecule that carries oxygen in red blood cells, is approximately 5 nm in diameter, DNA 2.5, while a quantum dot is about the same size as a small protein (<10 nm) and some viruses measure less than 100 nm.

Devices smaller than 50 nm can easily enter most cells, while those smaller than 20 nm can move out of blood vessels as they circulate through the body. Because of their small size, nanoscale devices can readily interact with biomolecules on both the surface of cells and inside of cells. By gaining access to so many areas of the body, they have the potential to detect disease and deliver treatment in new ways. Nanotechnology offers the opportunity to study and interact with cells at the molecular and cellular scales in real time, and during the earliest stages of the development of a disease.

And since nanocomponents can be made to share some of the same properties as natural nanoscale structures, it is hoped to develop artificial nanostructures that sense and repair damage to the organism, just as naturally-occurring biological nanostructures such as white blood cells do. Cancer research illustrates many of the medical potentials of nanotechnologies in the longer term. It is hoped that nanoscale devices and processes will help to develop:

- Imaging agents and diagnostics that will allow clinicians to detect cancer in its earliest stages,
- Systems that will provide real-time assessments of therapeutic and surgical efficacy for accelerating clinical translation,

— Multifunctional, targeted devices capable of bypassing biological barriers to deliver multiple therapeutic agents directly to cancer cells and those tissues in the microenvironment that play a critical role in the growth and metastasis of cancer,

— Agents that can monitor predictive molecular changes and prevent precancerous cells from becoming malignant,

— Novel methods to manage the symptoms of cancer that adversely impact quality of life,

— Research tools that will enable rapid identification of new targets for clinical development and predict drug resistance.

This may be the most profitable application of nanotechnology in medicine, and even generally, over the next two decade . Drugs need to be protected during their transit through the body to the target, to maintain their biological and chemicals properties or to stop them damaging the parts of the body they travel through.

Once a drug arrives at its destination, it needs to be released at an appropriate rate for it to be effective. This process is called encapsulation, and nanotechnology can improve both the diffusion and degradation characteristics of the encapsulation material, allowing the drug to travel efficiently to the target and be released in an optimal way. Nanoparticle encapsulation is also being investigated for the treatment of neurological disorders to deliver therapeutic molecules directly to the central nervous system beyond the blood-brain barrier, and to the eye beyond the blood-retina barrier.

Damaged tissues and organs are often replaced by artificial substitutes, and nanotechnology offers a range of new biocompatible coatings for the implants that improves their adhesion, durability and lifespan. New types of nanomaterials are being evaluated as implant coatings to improve interface properties. For example, nanopolymers can be used to coat devices in contact with blood (e.g. artificial hearts, catheters) to disperse clots or prevent their formation.

Nanomaterials and nanotechnology fabrication techniques are being investigated as tissue regeneration scaffolds. The ultimate goal is to grow large complex organs. Examples include nanoscale polymers moulded into heart valves, and polymer nanocomposites for bone scaffolds. Commercially viable solutions are thought to be 5 to 10 years away, given the scientific challenges related to a better understanding of molecular/cell biology and fabrication methods for producing large threedimensional scaffolds.

Nanostructures are promising for temporary implants, e.g. that biodegrade and do not have to be removed in a subsequent operation. Research is also being done on a flexible nanofiber membrane mesh that can be applied to heart tissue in open-heart surgery. The mesh can be infused with antibiotics, painkillers and medicines in small quantities and directly applied to internal tissues. Subcutaneous chips are already being developed to continuously monitor key body parameters including pulse, temperature and blood glucose.

Another application uses optical microsensors implanted into subdermal or deep tissue to monitor tissue circulation after surgery, while a third type of sensor uses MEMS (microelectromechanical system) devices and accelerometers to measure strain, acceleration, angular rate and related parameters for monitoring and treating paralysed limbs, and to improve the design of artificial limbs. Implantable sensors can also work with devices that administer treatment automatically if required, e.g. fluid injection systems to dispense drugs. Initial applications may include chemotherapy that directly targets tumors in the colon and are programmed to dispense precise amounts of medication at convenient times, such as after a patient has fallen asleep. Sensors that monitor the heart's activity level can also work with an implantable defibrillator to regulate heartbeats.

Nano and related micro technologies are being used to develop a new generation of smaller and potentially more powerful devices to restore lost vision and hearing. One approach uses a miniature video camera attached to a blind person's glasses to capture visual signals processed by a microcomputer worn on the belt and transmitted to an array of electrodes placed in the eye. Another approach uses of a subretinal implant designed to replace photoreceptors in the retina. The implant uses a microelectrode array powered by up to 3500 microscopic solar cells. For hearing, an implanted transducer is pressure-fitted onto a bone in the inner ear, causing the bones to vibrate and move the fluid in the inner ear, which stimulates the auditory nerve.

An array at the tip of the device uses up to 128 electrodes, five times higher than current devices, to simulate a fuller range of sounds. The implant is connected to a small microprocessor and a microphone in a wearable device that clips behind the ear. This captures and translates sounds into electric pulses transmitted by wire through a tiny hole made in the middle ear.

Food and Agricultural Applications

Nanotechnology is rapidly converging with biotech and information technology to radically change food and agricultural systems. Over the next two decades, the impacts of nano-scale convergence on farmers and food could even exceed that of farm mechanisation or of the Green Revolution according to some sources such as the ETC group. Food and nutrition products containing nano-scale additives are already commercially available.

Likewise, a number of pesticides formulated at the nanoscale are on the market and have been released in the environment. The US leads, followed by Japan and China. HKC expects the nanofood market to surge from $2.6 billion in 2003 to $7.0 billion in 2006 and to $20.4 billion in 2010.

Companies not associated with food production in the public mind are already supplying nano-enabled ingredients to the industry. BASF, for example, exploits the fact that many vitamins and other substances such as carotinoids are insoluble in water, but can easily be mixed with cold water when formulated as nanoparticles. Many lemonades and fruit juices contain these specially formulated additives, which can also be used to provide an "attractive" colour. Expected breakthroughs in crop DNA decoding and analysis could enable agrifirms to predict, control and imnrove agricultural production.

And with technology for manipulating the molecules and atoms of food, the food industry would have a powerful method to design food with much greater capability and precision, lower costs and improved sustainability. The combination of DNA and nanotechnology research could also generate new nutrition delivery systems, to bring active agents more precisely and efficiently to the desired parts of the human body. Nanotechnology will not only change how every step of the food chain operates but also who is involved.

At stake is the world's $3 trillion food retail market, agricultural export markets valued at $544 billion, the livelihoods of farmers and the well-being of the rest of us. Converging technologies could reinvigorate the battered agrochemical and agbiotech industries, possibly igniting a still more intense debate—this time over "atomically-modified" foods. The most cited nano-agricultural developments are:

— *Nanoseeds*: In Thailand, scientists at Chiang Mai University's nuclear physics laboratory have rearranged the DNA of rice by drilling a nano-sized hole through the rice cell's wall and membrane and inserting a nitrogen atom. So far, they've been able to change the colour of the grain, from purple to green.

— *Nanoparticle pesticides*: Monsanto, Syngenta and BASF are developing pesticides enclosed in nanocapsules or made up of nanoparticles. The pesticides can be more easily taken up by plants if they're in nanoparticle form; they can also be programmed to be "time-released."

— *Nanofeed for Chickens*: With funding from the US Department of Agriculture (USDA), Clemson University researchers are feeding bioactive polystyrene nanoparticles that bind with bacteria to chickens as an alternative to chemical antibiotics in industrial chicken production.

— *Nano Ponds*: One of the USA's biggest farmed fish companies, Clear Spring Trout, is adding nanoparticle vaccines to trout ponds, where they are taken up by fish.

— *"Little Brother"*: The USDA is pursuing a project to cover farmers' fields and herds with small wireless sensors to replace farm labour and expertise with a ubiquitous surveillance system.

— *Nano foods*: Kraft, Nestlé, Unilever and others are employing nanotech to change the structure of food - creating "interactive" drinks containing nanocapsules that can change colour and flavour (Kraft) and spreads and ice creams with nanoparticle emulsions to improve texture. Others are inventing small nanocapsules that will smuggle nutrients and flavours into the body (what one company calls "nanoceuticals").

— *Nano packaging*: BASF, Kraft and others are developing new nanomaterials that extend food shelf life and signal when a food spoils by changing colour.

— *Food safety*: Scientists from the University of Wisconsin have successfully used single bacterial cells to make tiny bio-electronic circuits, which could in the future be used to detect bacteria, toxins and proteins.

Nanosensors can work through a variety of methods such as by the use of nanoparticles tailor-made to fluoresce different colors or made from magnetic materials can selectively attach themselves to food pathogens. Handheld sensors employing either infrared light or magnetic materials could then note the presence of even minuscule traces of harmful pathogens.

The advantage of such a system is that literally hundreds and potentially thousands of nanoparticles can be placed on a single nanosensor to rapidly, accurately and affordably detect the presence of any number of different bacteria and pathogens. A second advantage of nanosensors is that given their small size they can gain access into the tiny crevices where the pathogens often hide, and nanotechnology may reduce the time it takes to detect the presence of microbial pathogens from two to seven days down to a few hours and, ultimately, minutes or even seconds.

Nanotechnology and Textile Industry

The textile industry could be affected quite significantly by nanotechnology, with some estimates talking of a market impact of hundreds of billions of dollars over the next decade. Nanoscience has already produced stain- and wrinkle-resistant clothing, and future developments will focus on upgrading existing functions and performances of textile materials; and developing "smart" textiles with unprecedented functions such as:

— sensors and information acquisition and transfer,
— multiple and sophisticated protection and detection,
— health-care and wound-healing functions,
— self-cleaning and repair functions.

This last function illustrates how nanotechnology could impact areas outside its immediate application. US company Nano-Tex is already marketing its NanoCare stain- and wrinkle-resistant technology, and NanoFresh is expected soon. Scientists at the Hong Kong Polytechnic University have built a nano layer of particles of titanium dioxide, a substance that reacts with sunlight to break down dirt and other organic material. This layer can be coated on cotton to keep the fabric clean. Clothes simply need to be exposed to natural or ultraviolet light for the cleaning process to begin.

Once triggered by sunlight, clothing made out of the fabric will be able to rid itself of dirt, pollutants and micro-organisms. The whole laundry industry would be affected if the technology proves to be economically viable. Research involving nanotechnology to improve performances or to create new functions is most advanced in nanostructured composite fibers employing nanosize fillers such as nanoparticles (clay, metal oxides, carbon black), graphite nanofibers (GNF) and carbon nanotubes (CNT). The main function of nanosize fillers is to increase mechanical strength and improve physical properties such as conductivity and antistatic behaviours.

Being evenly distributed in polymer matrices, nanoparticles can carry load and increase the toughness and abrasion resistance; nanofibers can transfer stress away from polymer matrices and enhance tensile strength of composite fibers. Additional physical and chemical performances imparted to composite fibers vary with specific properties of the nanofillers used. Although some of the filler particles such as clay, metal oxides, and carbon black have previously been used as microfillers in composite materials for decades, reducing their size into nanometer range have resulted in higher performances and generated new market interest.

— *Carbon nanofibers and nanoparticles:* Carbon nanofibers and carbon black nanoparticles are among the most commonly used nanosize filling materials. Carbon nanofibers can effectively increase the tensile strength of composite fibers due to their high aspect ratio, while carbon black nanoparticles can improve abrasion resistance and toughness. Both have high chemical resistance and electric conductivity.

— *Clay nanoparticles:* Clay nanoparticles or nanoflakes possess electrical, heat and chemical resistance and an ability to block UV light. Composite fibers reinforced with clay nanoparticles exhibit flame retardant, anti-UV and anticorrosive behaviours.

— *Metal oxide nanoparticles:* Certain metal oxide nanoparticles possess photocatalytic ability, electrical conductivity, UV absorption and photooxidising capacity against chemical and biological species. Research involving these nanoparticles focuses on antimicrobial, self-decontaminating and UV blocking functions for both military protection gear and civilian health products.

— *Carbon nanotubes :* Potential applications of CNTs include conductive and high-strength composite fibers, energy storage and energy conversion devices, sensors, and field emission displays. One CNT fiber already exhibits twice the stiffness and strength, and 20 times the toughness of steel wire of the same weight and length. Moreover, toughness can be four times higher than that of spider silk and 17 times greater than Kevlar fibers used in bullet-proof vests, suggesting applications in safety harnesses, explosion-proof blankets, and electromagnetic shielding.

— *Nanotechnology in textile finishing:* Nanoscale emulsification, through which finishes can be applied to textile material in a more thorough, even and precise manner provide an unprecedented level of textile performance regarding stain-resistant, hydrophilic, anti-static, wrinkle resistant and shrinkproof properties.

Nanosize metal oxide and ceramic particles have a larger surface area and hence higher efficiency than larger size particles, are transparent, and do not blur the colour and brightness of the textile substrates. Fabric treated with nanoparticles TiO_2 and MgO replaces fabrics with active carbon, previously used as chemical and biological protective materials.

The photocatalytic activity of TiO_2 and MgO nanoparticles can break down harmful chemicals and biological agents. Finishing with nanoparticles can convert fabrics into sensor-based materials. If nanocrystalline piezoceramic particles are incorporated into fabrics, the finished fabric can convert exerted mechanical forces into electricai signals enabling the monitoring of bodily functions such as heart rhythm and pulse if they are worn next to skin.

— *Self assembled nanolayers:* In the longer-term future, self-assembled nanolayer (SAN) coating may challenge traditional textile coating. Research in this area is still in the very early stages, but the idea is to deposit a coating less than one nanometer thick on the textile, and then to vary the number of successive nanolayers to modulate the desired physical properties of the finished article.

Energy Security and Supply

Breakthroughs in nanotechnology could provide technologies that would contribute to world-wide energy security and supply. A report published by Rice University (Texas) in February 2005 identified numerous areas in which nanotechnology could contribute to more efficient, inexpensive, and environmentally sound technologies than are readily available. Although the most significant contributions may be to unglamorous applications such as better materials for exploration equipment used in the oil and gas industry or improved catalysis, nanotechnology is being proposed in numerous energy domains, including solar power; wind; clean coal; fusion reactors; new generation fission reactors; fuel cells; batteries; hydrogen production, storage and transportation; and a new electrical grid that ties all the power sources together. The main challenges where nanotechnology could contribute are:

— Lower the costs of photovoltaic solar energy tenfold,

— Achieve commercial photocatalytic reduction of CO_2 to methanol,

— Create a commercial process for direct photoconversion of light and water to produce hydrogen,

— Lower the costs of fuel cells between tenfold and a hundredfold and create new, sturdier materials,

— Improve the efficiency and storage capacity of batteries and supercapacitors between tenfold and a hundredfold for automotive and distributed generation applications,

— Create new lightweight materials for hydrogen storage for pressure tanks, liquid hydrogen vessels, and an easily reversible hydrogen chemisorption system,

— Develop power cables, superconductors or quantum conductors made of new nanomaterials to rewire the electricity grid and enable long-distance, continental and even international electrical energy transport, also reducing or eliminating thermal sag failures, eddy current losses and resistive losses by replacing copper and aluminium wires,

— Develop thermochemical processes with catalysts to generate hydrogen from water at temperatures lower than 900C at commercial costs,

— Create superstrong, lightweight materials that can be used to improve energy efficiency in cars, planes and in space travel; the latter, if combined with nanoelectronics based robotics, possibly enabling space solar structures on the moon or in space,

— Create efficient lighting to replace incandescent and fluorescent lights,

— Develop nanomaterials and coatings that will enable deep drilling at lower costs to tap energy resources, including geothermal heat, in deep strata,

— Create CO_2 mineralisation methods that can work on a vast scale without waste streams.

Solving these challenges will take many years, but commercial and public research institutes are already exploiting nanotechnology for energy applications. Bell Labs, for example, is exploring the possibility of producing a microbattery that would still work 20 years after purchase by postponing the chemical reactions that degrades traditional batteries.

The battery is based on a Bell Labs discovery that liquid droplets of electrolyte will stay in a dormant state atop microscopic structures called "nanograss" until stimulated to flow, thereby triggering a reaction producing electricity. Other researchers hope to dispense with batteries completely by developing nanotubes-based "ultra" capacitors powerful enough to propel hybrid-electric cars.

Compared with batteries, ultracapacitors can put out much more power for a given weight, can be charged in seconds rather than hours, and can function at more extreme temperatures. They're also more efficient, and they last much longer. The technology is in it earlier stages: the world-wide market was only $38 million in 2002, the most recent year for which figures are available, but researcher firm Frost & Sullivan predicts total 2007 revenues for ultracapacitors of $355 million. Photovoltaics is another area where nanotech is already providing products that could have a significant impact. Three US-based solar cell start-ups (Nanosolar, Nanosys and Konarka Technologies), and corporate players including Matsushita and STMicroelectronics are striving to produce photon-harvesting materials at lower costs and in higher volumes than traditional crystalline silicon photovoltaic cells.

Nanosolar has developed a material of metal oxide nanowires that can be sprayed as a liquid onto a plastic substrate where it selfassembles into a photovoltaic film. A roll-to-roll process similar to high-speed printing offers a high-volume approach that does not require high temperatures or vacuum equipment. Nanosys intends its solar coatings to be sprayed onto roofing tiles. And Konarka is developing plastic sheets embedded with titanium dioxide nanocrystals coated with light-absorbing dyes.

The company acquired Siemens' organic photovoltaic research activities, and Konarka's recent $18 million third round of funding included the world's first- and fifth-largest energy companies, Electricité de France and ChevronTexaco. If nanotech solar fabrics could be applied to, e.g., buildings and bridges, the energy landscape could change in important ways. Integrated into the roof of a bus or truck, they could split water via electrolysis and generate hydrogen to run a fuel cell. Losers would include current photovoltaic-cell makers and battery manufacturers who failed to react to the new challenge.

Such developments however depend on solving a number of fundamental problems at the nanoscale, but researchers are making fast progress using nanoscale design, include accelerating the kinetics of reactions through catalysis, separating the products at high temperature, and directing products to the next reaction step.

Nanotech Companies

Most nanotech companies are in the US, mainly because of the more developed venture capital market (over half the venture capital investors in nanotechnology are from the US). Statistics for universities and research institutes also shows a strong, but less marked, US bias. These figures should be treated with caution, since new companies are created all the time and some do not remain active very long. Moreover, the lack of any clear nanotech strategy even in companies heavily involved in nanotechnology means that tomorrow's winners will not necessarily be today's heavy investors. A survey of executives responsible for nanotech at 33 companies with over $5 billion annual revenue found that they have not converged towards any particular model for organising and governing their nanotechnology initiatives.

Forty-two percent of represented companies have centralised nanotechnology programmes, but an equal share pursue decentralised activity with no co-ordination. At 45% of companies, the R&D organisation "owns" nanotech; ownership varies widely across the rest. Barely half of interviewees' firms have a stated nanotech strategy today. When a strategy does exist, it is frequently a platitude like "survey the field and move quickly." Fewer than half of interviewees rate their companies' current approaches to nanotech as "very effective." Pharmaceutical companies are least likely to have an explicit nanotechnology strategy; they also invest the lowest level of people and funding compared with other sectors.

Asian companies across industries show the highest levels of staffing, funding, and executive sponsorship for nanotech. These results are all the more surprising given the size of the companies and the sums of money involved. The median corporation had 55 people working on nanotechnology, allocated $33 million in R&D funding in 2004 to nanoscale research, and has partnerships with universities, start-ups, and public sector agencies on multiple nanotech projects. Interviewees expect double-digit increases on each front through 2006. The roles of the different players in the nanotech sector are no different from those elsewhere:

— large organisations, with the resources to investigate longer-term technologies, seek applications to improve margins, lower costs or increase market share,

— start-ups, seeking to apply technologies in order to capture market share or disrupt existing markets, attract the attention of acquisition-hungry incumbents,

— economic blocs compete for supremacy, mindful of the economic benefits that strength in many of the applications of nanotechnology will bring,

— public agencies attempt to capture the maximum number of links in the value chain.

The long-term outcome is also likely to be similar, with, as happened in microcomputing, one or two new large companies emerging and most of the other viable startups being absorbed by large firms. Small companies are likely to target emerging technologies, seeking new generations of products, of which four generations were identified in 2004 by Mihail Roco, Chairman of the Federal Subcommittee on Nanoscale Science Engineering and Technology which oversees the National Nanotechnology Initiative.

An OECD survey published in 2004 indicates that many countries have developed definitions of nanotechnology as a field of science and technology, and explicitly recognise nanotechnology as a multi- or inter-disciplinary field that draws upon work in the physical science, life sciences and engineering. The survey underlines the lack of progress in developing a statistical definition of nanotechnology that can be used for collecting data on R&D expenditures, human resources, firm creation, etc.

The organisation of government support for nanotechnology reflects its multi-disciplinary nature, with funding for nanotechnology R&D generally channelled through a number of ministries and research councils with responsibility for different fields of application (e.g., environment, industry, health) or fields of science and technology (e.g., physics, life sciences, engineering). Some countries have begun to take steps to centralise management of their R&D programmes, even if programme implementation remains distributed.

In most cases, co-ordination also entails development of a national strategy for nanotechnology development. The R&D programmes vary considerably in size and scope. In many countries, programmes are aimed at developing world-class R&D capability in nanotechnology, recognising its importance in a number of industrial fields and in addressing a number of social needs. Japan, for example, has a range of programmes aimed at basic research, nanomaterials and nano-electronic devices.

Canada has established the National Institute of Nanotechnology as an integrated research institute with 150 researchers from various disciplines and a business incubation facility. Denmark has established three new research centres, two of which focus on interdisciplinary approaches to nanoscience, and one of which will address nano systems engineering. In addition to these broad-based efforts, some countries (including those mentioned above) have established more focused programmes as well, linking R&D to specific national needs. The Netherlands is financing three programmes dealing respectively with nanotechnology, microsystems, materials science and microelectronics; electronic devices, circuits and systems; and molecular nanotechnologies.

Norway is concentrating on sensors and smart materials, microtechnology, energy, environment, and new process technology. It also has a programme aimed at stimulating innovation and growth in the biomedical industry, based on the production of new materials. Poland's R&D prioritises nanomaterials processing, nanometals for construction and functional applications, and polymers. Support for nanotechnology is not limited to R&D. Canada, for example, identifies a number of programmes at the federal and provincial levels for major infrastructure support and training. Denmark funds education programmes at a number of universities.

In Japan, METI supports the Nanotechnology Business Creation Initiative, with 300 corporations, to promote business-matching. MEXT operates a Nanotechnology Support Project which makes specialised facilities available to nanotechnology researchers. Other programmes to support international exchanges of young researchers, entrepreneurship, technology licensing and industrial R&D are also expected to support innovation in nanotechnology. Poland has also supported nanotechnology education programmes and is creating a virtual institute to strengthen collaboration among nanotechnology researchers in Poland and with researchers in other countries.

The UK's Micro and Nanotechnology Manufacturing Initiative includes funding for a new network of micro and nanotechnology facilities. It is open to public and private companies, research institutes and universities. Two other programmes are worth mentioning in addition to those covered by the OECD survey. In 2003, the United States passed the 21st Century Nanotechnology Research and Development Act, authorising $3.7 billion in federal subsidies for three years beginning in 2005. This is for projects supported by the National Nanotechnology Initiative (NNI), a federal R&D programme established in 2001. Government funding for the NNI itself is projected to be $886 million for 2005, roughly 3% of overall US government R&D expenditure. The EU's Sixth Research Framework Programme (FP6) includes nanotechnologies and nano-sciences, knowledge-based multifunctional materials and new production processes and devices among its priorities, with total Community support of around □1 billion over 2002-2006. The programme's main objectives are the development of a successful European nanotechnology industry, and the application of nanotechnologies in existing industrial sectors. Additional nanotechnology research is supported by other parts of FP6. The follow-up, FP7, calls for almost 5 billion to be spent on nanotechnology over 2007-2013.

Following risks are key to consider will depend on the perspective of the particular organisation involved in nanotechnologies:

- business risks involved with marketing of nanotechnology enabled products,
- risks related to the protection of intellectual property,
- political risks regarding the impact on the economical development of countries and regions,
- risks regarding privacy when miniature sensors become ubiquitous,
- environmental risks from the release of nanoparticles into the environment,
- safety risks from nanoparticles for workers and consumers,
- futuristic risks like human enhancement and self replications of nano machines.

The catch-all term "nanotechnology" is not sufficiently precise for risk governance and risk management purposes. From a risk-control point of view it will be necessary to systematically identify those critical issues, which should be looked at in more detail. This risk identification process is a task for all parties involved and it should remain a dynamic process which always takes into account new scientific, technological, societal and legal trends. Almost all safety concerns that have been raised about nanotechnologies are related to "free" rather than fixed engineered nanoparticles. The risk and safety discussion related to free nanoparticles will concern only a fraction of the applications of nanotechnologies.

In most applications nanoparticles will be embedded in the final product and therefore not come into direct contact with workers, consumers or the environment. They are unlikely to raise concerns because of their immobilisation. Exceptions are possible when the products or materials within which nanoparticles are enclosed are discarded, burned or otherwise destroyed (e.g. in an accident). Looking at the manufacturing processes involved, they are similar to conventional well-established chemical and engineering processes.

Building on established previous experience can be a guideline for risk assessment purposes, but the approach to health and safety issues needs to be modified to address the special characteristics of nanoparticles. In the early phase of commercialisation most applications of nanotechnology will improve existing products, rather than generating new products. In themselves, most areas of nanotechnology are not likely to present novel safety risks. As with all new technologies new risks might appear that we have not thought about yet, underlining the need for continuous and dynamic risk reviews.

Human Health and the Environment

A fair assessment of the risks of any new technology must also consider positive contributions to increased safety. The basic innovations that come from nanotechnologies have the potential to contribute to human health and environmental safety in many ways. They have the potential to contribute to solve urgent issues like the provision of clean drinking water or more efficient energy conversion and energy storage.

The potential of nanotechnologies regarding economic benefits, the potential to create jobs, wealth and well being is very high. At the moment, public awareness about nanotechnology is limited. What happens over the next few years will determine how the public comes to view it. A transparent discussion of benefits and risks will help people reach a considered, balanced view. This will enable a greater public acceptance, which, in turn, will enable society as a whole to profit from these fundamental technological developments while, at the same time, the risks are kept under control. Especially in the field of medicine there are quite a few technological developments that promise enhanced diagnostic possibilities, new ways to monitor patients, new ways to treat diseases like cancer and to reduce side effects.

The potential benefits for our environment range from resource-efficient technologies reducing waste to new ways to transform and detoxify a wide variety of environmental contaminants, such as chlorinated organic solvents, organochlorine pesticides, and PCBs.

The term "manufactured nanoparticle" is used to refer to particles that have a physical size of less than 100 nm in at least two dimensions and that are deliberately produced rather than merely emerging as a by-product in activities not targeted for the production of these particles such as combustion processes or welding.

While a more rigorous definition would have to take more parameters such as size distribution, diffusion diameter into account, the term nanoparticles shall be used in a rather broad sense here, including agglomerates and aggregates of the primary particles. Nanoparticles exist in various forms such as powders, suspensions or dispersed in a matrix. In theory manufactured nanoparticles can be produced from nearly any chemical; however, most nanoparticles that are currently in use have been made from transition metals, silicon, carbon (carbon black, carbon nanotubes; fullerenes), and metal oxides. Quite a few of these nanoparticles have been produced for several decades on an industrial scale, but various new materials such as carbon nanotubes, fullerenes or quantum dots that have only been discovered within the last two decades.

Table 3. Examples of manufactured nanoparticles

Type	Examples for use
Metal oxides	
– silica (SiO_2)	– Additives for polymer composites
– titania (TiO_2)	– UV-A protection
– aluminia (AL_2O_3)	– Solar cells
– iron oxide (Fe_3O_4, Fe_3O_3)	– Pharmacy/medicine
– zirconia (ZrO_2)	– Additives for scratch resistance coatings
– zinc dioxide (ZNO_2)	
Fullerenes	
– C_{60}	– mechanical and trbological applications/additives to grease
Carbon Nanotubes	
– Single-wall carbon	– Additives for polymer composites nanotubes (mechanical performance, conductivity)
– Multiwall carbon	– Electronic field emitters nanotubes
	– Batteries
	– Fuel cells
Compound Semiconductors	
– CdTe	– Electronic an optical devices
	– GaAs
Organic Nanoparticles	– Micronised drugs and chemicals (vitamins, pigments, pharmaceuticals)
	– Polymer dispersions
Metals	
– Au	– Catalytic applications
– Ag	– Optoelectronics
– Ni	– Wound dressings

The development of nanomaterials is rapidly progressing and the variety of "makes" is increasing with considerable speed. The following list gives a few examples of manufactured nanoparticles that are of commercial interest: To fully exploit the properties of nanoparticles technologically, not the composition is important, but also parameters like the exact size, morphology and surface coatings.

Regulatory Considerations

Nanotechnology exploits properties not generally seen in large-scale solids of the same chemical composition, and that these same properties have led to health and safety concerns. For example, the high surface reactivity of nanoparticles and the ability to cross cell membranes might have negative human health impacts. On the other hand, not all nanoparticles, and not all uses of nanotechnology, will necessarily lead to new human health or environmental hazards. A distinction can be already be made, for example, between free and fixed nanoparticles.

Fixed nanoparticles are less likely to pose a problem because they are immobilised within a matrix and cannot freely move or disperse within the human body or the environment. In other words, there is likely to be low human exposure. It may be possible to assess many products involving nanoparticles from the chemicals industry using existing mechanisms or techniques for risk assessment, but it may often be necessary to adapt existing techniques or devise new risk assessment methods.

In any case it will be important to address safety issues in a proactive way in order to avoid public uneasiness about the new technology as a result of a lack of information and attention to safety aspects which could lead to limitations on the safe development of a promising technology. The International Risk Governance Council

(IRGC) discussed nanotechnology at a meeting of its Scientific and Technical Council in February 2005, agreeing that it is a broad technology which raises important long-term issues but arguing that grouping all nanoscale R&D and potential products within the single term "nanotechnology" makes it difficult to distinguish between technologies with different risk governance issues.

The situation is complicated by the fact that some possibly harmful commercial applications, such as in cosmetics, already exist and are subject to little new control, while potentially beneficial technologies may be retarded. Drug delivery, which may turn out to be the most important area economically, will take some time to come to market because of the time needed to complete approval processes.

2

Molecular Applications

The design of protein systems is complex. Indeed, chemists cannot yet predict the three-dimensional conformation of a natural protein from its amino acid sequence, an ability that might seem requisite to the design of new proteins. Two considerations suggest that this obstacle is surmountable: first, the continuing improvement in protein science and, second, the difference between natural science and design engineering. Regarding the first, computer simulation of protein molecules in solution shows promise.

As computer technology and chemical knowledge improve, simulations will increase in accuracy, speed, and size. Improvement promises new insight into protein behaviour and may permit the designer to modify (simulated) molecules quickly and to observe their behaviour directly. Regarding the second consideration, natural scientists seek a more general understanding than design engineers require. Science seeks the ability to predict the conformations of all natural polypeptides. In attempting this, protein chemists can search for a minimum-energy chain conformation or can attempt to follow the chain-folding mechanism to find the final conformation. Prediction will be easier if the natural conformation has outstanding stability or if its folding mechanism proceeds in a sequence of strongly preferred steps. Unfortunately, natural selection accepts polypeptides that have natural conformations of low stability (in energetic terms) so long as they exhibit long lifetimes on the cellular time scale. Similarly, natural selection accepts any folding process so long as the chain reaches its natural conformation with essentially 100% yield.

Moreover, random mutations are unlikely to enhance the stability of a particular conformation. Thus, natural proteins tend to accumulate disruptive changes until they reach the threshold of poor stability or reduced yield of the natural conformation; only then does natural selection come into play. Thus, it is little wonder that chemists cannot yet predict the conformations of natural proteins; they are not designed to fold predictably. Engineers (in contrast to scientists) need not seek to understand all proteins but only enough to produce useful systems in a reasonable number of attempts.

An engineer designing a protein that has 1000 amino acids may choose among some 101300 different amino acid sequences. It might be that only one in 109 (or even 10700) randomly selected sequences would yield a predictable conformation, yet this tiny fraction represents a vast number of proteins. Through use of strategically placed charged groups, polar groups, disulfide bonds, hydrogen bonds, and hydrophobic groups, the engineer should be able to design proteins that not only fold predictably to a stable structure (sometimes) but that serve a planned function as well.

Even a low success rate will lead to an accumulation of successful designs. Thus, the difficulties encountered in predicting the conformations of natural proteins do not seem insurmountable obstacles to protein engineering. Computer modelling and chemical understanding of biological targets have already found use in pharmaceutical design, and an artificial 34-residue polypeptide designed to interact with RNA has been synthesised and found active. It has been proposed to give microcircuitry special sensitivities by adsorbing engineered proteins onto selected surfaces.

The promise of enzyme design in chemical engineering is evident. As protein science has great promise and difficulties in understanding natural proteins need not block engineering, the substantial pay-offs for improved capabilities should lead to development of protein design technology. It would be foolish to underestimate the time and effort that will be required to develop basic design capabilities and then a broad family of working molecular devices; still, the path seems clear to achieving the capabilities exhibited by existing biochemical systems, by copying their features if need be. A comparison of biochemical to macroscopic components will show the possibilities of the former by analogy to the latter. With structural members, moving parts, bearings, and motive power, versatile mechanical systems can be built. Molecular assemblages of atoms can act as solid objects, occupying space and holding a definite shape.

Thus, they can act as structural members and moving parts. Sigma bonds that have low steric hindrance can serve as rotary bearings able to support ~ 10^{-9} N. A line of sigma bonds can serve as a hinge. Conformation-changing proteins (such as myosin) can serve as sources of motive power for linear motion; the reversible motor of the bacterial flagellum can serve as a source of motive power for rotary motion. The existence of this range of components in nature indicates that power-driven mechanical systems can be constructed on a molecular scale. By analogy with macroscopic devices, feasible molecular machines presumably include manipulators able to wield a variety of tools.

Thermal vibrations in typical structures are a modest fraction of interatomic distances; thus, such tools can be positioned with atomic precision. As present microtechnology can lay down conductors on a molecular scale (10 nm) and molecular devices can respond to electric potentials, such devices can be controlled by human operators or macroscopic machines.

Further, by analogy with biological sensors, molecular scale instruments can evidently produce macroscopic signals, indicating the feasibility of feedback control in molecular manipulations. Together, these arguments indicate the feasibility of devices able to move molecular objects, position them with atomic precision, apply forces to them to effect a change, and inspect them to verify that the change has indeed been accomplished. It would be foolish to minimise the time and effort that will be required to develop the needed components and assemble them into such complex and versatile systems. Still, given the components, the path seems clear.

Ordinary chemical synthesis relies on thermal agitation to bring reactant molecules in solution together in the correct orientation and with sufficient energy to cause the desired reaction. Enzyme-like molecular machines can hold reactants in the best relative positions as bonds are strained or polarised. Like some enzymes, they can do work on reactant molecules to drive reactions not otherwise thermodynamically favoured.

These are clearly techniques of great power, yet the synthetic capabilities of systems based on polypeptide chains might seem limited by amino acid properties. However, enzymes show that other molecular structures bound to the polypeptide can extend protein capabilities. The range of such tools is large and greater than found in nature. Thus, the synthetic capabilities of enzymes set only a lower bound on the capabilities of engineered protein systems.

Indeed, as tool-wielding protein systems can control the chemical environment of a reaction site completely, they should be able, at a minimum, to duplicate the full range of moderate-temperature synthetic steps achieved by organic chemists. Further, where chemists must resort to complex strategies to make or break specific bonds in large molecules, molecular machines can select individual bonds on the basis of position alone.

Conventional organic chemistry can synthesise not only one-, two-, and three-dimensional covalent structures but also exotic strained and fused rings. With the addition of controlled site-specific synthetic reactions, a broad range of large complex structures can doubtless be built. Still, the synthetic abilities of protein machines will be limited by their need for a moderate temperature aqueous environment. These limits may be sidestepped by using the broad synthetic capabilities outlined above to build a second generation of molecular machinery whose components would not be coiled hydrated polypeptide chains but compact structures having three-dimensional covalent bonding.

There is no reason why such machines cannot be designed to operate at reduced pressure or extreme temperatures; synthesis can then involve highly reactive or even free radical intermediates, as well as the use of mechanical arms wielding molecular tools to strain and polarise existing bonds while new molecular groups are positioned and forced into place. This may be done at high or low temperature as desired. The class of structures that can be synthesised by such methods is clearly very large, and one may speculate that it includes most structures that might be of technological interest. The development path described above should lead to advanced molecular machinery capable of general synthesis operations.

As the results of this path can be shown to have consequences for the present, it is of interest to discuss the degree of confidence that should be placed in its feasibility. It might be argued that complex protein or nonprotein machines are impossible or useless, on the grounds that, if they were possible and useful, organisms would be using them.

A similar argument would, however, conclude that bone is a better structural material than graphite composite, that neurons can transmit signals faster than wires, and that technology based on the wheel is impossible or useless. Nature has been constrained less by what is physically possible than by what could be evolved in small steps. Thus, the absence of a proposed kind of molecular machinery in organisms in no way suggests its infeasibility.

To deny the feasibility of advanced molecular machinery, one must apparently maintain either

— that design of proteins will remain infeasible indefinitely, or

— that complex machines cannot be made of proteins, or

— that protein machines cannot build second-generation machines.

In light of the expected improvements in computation, the simplified task of design engineers, the possibilities offered by sheer trial-and-error modification of natural proteins, and the progress already made in protein design, the first seems difficult to maintain.

Further, even if protein design were to prove intractible, this would in no way preclude developing an alternative polymer system with predictable coiling and using it as a basis for further development. In light of the presence of the needed components for mechanical devices in the cell, the second seems difficult to maintain. Indeed, the cytoskeleton provides a fair counterexample.

In light of the results of synthetic organic chemistry and the ability of molecular machines to make reactions site specific, it seems difficult to maintain that nonprotein machine components cannot be built and assembled. Each of these development steps seems closely analogous to past steps taken by nature or by technology. Each of these steps can be accomplished in many ways.

To argue their infeasibility would seem to require some general principle precluding success, and it is difficult to see what such a principle might be like. Thus, the claim that advanced molecular technology can be developed seems well founded. Although the existence of molecular machinery in cells indicates the feasibility of some sort of artificial molecular machinery, errors in assembly might limit the synthesis of structures of great complexity. In the cell, molecular machinery uses DNA to direct the assembly of DNA and other molecules.

In some eukaryotic cells, DNA directs DNA synthesis with an error rate of ~ 10^{-11} per nucleotide added. The possibility of low error rates is not surprising. For synthesis systems permitting error detection and correction (such as DNA synthesis), the net error rate in assembly can be reduced to roughly the product of the raw error rate in assembly and the rate at which errors are falsely identified as correct. As no uncertainty principle prohibits accurate discrimination between objects of different kinds (such as correctly and incorrectly assembled molecular structures), no limits to the detection and correction of errors are apparent.

Storage and Processing of Information

Molecular technology has obvious application to the storage and processing of information. A crude approach would involve literal "molecular machinery" patterned on the Babbage machine. In a more subtle approach, bits could be represented by protons, bound electrons, reactive groups, or conformation changes and transferred by movement of protons or of well-localised electrons, excitons, or phonons. The range of plausible device speeds is suggested by the 10^{-6}-sec turnover time for a fast enzyme, by the 10^{-13}-sec scale of collisional interactions, and by the 10^{-16} sec taken for an electron to cross an interatomic distance at a typical Fermi velocity. It seems highly likely that a cubic cell 0.1 micrometers on a side can hold a bit or perform a logic operation and, at the same time, transmit bits through itself to provide communication from cell to cell in a lattice. If so, then computers can be built with at least 10^{15} active elements per cubic centimeter.

Elements so small will be sensitive to radiation damage; to be reliable, systems will require a large measure of redundancy. Concern might be raised about the cost of such intricately patterned matter, either because of labor or energy requirements. It seems clear, however, that molecular-scale production systems can be completely automated.

Thus, labor costs of production can approach zero. The energy needed to produce molecularly engineered material will generally be greater than the energy needed to produce ordinary materials of similar bulk composition, but analogy suggests that the energy cost need not be vastly greater than for the production of biological materials. In many cases, the unique value of the products would make such energy costs unimportant, even if energy costs remained high.

Molecular devices can interact directly with the ultimate molecular components of the cell and thus serve as probes of unique value in studying processes within the cell. Further, molecular devices can characterise a frozen cell in essentially arbitrary detail by removal and characterisation of successive layers of material. Although the amount of data involved is large, the physical bulk of a device able to store and manipulate this amount of data will be quite small.

The change of temperature and water distribution during freezing modifies cell structures in several ways, primarily by physical displacement of structures by ice crystals and denaturation of proteins by concentration of solutes in the residual liquid. With frozen tissue, knowledge of normal structures and analysis of frozen structures should permit quite accurate reconstruction of the nature of the tissue before freezing. Such procedures would have special utility in analysing the structure of tissue in the brain. Unlike, say, muscle or liver tissue, the function of brain tissue depends on the detailed three-dimensional structure of intertwined cells and their interfaces.

The freezing process is far too slow to stop such dynamic processes as action potentials and synaptic transmission; short-term memory, however, is suspected to involve chemical modification of the neurons, and long-term memory is believed to involve the growth and modification of neuronal structures, particularly synapses. At the modest freezing rates possible in substantial pieces of tissue, ice crystals may be expected to nucleate and grow in the intercellular fluid, displacing the cell membranes as they do so. Electron micrographs, however, show that synapses (like many intercellular junctions) involve complementary structures on both sides of the intercellular gap, which should provide information enough to reconstruct the pre-freezing configurations of the cells almost regardless of ice crystal locations.

The ability to reconstruct the prefreezing structure of tissue, when combined with the general synthetic capabilities outlined above, will make feasible the physical restoration of tissue damaged by ordinary freezing through characterisation, reconstruction, and restoration of successive segments of frozen material. Although restored to a frozen condition, such tissue would lack the characteristic damage caused by the freezing process. As many tissues can survive the gross insult of ordinary freezing, it seems likely that most could survive freezing followed by repair. The remaining mode of damage would seem to be denaturation of proteins sensitive to cold alone during the thawing process. Should cell components of some species prove sensitive to short periods of cold, they could presumably be modified to resemble those of hardier species without changing either cell function or DNA.

The existence of a path to an advanced molecular technology has implications for the present. As with all technologies, long-range promise should tend to increase interest in undertaking the early steps, even beyond the interest springing from more immediate benefits. The longer the expected wait, however, the less the interest.

Molecular engineering of materials and devices can extend the capabilities of technology many fold in many areas. The implications of the feasibility of molecular technology are important to present day speculations concerning the probable behaviour of extraterrestrial technological civilisations.

Similarly, those concerned with the long-range future of humanity must concern themselves with the opportunities and dangers arising from this technology. Finally, the eventual development of the ability to repair freezing damage has consequences for the preservation of biological materials today, provided a sufficiently long-range perspective is taken.

Self Replicating Systems

Design concepts for the use of self replicating systems in space exploration have been discussed for several years. In the NASA LMF (Lunar Manufacturing Facility), a small cross section of conventional manufacturing technology, along with facilities for mining and refining lunar soil, would have been packed into a "seed" of perhaps a hundred tons and then launched to the moon. The obvious advantage of such a facility is the reduced need to launch further equipment manufactured with earth-bound systems: equipment required on the moon could be made as needed using the available lunar material, eliminating further launch costs. These proposals draw on a body of theoretical work, started by von Neumann, on the design of self replicating systems. A wide range of methods have been considered.

The von Neumann architecture for a self replicating system is perhaps the ancestral and archetypical proposal. Von Neumann's proposal consisted of two central elements: a Universal Computer and a Universal Constructor (Figure 1). The Universal Computer contains a programme that directs the behaviour of the Universal Constructor. The Universal Constructor, in turn, is used to manufacture both another Universal Computer and a Universal Constructor. Once finished, the newly manufactured Universal Computer was programmed by copying the programme contained in the original Universal Computer, and programme execution would then begin.

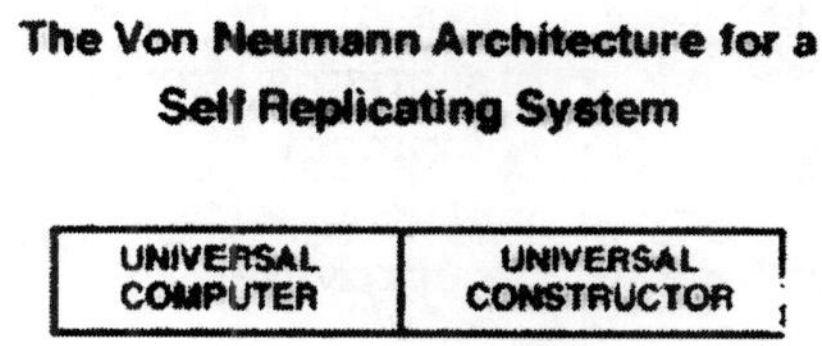

Figure 1. Von Neumann Self Replicatin System

This is rather an abstract proposal and covers a wide variety of specific implementations. Furthermore, both the design of the system and the environment in which it is intended to operate must be specified. The range of systems that would successfully operate on the ocean floor would be different from those that would operate in either deep space or an abstract mathematical space that had no physical existence. Von Neumann worked out the details for a Constructor that worked in a theoretical two-dimensional cellular automata world.

The Constructor had an arm, which it could move about; and a tip, which could be used to change the state of the cell on which it rested. Thus, by progressively moving the arm and changing the state of the cell at the tip of the arm, it was possible to create "objects" that consisted of regions of the two-dimensional cellular automata world which were fully specified by the programme that controlled the Constructor. While this solution demonstrates the theoretical validity of the idea, von Neumann's kinematic constructor has had perhaps a greater influence, for it is a model of self replication which can more easily be adapted to the three-dimensional world in which we live.

The kinematic constructor was a robotic arm which moved in three-space, and which grasped parts from a sea of parts around it. These parts were then assembled into another kinematic constructor and its associated control computer. An important point to notice is that self replication, while important, is not by itself an objective. A device able to make copies of itself but unable to make anything else would not be very valuable.

Von Neumann's proposals centered around the combination of a Universal Constructor, which could make anything it was directed to make, and a Universal Computer, which could compute anything it was directed to compute. This combination provides immense value, for it can be re- programmed to make any one of a wide range of things. It is this ability to make almost any structure that is desired, and to do so at low cost, which is of value. The ability of the device to make copies of itself is simply a means to achieve low cost, rather than an end in itself.

The positional capability might be provided by one or more small robotic arms, or alternatively might be provided by any one of a wide range of devices that provide positional control. The emphasis, though, is on a positional device that is very small in scale: perhaps 0.1 microns (100 nanometers) or so in size. As an aside, current SPM (Scanning Probe Microscope) designs employ piezoelectric elements for positional control. A rather obvious question to ask is: why prefer mechanical positioning systems over piezoelectric or other electrostatic devices?

The reasons for using basically mechanical devices at the molecular scale are similar to the reasons that mechanical devices are employed at the macroscopic scale: the desire for compactness and high positional accuracy (e.g., high stiffness). This weighs against electrostatic and piezoelectric devices. Molecular mechanical devices, on the other hand, can employ very stiff materials and, with appropriate design, can have joints that can rotate easily but which at the same time provide high stiffness in other degrees of freedom The "tip chemistry" is logically similar to the ability of the Von Neumann Universal Constructor to alter the state of a cell at the tip of the arm, but here the change in "state" must correspond to a real world change in molecular structure.

That is, we must specify a set of well defined chemical reactions that take place at the tip of the arm, and this well defined set of chemical reactions must be sufficient to allow the synthesis of the class. of structures of interest. The assembler, as defined here, is not a specific device but is instead a class of devices. Specific members of this class will deal with specific issues in specific ways.

Today, diamond is often synthesised at relatively low temperature and pressure using CVD (Chemical Vapor Deposition). In this process a highly reactive low-pressure gas is passed over the growing diamond surface. The gas typically includes atomic hydrogen and various species of hydrocarbons. The growing diamond surface is usually terminated with hydrogen. The growth mechanisms have been the subject of fairly extensive studies. A fairly common mechanism for growth involves (1) the abstraction of one or more hydrogen atoms from the surface, leaving one or more dangling bonds, followed by (2) reaction of the dangling bond(s) with a carbon containing species (e.g., CH_3, C_2H_2, etc). This cycle of abstraction and deposition is repeated indefinitely. Obviously, if we wish to make an atomically precise diamondoid structure, we cannot rely on reactive molecules in a gas.

A gas molecule can react with the surface at any location, and so the synthesis process is statistical and largely uncontrolled. If we are to achieve atomically precise control over the product, we need highly precise positional control over the reactants. The first thought would be to mount a highly reactive molecule on the tip of a positional device. For example, hydrogen abstraction can take place when an atomic hydrogen in the reactive gas strikes a hydrogen bonded to the growing surface. In some cases, the result will be an H_2 molecule leaving the surface and a dangling bond at the site where the H was removed. Unfortunately, atomic hydrogen is difficult to hold without making it inert.

Bonded to the tip of a positional device, a hydrogen atom is non-reactive. If it is not bonded to some structure, then it is difficult to control its position with the required precision. What we desire in a hydrogen abstraction tool is a structure which (a) has one end which is fairly stable, and so can be bonded into a larger "handle," and (b) has a highly reactive end that has a high affinity for hydrogen.

The tip atom is a radical. If the tip atom were bonded to hydrogen, the resulting bond would be very strong: about 130 kcal/mole. Quantum chemical calculations strongly support the idea that this tool will be able to easily abstract hydrogen from most diamond surfaces, and in particular that the barrier to the abstraction will either be small or non-existent. The base of the tool would be bonded into an extended diamondoid "handle" which could then be mechanically grasped and positioned.

This tool could be used to remove hydrogen in a site-specific fashion from a diamondoid work-piece, thus setting the stage for a carbon deposition tool to bond one or more carbon atoms at that site. Once the tool had performed its task it could either be thrown out and a new tool created from an appropriate pre-cursor, or the tool could be "refreshed" by removal of the abstracted hydrogen atom.

Several proposals for carbon deposition tools have been made. The general idea, however, is to use tools which bond a gas-phase growth species to a positionally controlled tip, and then to employ a reaction mechanism similar to that which would occur for the gas-phase species during deposition on the surface. It is useful to note that positional control also provides a convenient and very controlled mechanism for providing the activation energy sometimes needed: it is possible to apply mechanical force (push). This option is not normally available in chemistry and so opens up a rich new set of reaction mechanisms. Molecular mechanical systems can be modelled with sufficient accuracy using, appropriately enough, molecular mechanics. Chemical reactions involving the deposition or removal of individual atoms or small clusters of atoms can be modelled by using ab initio quantum chemistry programmes.

A wide range of molecular structures can be modelled using the software tools of computational chemistry. This lets us think about, design, and model the molecular structures that will be needed in future molecular manufacturing systems. Such "computational experiments" will speed the development of such systems. Just as Boeing can build better airplanes more quickly by first "building" and "flying" them in a computer, so too the development of molecular manufacturing will happen more quickly and with fewer false starts if we use the available computational resources to speed the design and analysis of such systems.

Developments of Molecular Manufacturing

Molecular manufacturing is coming soon. Because it will be so useful, there will be strong pressure to develop it as soon as possible, and past a certain point it could happen quite rapidly. Macro-scale integrated nanotechnology manufacturing systems will improve product functionality, product design time and manufacturing speed and cost by orders of magnitude.

This advance may profoundly affect economics and geopolitics, creating enormous benefits and risks. It will be difficult to prepare adequately for such a powerful technology. For all these reasons, molecular manufacturing technologies should be a current topic in high-level policy and planning. The word "nanotechnology" means several different things. Today's nanoscale technology research is mainly concerned with building small structures that have novel properties. Such research adds steadily to the technological toolbox, leading to improved products and occasionally to new industries.

Broadly speaking, such nanoscale technologies create risks comparable to other material science work. The second kind of nanotechnology is the science-fictional kind, in which nanobots can go anywhere and do anything but generally do not conform to reality. The third kind of nanotechnology, which will lead to molecular manufacturing. Molecular manufacturing, which is sometimes called molecular nanotechnology (MNT), will combine chemistry and fabrication to produce precise machines and manufacturing systems at the nanometer scale. Much of the basic science work has already been done; what remains is the engineering to create a working device and then integrate many devices into a humanscale "nanofactory"

Although most nanotechnology projects today focus on nanoscale technology, development of molecular manufacturing will surely become a priority within a few years. Full capability for this may not be developed for a decade or longer, but preparation for it should probably start now. The economic value-and military significance-of a nanofactory will be immense. Even a primitive model will be able to convert CAD files to products in a few hours.

Duplicate nanofactories will cost the same as any other nano-built product.

The capital cost of manufacturing will be negligible by today's standards, and manufacturing capacity can be doubled in a matter of hours. Nanocomputers will quickly replace semiconductor technologies; whoever controls this technology will be able to produce more computers than the rest of the world combined.

The ability to fit a supercomputer (or sophisticated robotics) into every piece of equipment, at no extra manufacturing cost, will enable new kinds of products and weapons. A nanotechnology-built surgical robot with a full sensor suite could be smaller than a hypodermic needle.

Development and deployment of new weapons systems could be far faster and cheaper. Even the initial products of a nanofactory would be worth hundreds of billions of dollars, and the potential for extremely rapid advancement of nanotechnology fabrication capability means that no economic or political unit can afford to allow a competitor to control the technology. Much evidence has accumulated to indicate that molecular manufacturing is possible.

A decade ago, Nanosystems studied the required chemistry and engineering in detail; not a single significant error has been found so far. Cells, natural self-replicating machines, make a variety of minerals including magnetite and silica-and they do this under water, using chemical techniques four billion years old. Mechanically guided covalent chemistry has already been accomplished with a scanning probe microscope. There is little doubt that a small self-duplicating system can be built. There is strong theoretical support for basing such a system on mechanochemistry.

And given the variety of buckytubes, buckyballs, buckyhorns, and other graphitic and diamondoid shapes that have been manufactured or found in nature, it's likely that a self-duplicating nanoscale machine based on 3D covalent carbon mechano-chemistry will be relatively straightforward to design. A goal or milestone of molecular manufacturing is a "fabricator": a self-contained mechanical system capable of fabricating duplicates of itself from simple chemicals.

Several researchers have investigated the requirements of a fabricator, and Robert Freitas and Ralph Merkle are due to publish two books on the topic in 2003 and 2004. A single fabricator is not very useful, since it can only make very small products. However, if a nanofactory containing many fabricators can combine the tiny products (nanoblocks) into a single large product, the result would be extremely useful. It has been claimed that this will take years to achieve, blunting the utility of molecular manufacturing. However, work by the author demonstrates that a useful nanofactory can be pre-designed, so that building and debugging the design might take only a few months.

Once the first fabricator is built, a fully functional nanofactory-and the nanofactory's products-may follow in well under a year. Although design at the atomic level will not be easy, a nanotechnology product designer will not need to worry about that-just as a software engineer does not think about the transistors in the computer.

A small and pre-tested set of nanomachines, built into nanoblocks, can be combined in many ways to make a vast array of products. By designing with nanoblocks instead of atoms, a product designer loses little flexibility, and gains simplicity and reliability. Nanoblocks can be fastened together in a process called "convergent assembly." The joining process uses a single motion, requiring only simple robotics, and the joints retain most of the strength of the base material.

A single nanoblock is big enough to contain a fabricator, computer, or motor, and small enough to be built by a single fabricator in a few hours. A nanofactory built of nanoblocks can build and assemble nanoblocks into a huge range of products-including duplicates of itself. Such a powerful technology introduces many risks.

One obvious risk is an unstable arms race. Rapid development of new weapons technologies means less opportunity for surveillance and more uncertainty about the enemy's future capabilities. Weapons could be more powerful and far "smarter"-imagine the combined capability of a million unmanned aerial vehicles with on-board pattern matching and navigation capability. Many factors tempt a preemptive strike if a temporary advantage is gained in a molecular manufacturing arms race.

The likely outcome of a policy of preemption would be either global domination requiring Draconian measures including denial of technology, or a series of increasingly destructive high-tech conflicts. Once weapons, or the systems that produce them, are dispersed, preventing guerrilla use of them would require inspection of literally every cubic millimeter, or continuous surveillance of entire populations.

Availability of unregulated molecular manufacturing could create several serious problems. Criminal and terrorist activity would benefit from smaller, more capable products. Small, widely available, cheap surveillance devices would allow an unprecedented invasion of privacy by governments, criminals and neighbours.

Cheap microscopic products can lead to widespread microscopic litter, with possible environmental or health consequences. Small self-contained foraging self-replicating systems appear to be theoretically possible, and might be released by terrorists, saboteurs or even irresponsible hobbyists.

Though probably less dangerous than all-out war with nanotechnology-built weapons, such devices could be significantly more destructive than invasive biological species because they would have no natural enemies. Many of these problems can best be addressed by widespread environmental monitoring, but the required systems may not be deployed quickly or universally. Molecular manufacturing may cause substantial economic disruption.

Several of today's sectors, including manufacturing, shipping and raw materials, would be disrupted or outmoded. Fully automated self-duplicating factories would reduce the value of both capital and labour, and drive down the cost of goods. Large disparity between cost and value would provide strong incentive for protectionism and anticompetitive policy, resulting in widespread black markets. The entertainment industry is already experiencing similar problems; molecular manufacturing may extend them to most manufactured products.

Simplistic attempts to regulate molecular manufacturing could create more problems than they solve. Attempts to restrict proliferation may generate oppressive or even abusive regulation. Today, billions of people live in sickness or poverty for lack of a few basic products like water filters, mosquito netting and computers. All of this would be easy to produce with nanotechnology-based manufacturing, but US attempts to block a WTO effort to provide affordable pharmaceuticals to poor nations indicate that the same could happen with MNT.

A population denied access to lifesaving benefits of cheap molecular manufacturing due to protectionist economic policy or paranoid security policy would have a strong incentive to steal, duplicate or "crack" the technology. Multiple independent programmes to develop molecular manufacturing would multiply many of the risks, including the risk of necessary regulations and technical restrictions being bypassed. Since nanofactories will be self-contained, incredibly valuable and easily concealed, a black market in nanofactories would be difficult to prevent.

Ultimately, control of the technology could be lost, and regions with excessive regulation may be sidelined. In developing molecular manufacturing, it may be that the safest course is a single, international development effort, leading to a technology that can be widely distributed and carefully administered-with tight technological controls in place to limit its use.

This would provide an infrastructure for rapid humanitarian relief with basic products, profit making with other products, and perhaps even arms control-if nations could be restrained from developing independent, unmonitored molecular manufacturing capability. If this is in fact the best approach, the need for action is even more urgent.

A nation with an entrenched development programme may be less likely to join or support an international development effort. It will not be easy to convince military and political leaders, captains of industry, and environmental and social watchdogs that the best course of action involves giving up some control in order to retain some control. Development of molecular manufacturing appears inevitable for two reasons.

The first is its immense value. Even if public pressure prevented it from being used in consumer goods, various militaries would not hesitate to develop it as a tremendous aid to military capability. In conventional conflicts, the improvements in logistics, miniaturisation, development and cost would give an overwhelming advantage to the possessor of such technology, both in preparation and in actual combat.

The second reason is the increasing ease of development. Enabling technologies are improving each year. New families of structural chemicals are being discovered. New fabrication technologies, new nanoscale imaging technologies, and increased computer power for mechanochemical simulation will rapidly decrease the difficulty of building a fabricator-and thus a nanofactory.

Today, a successful programme might require billions of dollars and several years. A decade from now it might be possible for only $100 million, within the reach of many corporations and nations. At that point, if molecular manufacturing is not already widely available, it will be developed in multiple labs around the world-and will be almost impossible to control. By encompassing all phases of production from chemical processing to final assembly, molecular manufacturing can be far more flexible than any other single technology, with the possible exception of programmable computers.

A few other technologies may be equally dangerous, but are easier to control. Nuclear technology can only be used for a few things-bombs, power generation, cancer treatment-so it has been possible for a fairly small international effort to keep control of various aspects of this technology. Biotechnology is flexible in its domain, but biotech products have been difficult to engineer. Conventional rapid prototyping systems will improve gradually; it will be a while before they can make complete products, and even longer before they can cheaply duplicate themselves.

A single technology with the programmability and speed of digital computers, the chemical flexibility of biotechnology, the military potential of nuclear technology or airplanes and the utility of very advanced rapid prototyping will bring many changes. The variety of potential problems, in economic, military, political, humanitarian and environmental spheres, indicates that no simple solution can work. A balance must be struck between national defence and arms control, between capitalist practice and social needs, and between unrestricted private use and oppressive restriction. These issues will not be easy to solve.

The final stages of development will occur too quickly for solutions to evolve. If a welldesigned plan is not in place before this happens, one or more serious risks will very likely lead to military destruction, social or economic disruption, or unnecessary human suffering on a large scale. Each major risk should be studied in detail. Public education and discussion should take place. Policy makers need to be informed. There is very little doubt that molecular manufacturing will be developed in the next three decades, and it may be within ten years. It seems likely that some sort of international administration will be necessary.

Any large administrative body, especially one requiring complex international cooperation, will take time to design, fund and create. All this may require more than a decade. A large international development effort may also be necessary, and would have to begin even sooner. These factors indicate that preparation for molecular manufacturing technology should become a current topic in high-level policy and planning.

Molecular manufacturing relies on two counterintuitive ideas: first, that mechanical operations can reliably be carried out at the nanoscale; second, that handling of individual molecules can be scaled up to produce useful quantities of product. The development of molecular manufacturing can be an incremental process from today's capabilities. There are many strategies, techniques, and tools that may contribute to its development. Three milestones can be identified for molecular manufacturing.

— Basic molecular manufacturing: Digital control of precise molecular assembly.

— Exponential molecular manufacturing: The ability to use molecular manufacturing systems to build additional usable molecular manufacturing systems, making it possible to produce large quantities of product.

— Integrated molecular manufacturing: The ability to combine the outputs of molecular manufacturing into large products.

The first milestone has almost been achieved already; the principle has been demonstrated in the laboratory. This level of technology may be used to make sensors, as well as a variety of research tools, and possibly to make limited but useful quantities of pharmaceuticals. The requirements to move from the first to the second milestone can be identified and preliminary design work can be started today. The ability to build large quantities of individually constructed molecularly precise products would be extremely valuable. Potential products include computers, pharmaceuticals, medical tools, and advanced materials.

Moving from the second to the third milestone would greatly increase the range of possible products. It has been argued elsewhere that this step might not be prohibitively difficult. However, the engineering details will depend on the molecular manufacturing technology being used, which could vary widely. After exploration of the range of options for developing these capabilities, several specific areas for study are suggested. These studies, which could be initiated today, would help to quantify the potential of the technology and the effort required to develop that potential.

The individual control of molecular composition and placement is often cited as a goal of nanotechnology. To date, many nanotechnology efforts have been content to achieve nanoscale-but not atomic-precision, or to build large quantities of small identical molecules. However, there are some technologies that are on the verge of achieving the goal. Liao and Seeman have built a nanomachine out of DNA that can guide the construction of any of several different strands of DNA; the product sequence can be chosen by "programming" the machine with other DNA strands. This is a demonstration of programmable molecular fabrication.

A planned extension to the machine would allow it to build longer and more interesting strands. Although this machine does not select from among multiple sites for the reaction, it does select from among multiple potential reactants, and its product has a precise and programmable molecular structure. Aono developed the ability to transport individual silicon atoms from one place to another in a covalent crystal, and was even able to automate this to make two-dimensional patterns. Several other researchers have also used electricity (fields and/or currents) with scanning probe microscopes to implement reactions at sites chosen with atomic precision.

Hersam has removed single selected hydrogen atoms from silicon at room temperature. Oyabu has removed and replaced single silicon atoms with purely mechanical force, but has not yet reported the ability to build multi-atom patterns. A strategy for easier atomically precise positioning is to separate the possible deposition sites. For example, a self-assembled repetitive grid could be used to create widely separated sites that might even be individually accessed optically for higher throughput.

A related strategy is to deposit large molecules into large receptors that are designed not to bond if misaligned. There are several possible ways to increase the throughput of molecular manufacturing without requiring it to build its own tools. If the manufacturing operation is done with a scanning probe microscope, then an array of MEMS microscopes like IBM's "millipede" could be used. If it is done with molecular tools similar to Liao and Seeman's, many tools could be created and used in parallel.

The productivity of individual control of molecules is limited by the small size of the molecules. A typical scanning probe microscope might weigh two kilograms, have a size of about 10 cm, and carry out ten automated operations per second. If each operation deposits one carbon atom, which masses about 2×10^{-26} kg, then it would take 10^{26} seconds or six billion years for that scanning probe microscope to fabricate its own mass! The speed with which a molecular manufacturing tool can create its own mass of product may be called "relative productivity." This depends on several factors: the mass of the tool, its frequency of operation, and the mass deposited per operation.

Roughly speaking, an object's mass will be about the cube of its size; hence, for each factor of ten shrinkage, the mass of the tool will decrease by 1,000. In addition, small things move faster than large things, and the relationship is roughly linear. Taken together, each factor of ten shrinkage of the tool will increase its relative productivity by about 10,000 times; relative productivity increases as the inverse fourth power of the size. If a tool could be shrunk by a factor of a million, from 10 cm to 100 nm, then its relative throughput could increase by 10^{24}, in which case it would take only 100 seconds to fabricate its own mass.

This assumes an operation speed of 10 million per second (which requires a linear speed of only 2 m/s over a 100 nm range). This is about ten times faster than the fastest known enzymes (carbonic anhydrase and superoxide dismutase). But a relative productivity of 1,000 or even 10,000 seconds would be sufficient for a very worthwhile manufacturing technology.

The following techniques all share a goal of controlling molecular joining and/or placement in order to build intricate, engineerable, functional, nanoscale, kinematic systems that are capable of building more of the same. In general, it is not required that every covalent bond in the final product be formed under direct mechanical control, or even at the time of the deposition process. Useful molecular building blocks can be pre-built by bulk chemistry. Also, crosslinking can be triggered optically or chemically after the manufacturing is completed to increase strength and stiffness.

The goal of building functional manufacturing systems implies that the newly built systems must be controllable. Many types of control can be broadcast, including chemicals, photons, pressure, and electric or magnetic fields. Electric current is harder to broadcast, but systems too small to be contacted via micromanipulation could self-assemble to electrodes. Electrical control may ultimately be the fastest and most flexible approach.

Although the techniques can be conveniently divided into groups according to the working conditions and bonding structure, the divisions between the groups are not absolute. For example, a system that used liquid xenon as a solvent would fall halfway between solution-phase and machine-phase. This reinforces the point that none of these approaches is entirely distinct from the rest; there is a continuum from today's well-established techniques to the most extreme machine-phase proposals.

Polymerisation Techniques

Ribosomes, which are made of RNA and protein, show that polymers can fold into functional shapes that carry out manufacturing operations. Polymer sequences can be controlled digitally by selecting the building blocks in the right sequence, as ribosomes do, or by flushing different building blocks past while controlling whether or not they stick, as DNA synthesisers do. Some polymers including DNA and RNA fold predictably, so their shapes can be engineered.

Seeman's machine selects short sequences to join rather than individual monomers, but a variant that could select monomers or could be constructed out of a few short repeated sequences would be able to build a copy of itself. Polymer chemistry is known to be quite versatile, and it should be possible to incorporate molecular actuators to select the polymer sequence; this would be faster and probably more reliable than using DNA strands to programme the device. Molecular actuators can be controlled and powered by light, electricity, or changes in the composition of the solution. Bulk controlled polymerisation techniques, such as DNA synthesis, often use two repeated steps: first they make the end of the polymer reactive by "deprotecting" it, then add a monomer that is protected from further deposition.

Nanoscale controlled polymerisation could control either the timing of the deprotection step or the monomer selection for the polymerisation step. Or the system could protect the addition site by steric hindrance. Alternatively, it could use a polymerisation reaction that is exothermic but has a high barrier, and accelerate the desired reaction-possibly by many orders of magnitude-by holding the monomer in place. The ratio of reaction rates of confined and unconfined monomers will approximate the error rate. Because there is only one reaction site and one choice-to add a monomer or not-extreme stiffness should not be required in polymer-based molecular manufacturing systems. Even minimally crosslinked polymers can implement a controllable, low-error system.

Implementing polymer exponential molecular manufacturing systems appears to be a fairly small step from existing and currently feasible non-exponential polymer-based polymer-building systems. Instead of building a linear chain that then folds into a shape, it may be possible to build the desired shape directly by depositing small molecular building blocks.

These building blocks could either form covalent bonds during deposition, or be held by hydrogen bonds (similar to self-assembly) and perhaps joined later by crosslinking. Making an atomically precise product does not require atomic precision in block positioning-only enough precision to select between adjacent block deposition sites.

Branched molecules, possibly including dendrimers, may be of interest as building blocks. This approach has not been much studied yet. It may be worth pursuing because exotic environments would not be needed, but 3D shapes and structures might be built directly rather than needing to be formed by folding.

Actuator molecules could either be placed individually or added by self-assembly once the structure was built. Any useful moving system needs to have parts moving relative to other parts. This has not been explored in systems of this class. As in MEMS, springs might be useful instead of sliding-surface bearings. A wider palette of materials might allow the spring designs to be more compact.

Precise covalent structures with nanoscale width might be able to bend more sharply without fatigue or plastic deformation. Another option might be to have monolayer bearings self-assemble in spaces left during construction. The techniques used in low-friction biological molecular moving parts (e.g. ATP synthase) might be useful once they are better understood.

This approach might make use of relatively large molecular building blocks. It would probably be possible to place large blocks with a relatively crude scanning probe microscope in order to build the first manufacturing system. Silicatein, an enzyme that builds silica, may be useful. Also, a polymer-based molecular machine system might be used if one had been developed previously.

Integrated Molecular Manufacturing

A far-term goal of molecular manufacturing research is to build not just a large mass of products, but large integrated products. Sufficiently large products would create the possibility of manufacture for direct human use, without further expensive manufacturing steps, and the integration of familiar user interfaces.

Several problems would have to be solved in order to achieve this. In any system containing huge numbers of nanoscale components, some will be defective. It appears that, at least for simple hierarchical designs, the use of simple redundancy at multiple levels can result in excellent aggregate reliability. If a device has less than a 3% chance of failing in a certain time period, then a group of eight devices plus one spare will have higher reliability than a single device.

Multiple levels of such redundancy can make the aggregate failure rate negligible at a modest cost in extra mass. To produce an integrated product, it helps to have the production stations fastened into a framework so that the position of each nanoscale partial product is known. The framework can also be used to deliver power and control, and separate the workspace from the feedstock and cooling channels. (Waste heat appears to be a significant but not insurmountable problem, which will presumably improve in less primitive designs.) With strong materials, the mass of the framework may be a fraction of the mass of the active components. To produce a heterogeneous product, the manufacturing systems must be individually controlled.

The instructions may be delivered through a simple hierarchical network, but probably must be processed locally. This would require nanoscale computers, which would be responsible for significant portions of the mass and power budget. (Commonly used molecular pieces could be built by special-purpose high-speed systems-mills-substantially reducing the required control inputs.)

Nanoscale subproducts must be joinable to make a large product. With the high speed implied by small size, each workstation could fabricate millions of mechanical features. This should make it possible to build mechanical fastening systems into each subproduct, facilitating the task of joining them. The reference technology was diamond deposition and diamondoid materials. The nanoscale fabricator was adapted from Merkle's work, which itself was intentionally primitive and simple. The mechanical positioning/reaction system was assumed to be actuated by ratchets, requiring many control inputs for each motion. Despite the handicaps imposed by primitive design, it was calculated that the proposed nanofactory might be able to build another nanofactory-even a version twice as big-in less than a day.

Technologies for Molecular Manufacturing

Several existing and projected technologies may be useful for development of the various approaches and stages of molecular manufacturing. The following is only a partial list. The technologies listed are useful for imaging, fabrication of nanoscale shapes and tools, and basic research into relevant nanoscale phenomena. Because many technologies can perform more than one function, they are not grouped into categories.

— *Computers:* Computers have become quite powerful and will continue to improve. Computational chemistry is becoming increasingly trusted. Estimates can be determined of physical properties of molecular structures. Eventually, multilevel integrated simulations might be useful in planning and evaluating larger systems. Computers can also be useful for some design processes. For example, recent work on protein folding to a desired shape used a repeated simulate-and-modify process to arrive at appropriate sequences. Appropriate DNA sequences for optimum folding to a desired shape also have been generated by computer. As more extensive mechanosynthetic capabilities are developed, the ability to automate them will become crucial to carrying out repeated operations without excess labour.

— *Scanning probe microscopes:* Scanning probe microscopes (SPMs) can image areas with atomic resolution, and also manipulate molecules and do chemistry. Most SPMs have only a single probe with three degrees of freedom, but Xidex Corp. is developing two-probe, six-degree-of-freedom systems that will be able to touch the tips together. This may be useful for research into mechanosynthetic reactions: A tip with an active molecule could be brought together with another tip acting as a receptive surface, at various repeatable angles and offsets, to test 'he effects of displacement and angle on the reaction. SPMs can work in air, water, or vacuum, at room temperature or cryogenic temperature. A deposition system that can create 15-nm lines of molecules has been developed, called dip-pen nanolithography (DPN).

— *Electron microscopes:* Electron microscopes can image with near-atomic resolution. They can be used to cut carbon nanotubes, even to trim outer tubes from multiwalled tubes. They can also deposit a variety of materials from gas feedstock (electron beam induced deposition, EBID). These deposits have a feature size as small as 10 nm and can form three-dimensional structures.

— *Sub-wavelength imaging:* FRET (fluorescence resonance energy transfer, which is very sensitive to nanoscale distance) can be used to determine relative positions. NanoSight has developed an imaging system that can be placed in an existing optical microscope and image 20 nm particles. AngstroVision has claimed to be developing 3D nm-scale imaging using visible light.

— *Ion etching systems:* Ion etching systems can achieve single-atom accuracy and can use tiltable workpieces. This may enable production of freestanding (undercut) kinematic structures from high-performance materials that might be useful for research into nanoscale machinery or even as nanoscale molecular manufacturing systems.

— *Engineered molecules and molecular composites:* DNA structures have been used to position carbon nanotubes to make a working transistor. Protein folding prediction is still problematic, but the inverse problem-design of sequences that will fold into a desired shape-is becoming reliable. Silica can be deposited from water; this deposition can be mediated in shirtsleeve conditions by the enzyme silicatein. A silicatein molecule attached to a positioning system might be useful in building silica structures to specified shapes.

Levins and Schafmeister have developed a new polymer that uses two bonds between each monomer for significantly increased stiffness and well-defined shape even without folding. This may make it easier to design and build desired molecular shapes. Schafmeister states that conventional amino acids can be incorporated into the polymer chain; this increases chemical flexibility at the expense of local stiffness. A vast number of other molecules may be suitable for forming nanoscale engineered structures. The essence of molecular manufacturing is very simple: the formation of precise molecular structures under direct mechanical guidance. Artificial examples of this are close to being demonstrated, and a set of fairly short steps may lead from there to the achievement of a useful manufacturing technology.

The mechanical component of molecular manufacturing does not require a classical mechanical engineering approach, but such an approach seems to be a good fit for the method-especially since the creation of designed molecules will make it relatively easy to specify their shape. Nanoscale structures are often assumed to be inherently floppy and unstable, but this will be less true for strongly crosslinked polymers or covalent solids than for weakly crosslinked biological molecules. It is worth investigating how small a mechanical structure implemented in various materials can be made before thermal noise or quantum effects spoil its applicability as a mechanical design element.

A related question is how to design nanoscale mechanical elements to be reliable machines in the face of thermal noise and surface forces, and how small such designs can be made. A major and underappreciated potential advantage of molecular manufacturing products over MEMS is that the use of atomically precise surfaces may eliminate wear and greatly reduce friction.

There are many possible approaches to molecular manufacturing: many materials in at least four basic processes (polymer, covalent in solvent, noncovalent in solvent, covalent in machine-phase). Most of the possibilities have never been studied. A study of the merits and potentials of a range of approaches and materials would be very useful.

Once the potential capabilities and products were better understood, a more detailed roadmap to their development could be produced. Although low friction and low wear have been demonstrated in a few cases, the mechanisms of nanoscale friction are not well understood.

The study of low-friction sliding interfaces would help in determining the performance limits of nanoscale machinery. The study should include wet as well as superclean interfaces, and stiff materials and surfaces as well as biological-style non-stiff, wetted, or bushy surfaces. Nanoscale and molecular actuators are being studied, but many of these studies are not directed at large-scale integration of the actuators into nanoscale machines. The complex construction promised by even basic molecular manufacturing indicates that multi-actuator systems soon may be desirable. It would be useful to do studies emphasising actuators that can be integrated with a variety of structures and that can be controlled via rapid, small, and independent channels.

The binding and positioning of molecules will be a key competency for molecular manufacturing. Antibodies seemingly can be developed to bind almost anything. Binding pockets for individual molecules have been made by taking "molds" of the molecules in plastic. It would be useful to further explore how to bind and transport molecules, especially how to design binding sites based mainly on steric properties (shape) that will be flexibly engineerable in molecular manufacturing approaches.

Reliability will be an important factor in the ability to make complicated automated manufacturing systems. The mechanosynthetic operations have not yet been selected, but it may be possible to estimate upper and lower bounds on classes of operation, or at least begin to understand what factors affect reliability. Preliminary arguments indicate that reliabilities between 10^9 and 10^{15} may be achievable. If and when massively parallel systems are built, fault tolerance will be required.

As results from the above studies become available, it will be possible to form preliminary estimates of the manufacturing throughput and product capabilities of a particular molecular manufacturing technology. It would be useful to start such studies today, for two reasons. First, preliminary answers to many of the above questions are already available for at least one technology. Second, attempts to quantify performance will show what other questions need to be studied.

Any estimate of the time and resources that would be required to develop any particular approach to any given level will necessarily be preliminary. However, it seems important to develop such estimates as soon as possible. Exponential molecular manufacturing may significantly impact the semiconductor and pharmaceutical industries, among others; and integrated molecular manufacturing may even be competitive as a general-purpose manufacturing technology. This implies that development of molecular manufacturing may have a very high payoff.

3

Photodynamic Therapy

In recent years, an increasing number of researchers have considered the possibility of using nanoparticles in photodynamic therapy (PDT). PDT is based on the concept that photosensitiser (PS) molecules can be preferentially localised in tumour tissues upon systemic administration. Reactive oxygen species, such as singlet oxygen ($^1O_2$), or free radicals are the main cytotoxic substances, which can irreversibly damage the treated tissues. It is generally accepted that singlet oxygen is the primary cytotoxic agent responsible for photobiological activity.

Other active oxygen species such as O_2^- and OH produced from photoexcited fullerene (C_{60}) in the presence of NADH and Fe(II) may also be responsible for photoinduced DNA cleavage under physiological conditions. Compared to current treatments including surgery, radiation therapy and chemotherapy, PDT offers the advantage of an effective and selective method of destroying diseased tissues without damaging the surrounding healthy tissues. Singlet oxygen, the $^1\Delta_g$ state of the dioxygen molecule, is capable of damaging nucleic acids, proteins, and lipids in the cellular environment. Thus, reactions of singlet oxygen with nucleotide bases and amino acids have been the subject of intensive research for several decades. The combination of nanomaterials with singlet oxygen has emerged as a new interdisciplinary research field.

Nanoparticles can be ideal carriers of PS molecules for PDT. Moreover, some nanomaterials, e.g. TiO_2, ZnO, and fullerenes as well as their derivatives, can generate singlet oxygen. Although this research area has not nearly received as much attention as the application of nanomaterials to electronics or catalysis, it represents a promising route to overcome many of the difficulties associated with traditional PDT.

Photosensitisation

Photosensitisation is a simple and controllable method for the production of $^1O_2$, requiring only oxygen, light of the appropriate wavelength, and a PS capable of absorbing and using the energy to excite oxygen to its singlet state. With the irradiation of light of appropriate wavelength, the PS in its S_0 state is excited to the S_1 state. The lifetimes of the S_1 state are in the nano second range which is too short to allow for significant interactions with the surrounding molecules.

The S_1 state decays via a radiative process or by non-radiative processes to the ground state or triplet excited state, T_1. The lifetimes of the T_1 state are in the micro- to milli-second range. This is long enough for a variety of quenching processes to compete favourably with phosphorescence.

Quenching mechanisms include energy transfer, charge transfer, H-abstraction and oxidative transfer (mostly methyl viologen). Triplet quenching involving dioxygen can be described by energy transfer, electron transfer and physical deactivation which give $^1O_2$, O_2^- and $^3O_2$ respectively. The photophysical process leading to $^1O_2$ generation and its competing reactions can therefore be presented as follows:

$$P(S_0) + h\upsilon \rightarrow P\ (S_1) \tag{1}$$

$$P(S_1) + P(S_0) \rightarrow h\upsilon_F\ k_F \tag{2}$$

$$P(S_1) + P(S_0)\ k_{IC} \tag{3}$$

$$P(S_1) + P(T_1)\ k_{ISC} \tag{4}$$

$$P(T_1) + P(S_0) \rightarrow h\upsilon_P\ k_P \tag{5}$$

$$P(T_1) + P(S_0)\ k_{nr} \tag{6}$$

$$P(T_1) + {}^3O_2 \rightarrow P(S_0) \rightarrow {}^1O_2\ k_{en} \tag{7}$$

$$P(T_1) + {}^3O_2 \rightarrow P^+ + O_2^-\ k_{et} \tag{8}$$

$$P(T_1) + {}^3O_2 \rightarrow P(S_0) + {}^3O_2\ k_{pq} \tag{9}$$

Based on the above equations, we can define the quantum yield of triplet formaticn as

$$\Phi_T = \frac{k_{ISC}}{k_F + k_{IC} + k_{ISC}} \tag{10}$$

and, furthermore, the proportion of triplet quenched by ${}^3O_2$ ($P_T\ {}^3O_2$) as

$$P_T{}^3O_2 = \frac{k_{en} + k_{et} + k_{pq}[O_2]}{k + (k_{en} + k_{et} + k_{qp}[O_2]} \tag{11}$$

The fraction of triplet excited sensitiser quenched by ${}^3O_2$ and leading to the formation of singlet oxygen $f\Delta\ {}^3O_2$ is given by:

$$f_{\Delta}{}^{1}O_2 = \frac{k_{en}}{k_{en} + k_{et} + k_{qp}} \tag{12}$$

We can therefore express the quantum yield of singlet oxygen formation as

$$\Phi_{\Delta} = \Phi_T f_{\Delta}{}^{T} P_T{}^{1}O_2 \tag{13}$$

An alternative way of expressing the quantum yield of singlet oxygen formation based on reactions (1)-(9) is given by

$$\Phi_{\Delta} = \Phi_T \frac{k_{en}[O_2]}{k + (k_{en} + k_{et} + k_{pq}[O_2]} = \Phi_T \, \Phi_{en} \tag{14}$$

where Φ_{en} is the efficiency of energy transfer. Singlet dioxygen is able to cause irreversible damage to various cell constituents including plasma, mitochondria, lysosomal and nuclear membranes, and protein modifications. In PDT, the complete eradication of diseased tissue is believed to be largely due to the shutdown of tissue vasculature that provokes blood stasis, thus starving the diseased tissue of oxygen and nutrients. Ultimately, the target tissue may be eradicated with either little or no damage to the surrounding normal tissues.

The PDT efficiency depends upon the chemistry of the PS, the pharmaceutical formulations, the physical localisation and the amount of PS the in treated tissue, the time of activation with light, the light doses and the absorption properties of the PS. The maximum transmittance of skin tissue is in the 700-800 nm region, and the development of a PS with a maximum absorbance in this region remains a major challenge.

Photofrin, one of the two FDA-approved sensitisers is usually irradiated at 630 nm, which limits the penetration of light through the tissue to just a few mm. Thus far, it has not been possible to develop more red-shifted PSs by using nanoparticles. During the past few decades, various types of PS molecules have been synthesised. Many organic dyes, porphyrins and derivatives, flavins and other biomolecules are efficient sensitisers.

Recently, it has also been found that several organometallic species, namely bis(cyclometallated) Ir(III) complexes (which can easily be attached to protein residues), possess very high quantum yields. There are two photosensitisers currently approved by the FDA for use in PDT: photofrin (actually a mixture of porphyrins, including protoporphyrin, haematoporphyrin, and hydroxyethyl-deuteroporphyrin); and verteporfin, a benzoprohyrin derivative. However, there are many problems for the clinical application of existing photosensitsers.

— Most PS molecules are hydrophobic and can aggregate easily in aqueous media where the PS aggregation will result in the decrease of its quantum yield (WD). Moreover, the aggregated PS cannot be simply injected intravenously.

— Selective accumulation of the PS molecules in deceased tissues is required to avoid collateral damage to healthy cells.

Although third generation PS have been prepared for selective targeting, their selectivity is not high enough for clinical application. Because of these problems, the construction of an effective PS carrier becomes critical and remains a major challenge to PDT. It is therefore not surprising that there is increasing interest in using nanoparticles as PS carriers. Nanomaterials are promising in that

— they could be made hydrophilic;

— possess enormous surface areas, and their surface can be modified with functional groups possessing a diverse array of chemical or biochemical properties;

— owing to their sub-cellular and sub-micron size, nanoparticles can penetrate deep into tissues through fine capillaries, cross the fenestration present in the epithelial lining (e.g. as in the liver), and are generally taken up efficiently by cells;

— since numerous strategies for the preparation of nanomaterials are already in place, PS-loaded nanoparticles can be desirously made by numerous different methods, e.g. chemical covalent grafting or self-assembly.

In PDT, nanotechnology focuses on formulating PS agents in biocompatible nanocomposites, such as nanoparticles, nanocapsules, micellar systems, and conjugates. These colloid particles have different structures, e.g. colloidal particles with a PS agent encapsulated within their matrix or adsorbed or conjugated onto the surface.

Tumor-seeking molecules can be simultaneously attached to the surface of nanoparticles for specific targeting. These PS-loaded nanoparticles have the ability of recognising and selectively adhering to the target moieties of the tumor-specific molecular receptors. A variety of different nanomaterials, such as inorganic oxides, metal, and organic compounds, have been used to prepare PS-loaded composites.

Ceramic-based Nanoparticles

There is an increasing interest in developing ceramic-based nanoparticles as carriers for drug delivery. Ceramic-based nanoparticles have several advantages over organic carriers: particle size, shape, porosity, and mono-dispersibility of these particles can be easily controlled during their preparation.

The ceramic-based nanoparticles are water-soluble and extremely stable, are known for their compatibility in biological systems, and are not subject to microbial attack. Furthermore, there is no swelling or porosity change occurring in these particles with change of pH. For conventional drug delivery, the carrier vehicle should release the encapsulated drug at the target tissue. The ceramic-based nanoparticles, owing to the aforementioned immunity to chemical or microbial attack, have shells that are difficult to collapse to release the encapsulated drug.

Consequently, this feature of ceramic-based nanomaterials may have limited its application in the delivery of common drugs. In contrast with conventional medical treatment, PDT is based on the generation of an active oxygen species as a cytotoxic agent. Hence, for PDT it is unnecessary to release the loaded PS molecules, except that a small void in the shell of the nanoparticles is needed for the diffusion of oxygen molecules.

Metallic Nanoparticles

In recent years, metallic nanoparticles and monolayer protected nanoclusters (MPCs) have been explored due to their potential applications in nanoelectronic and optical devices, catalysis, and chemical and biological sensors. MPCs usually possess a very small size ranging from ca. 1 to a few nanometers, and are of immense monodispersibility. On the surface of the MPC, the hydrophilicreagent tetraoctylammonium bromide (TOAB) was adsorbed, and this made the MPC soluble in polar solvents. The threecomponent (PS/gold/phase transfer reagent) MPC was shown to generate singlet oxygen with enhanced quantum yields of ca.50% as compared to the free Pc. The enhanced quantum yield can be attributed to the TOAB phase transfer reagent, which affects the excited singlet state of Pc as well as the triplet energy transfer to molecular oxygen to formsing let oxygen. In contrast to ceramic-based nanoparticles, metallic nanoparticles can be confined to an extremely small particle size.

These particles possess an enormous surface area, and hence can be loaded with a relatively large dose of PS. Moreover, instead of being confined to the core of the silica-based nanoparticles, PSs can be attached on the surface of the MPC. Consequently, the produced singlet oxygen is able to diffuse into the tumor cells much more easily. This kind of PS-protected MPC may be especially useful for the PS delivery in PDT.

Biodegradable nanoparticles have received much attention as possible drug-delivering agents. Their main advantages lie in high drug loading, the possibility of controlling the drug release, and a large variety of materials and manufacturing processes. Biocompatible polymers are predominantly favoured over small molecules for drug delivery systems because of the opportunities that polymers offer in achieving optimal medication effects. The chemical composition and architecture of polymers can be readily tailored to accommodate drugs with varying degrees of hydrophobicity, molecular weight, pH, etc. Furthermore, the surface properties, morphologies, and composition of polymer matrices can be easily optimised to achieve the desired biocompatibility, controlled polymer degradation and drug release kinetics.

Recently, studies in PDT have thus focused on the use of polymer-based nanoparticles for PS delivery and release systems, in particular those with biocompatible and biodegradable polymers. These systems are able to target different organs and control the release of the PS molecules by the incorporation of site-specific moieties.

The surface of particles can be modified with poly (ethylene oxide) to improve the carrier's biocompatibility and biodistribution. Different strategies have been developed for the preparation of polymer-based nanomaterials for the delivery of PS molecules in PDT.

Among these methodologies, the common method is the emulsion polymerisation or the interfacial polymerisation in water-in-oil or oil-in-water microemulsions. The resulting nanomaterials can be either nanospheres or nanocapsules (core-shell nanoparticles) depending upon the synthetic approach.

Among the various PSs investigated for PDT, phthalocyanines have been found to be highly promising. However, one of the problems in using phthalocyanines for PDT arises from their intrinsic tendency toward aggregation. This intermolecular association process promotes the non-radiative internal conversion [eqn. (6)], almost invariably causing a shortening of the triplet lifetime and a drastic reduction in the overall efficiency of singlet oxygen production.

As early as 1991, the preparation of tetrasulfonated zinc phthalocyanine ($ZnPcS_4$) or aluminium naphthalocyanine entrapped into poly (isobutylcyanoacrylate) or poly (ethylbutylcyanoacrylate) nanocapsules or nanospheres by interfacial polymerisation in water-in-oil emulsion was reported. The prepared nanocapsule sizes ranged from 150 to 250 nm, while the nanospheres had a broader size distribution from 10 to 380 nm.

The PS encapsulation efficiency was very high and could reach 100% when prepared under optimal experimental conditions. PS binding in the nanoparticles was between 75 and 80%. In a subsequent study with cultured V-79 hamster cells as a model, it was found that the nanoencapsulation enhanced the cellular localisation of the dyes providing a high level of in vitro phototoxic activity. Indeed, $ZnPcS_4$-loaded poly (isohexylcyanoacrylate) nanocapsules turned out to be more active than the free dye. Hexadecafluoro zinc phthalocyanine ($ZnPcF_{16}$), a second-generation sensitiser for PDT, was formulated in poly (ethylene glycol)-coated poly (lactic acid) nanoparticles (PEG-coated PLA-NP) by a 'salting-out' method.

The resulting nanoparticles possessed a large average diameter, up to nearly 1000 nm, and the PS loading was very low, only 0.61%. The photodynamic activity of the PS-loaded nanoparticles was tested in EMT-6 tumor-bearing mice and the tumor response was compared to that induced by the same dye formulated as a Cremophor EL emulsion. It was found that the formulation of the biodegradable nanoparticle improved the PDT response of the tumor while providing prolonged tumor sensitivity towards PDT. Recently, a similar method has been applied to the preparation of poly (D,L-lactide-co-glycolide) (50:50 and 75:25 PLGA) and poly (D,L-lactide) nanoparticles entrapped with the PS meso-tetra (hydroxyphenyl) porphyrin (p-THPP).

The resulting nanoparticles have an average particle size of 130 nm and the PS loading was improved to near 8%. The photocytotoxicity of these nanoparticles was also evaluated on EMT-6 mammary tumor cells and compared to free PS molecules. The most important photocytotoxicity was observed with 50:50 PLGA nanoparticles, allowing drug doses and short drug administration-irradiation intervals for local PDT. Blais's group constructed colloidal capsules entrapped with a second-generation PS molecule, meta-tetra (hydroxyphenyl) chlorin (mTHPC).

These nanoparticles were oil/water nanospheres made of poly (D,L-lactic acid) (PLA), or nanocapsules made of PLA coated with poly (ethylene glycol) (PLAPEG), or poloxamer 188 (polox PLA). The cellular uptake, localisation and phototoxicity of PS-loaded carriers have been studied in macrophage-like J774 cells and HT 29 human adenocarcinoma cells. It was found that the cellular uptake was reduced with mTHPC encapsulated into surface-modified nanocapsules - PLA-PEG and polox PLA - compared with naked PLA. However, the phototoxicity was much less affected and a protecting effect against plasma proteins was observed. As explained above, singlet oxygen is the main cytotoxic species in PDT, and hence a fundamental requirement for a PS carrier is that it should not significantly quench singlet oxygen. The nanoparticles were quite uniform and possessed a hydrodynamic diameter of 20-25 nm. The PAA matrix was found not to quench $^1O_2$, while the AFPAA was found to reduce the singlet oxygen productivity to onlv 60% compared with the free dye.

Nanoparticles with amine functionalised PAA and AFPAA matrixes were produced by the same research group, and it was suggested that the amine groups on the surface of the nanoparticles could react with the targeting moieties for tumor-specific molecular receptors. This result indicated that PAA would be an ideal candidate for developing polymer-based PS carriers for PDT. Recently, a new methodology has been developed to synthesise the PS-containing nanoparticles by using the PS unit-containing copolymer as a precursor.

The copolymer, namely poly (phthalocyanine- co-sebacic anhydride) (Pc-SA), was constructed by the polymerisation of Zn(II) phthalocyanine and sebacic anhydride units. The Pc-SA-*n* copolymer then aggregated into nanoparticles via a microphase inversion method. The resulting nanoparticles have an average hydrodynamic diameter of about 160 nm. The fluorescence quantum yield (Φ_f) of phthalocyanine containing polymers Pc-SA-*n* is close to that of free Pc. This nanoparticle degrades in alkaline media, and releases Pc from the Pc-SA-*n* nanoparticles, and has a decreased aggregation tendency giving ultimately monomeric species. The methodology is superior compared with the common microemulsion polymerisation method for the construction of PS-loaded, polymerbased nanocomposites in that the PS loading is relatively high and that it avoids the possible quenching and entrapping of the produced singlet oxygen by the polymer matrix.

Fullerene-porphyrin hybrids

Fullerene-porphyrin hybrids possess attractive properties, e.g. excellent photo-absorption, solubility, etc. Research has been focused on both the synthesis and properties of this relatively new type of hybrid material. C_{60} is an excellent electron acceptor in the ground state and can accept, reversibly, up to six electrons. When irradiating the fullerene-porphyrin hybrid, the porphyrin unit harvests the light and is excited to its T_1 state, which is subsequently quenched by the fullerene molecule. During the process, intramolecular electron transfer from the porphyrin to the C_{60} unit occurs, and a charge-separated state is formed:

$$C_{60} - P \xrightarrow{hv} {}^{1*}C_6 - P \rightarrow C_{60}^{-} - D^{\cdot+} \quad (15)$$

C_{60}-porphyrin in the charge-separated state increases the solubility of C_{60} in polar solvents. Moreover, the attached porphyrin can absorb light in the visible range much more effectively than the 'naked' C_{60} molecules. The efficiency of formation of the triplet excited state of fullerenes is highly dependent upon the environment. It has been shown that when C_{60} molecules aggregate the quantum yield of formation of the triplet state decreases considerably. Fullerene molecules are able to exist in a monodispersed state when confined inside the pore of a solid matrix such as molecular sieves.

In contrast with chemical modification, i.e. the attachment of organic functional groups, this method can keep the original molecular structure intact without perturbation of the π-system. By detecting its characteristic near-IR emission at λ_{max} = 1270 nm, it was found that singlet oxygen was effectively generated in both of the materials. Moreover, the triplet excited state of C_{60} (λ_{max} ~ 780 nm) had a lifetime of several minutes when this fullerene was incorporated inside zeolite LiY! On the other hand, the C_{60} triplet excited state lifetime is in the sub-millisecond range when C_{60} is incorporated into zeolites HY and MCM-41. Single wall carbon nanotubes, which are structurally similar to fullerenes, have also been embedded into the pores of mesoporous silica. Moreover, this composite is able to generate singlet oxygen in D_2O. Many similar methods have been developed to incorporate fullerenes into the micro- or meso-porous materials.

Semiconductor nanoparticles such as TiO_2, ZnO, etc., are known as effective photocatalysts. Recently, these materials were shown to be capable of generating singlet oxygen by monitoring the photooxidation of methyl oleate and 2,2,6,6- tetramethyl-4-piperidone. Xu et al.prepared the hypocrellin B-chelated TiO_2 composite (HB-TiO_2) and found that the chelate had a high efficiency of singlet oxygen generation under irradiation of visible light.

The generation of singlet oxygen in HB-TiO_2 was attributed to an energy transfer and electron transfer mechanism, i.e. electron transfer from the excited HBTiO_2 chelate to the conduction band of TiO_2 and energy transfer between the excited triplet state of the chelate and ground state oxygen:

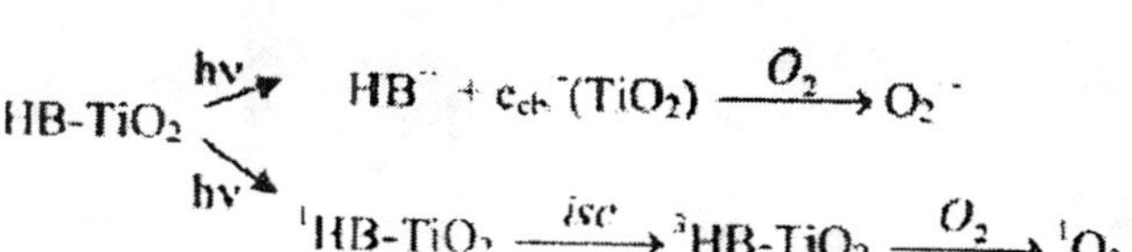

Feigelson et al.studied the photo-degradation of organic pollutants and found that the photocatalysed degradation was enhanced by the combined use of both dye and TiO_2, probably via the involvement of singlet oxygen.

Nanostructured Materials

Today, nanoparticles are distributed widely and are considered to be the building blocks in planet formation processes. Biological systems have built up inorganic-organic nanocomposite structures to improve the mechanical properties or to improve the optical, magnetic and chemical sensing in living species. As an example, nacre from the mollusc shell is a biologically formed lamellar ceramic, which exhibits structural robustness despite the brittle nature of its constituents.

Functional systems are characterised by complex sensing, self repair, information transmission and storage and other functions all based on molecular building blocks. Examples of these complex structures for structural purposes are teeth, such as shark teeth, which consist of a composite of biomineralised fluorapatite and organic compounds. These structures result in the unique combination of hardness, fracture toughness and sharpness, in Figure 1.

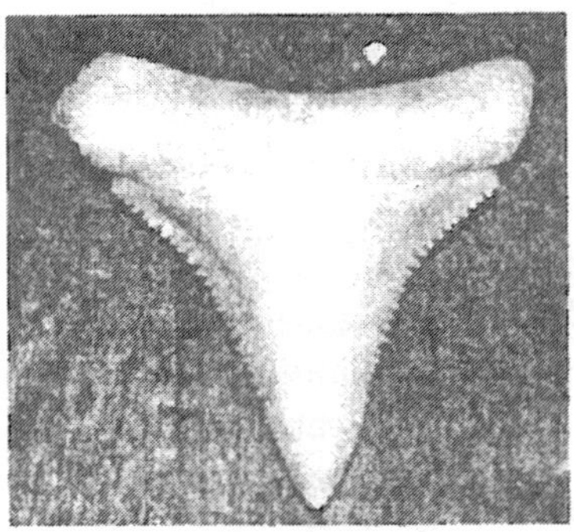

Figure 1. Example of a nanostructure found in nature: shark tooth with unique mechanical properties. The overall dimension of the tooth can reach several cm.

Another example for a biological nanostructure is opal which exhibits unique optical properties.

The self cleaning effects of the surfaces of the lotus flower have been attributed to the combined micro- and nanostructure which in combination with hydrophobic groups give the surface a water and dirt repellent behaviour. In the past few years, numerous companies have realised products resembling the surface morphology and chemistry of the lotus flower such as paint, glass surface and ceramic tiles with dirt repellent properties. The realisation that nature can provide the model for improved engineering has created a research field called bio-mimicking or bio-inspired materials science. It has been possible to process these ceramic-organic nanocomposite structures which provide new technological opportunities and potential for applications.

The biomimetic growth of synthetic fluorapatite in the laboratory and promising new technical applications of these nanomaterials are envisioned. Other man-made nanostructures were manufactured for their attractive optical properties, such as the colloidal gold particles in glass as seen in medieval church windows. While plentiful man made materials with nanostructures have been in use for a long time (partially without knowing it) a change of the scientific and technological approach can be identified over the past two decades.

This change can be related to a few key ideas and discoveries: the idea of assembling nanostructures from atomic, molecular or nanometer sized building blocks, the discovery of new forms of carbon, i.e., fullerenes and carbon nanotubes, and the development of scanning probe microscopy, such as scanning tunneling microscopy (STM) and atomic force microscopy (AFM). With the visionary goals many researchers worldwide have worked intensively on the development of novel or improved synthesis methods, new and better characterisation techniques and the measurement and the design of the properties of nanostructured materials. In this paper some aspects of the immensely wide field will be described. However, as the field of nanostructured materials is very broad including all classes of materials as well as composites it is not possible and not attempted to consider all developments and all research groups and industries.

Synthesis Method

The microstructure and properties of nanostructured materials depend in an extreme manner on the synthesis method as well as on the processing route. Therefore, it is of utmost importance to select the most appropriate technique for preparation of nanomaterials with desired properties and property combinations.

Synthesis techniques can be divided into bottom-up and top-down approaches. The top-down approach starts with materials with conventional crystalline microstructures, typically metals and alloys, and defects such as dislocations and point defects are introduced by severe plastic deformation such as in equal channel pressing. The recrystallisation of the material leads to finer and finer grain sizes and under certain processing conditions to nanostructured materials.

The advantage of these approaches is the fact that bulk nanostructured materials with theoretical density can be prepared. An alternative to obtain theoretical dense materials is the pulsed electrodeposition method developed by Erb and El-Sherik which yields nanocrystalline strips, however, only with thicknesses of several hundred microns. The bottom-up approach includes many different techniques which are based on liquid or gas phase processes. Classically, wet chemical processes such as precipitation and sol-gel have been employed to obtain nanoparticles, however, with the disadvantage of severe agglomeration. In the gas phase metallic and ceramic nanoparticles have been synthesised by using Inert Gas

Condensation, Flame Pyrolysis and chemical vapour based processes. The major microstructural features in preparing nanoparticles for subsequent use are: nanometer sized primary particles with narrow size distributions, minimum amount of agglomeration, good crystallinity, etc. Two techniques, chemical vapour synthesis (CVS) in the gas phase and electrodeposition under oxidising conditions (EDOC) in the liquid phase, together with the resulting microstructures will be presented in more detail and the advantages and disadvantages be discussed.

CVS is based on chemical vapour deposition (CVD) for the synthesis of thin films and coatings by the decomposition of metalorganic precursors. Whether thin films are deposited by heterogeneous „nucleation or nanoparticles are formed in the gas phase by homogeneous nucleation is determined by the residence time of the precursor in the hot zone of the reactor.

The most important parameters determining the growth regime and the particle size are the total pressure, the precursor partial pressure and the temperature of the reaction zone. When two precursors are used, the precursor delivery can be modified in the following way:

— two precursors are introduced simultaneously into the reaction zone yielding doped nanoparticles (i.e. alumina doped zirconia);

— two precursors are introduced into two concentric reaction tubes, reacted to form nanoparticles and then mixed in the gas phase to yield a nanocomposite structure (i.e., alumina mixed with zirconia) and

— in the first reaction zone the first precursor is decomposed to form nanoparticles by homogeneous nucleation which are subsequently coated in a second reaction zone by introducing the second precursor under conditions which favour CVD deposition (i.e., alumina surface coated zirconia).

Figure 2 shows a high resolution electron image of polymer coated titania nanoparticles where the crystalline titania core can be clearly distinguished from the amorphous organic shell on several grains.

The modification of the surfaces of nanoparticles allows the improvement of dispersibility in various aqueous and organic solvents which is important for many ceramic processing steps and for technical applications of dispersions. Additionally, the inorganic core/polymer shell structure allows the preparation of polymer nanocomposites with excellent separation between the inorganic nanoparticles.

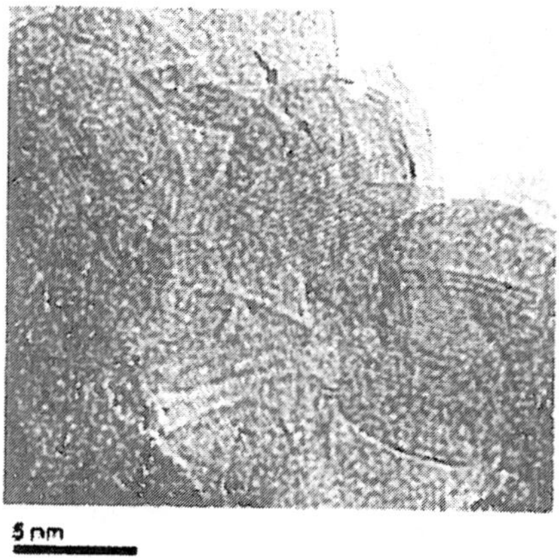

Figure 2. High resolution TEM of titania nanoparticles (crystalline core) coated with an amorphous polymeric shell

A further variation by exact control of all synthesis parameters allows the growth of thick nanocrystalline coatings on dense and porous substrates. Depending on the substrate temperature the porosity of the coating can be changed over a wide range up to theoretical density. This intermediate stage, called CVD/CVS, has been successfully used to deposit a nanocrystalline coating of yttrium stabilised zirconia on porous anode substrates for high temperature solid oxide fuel cell applications.

The molecular dynamics (MD) simulation technique to obtain details of the processes during particle formation, agglomeration, and sintering. As the nanoparticles contain only a limited number of atoms, it is possible to study diffusion and rearrangement processes leading to aggregation and particle growth. Atomistic simulations are extremely useful in describing the initial stages of sintering and equilibrium particle morphologies which determine the final structure and properties of nanoparticles prepared in the gas phase.

Figure 3 shows the time evolution of Ge-nanoparticles, the aggregation and sintering during condensation in an Ar-gas. In order to be able to simulate this process, high concentrations of atoms in the gas phase have to be employed in order to be able to adapt the time scale to the computing capabilities. A scaling law was established which allows the comparison to experimental conditions. MD-simulations have been employed for many other processes in nanocrystalline materials such as the calculation of the elastic properties of nanocrystalline nickel and the „plastic and superplastic deformation of nanocrystalline metals and the atomistic structure and energies of grain boundaries in nanocrystalline metals.

The EDOC process was developed to synthesise nanocrystalline oxides with improved properties as compared to oxides obtained by precipitation and sol-gel routes. In particular, it was attempted to improve the control on size and size distribution, the dispersibility and the possibility to modify the surfaces of the nanocrystalline powders. In the EDOC process an anode, i.e., metallic Zn, is dissolved in an organic electrolyte with an organic conducting salt by applying a voltage. The Zn^{2+}-ions migrate to an inert cathode, are discharged and subsequently oxidised by means of bubbling air through the electrolyte, thus forming ZnO-nanoparticles. The conducting salt has the additional role to prevent continued growth of the nanoparticles and their agglomeration.

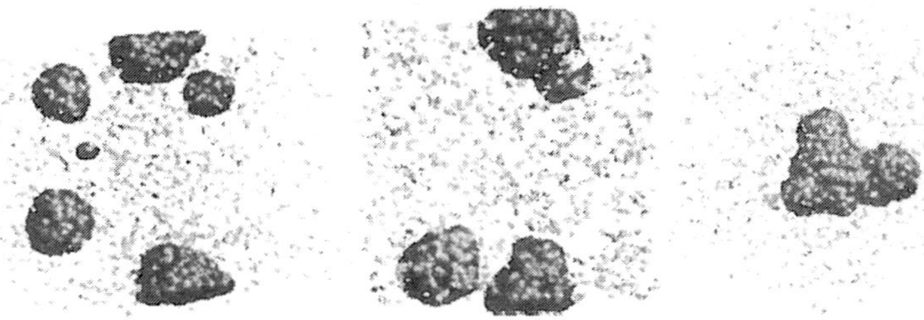

Figure 3. Result of a Molecular Dynamics (MD) simulation showing the evolution of Ge-nanoparticles in Argas for 0,96 ps a), 1,29 ps b) and 3.36 ns c)

After filtration, the nanoparticles can be further modified or functionalised by exchanging the organic shell by other molecules to adapt the surface chemistry to other chemical environments. Other metal oxides have been prepared by EDOC, such as SnO_2, TiO_2, and ZrO_2 as well as doped oxides. Compared to other wet chemical processes, the EDOC nanopowders exhibit superior dispersibility in solvents. In many processes, the microstructure, the morphology, the size and size distribution, the agglomeration and the elemental distribution on the scale of the nanoparticles can be controlled. In addition, it is possible to control the surface chemistry and thus to control the reactivity of the nanomaterials with the environment. The availability of versatile synthesis techniques is the prerequisite for materials design on the nanometer scale.

Characterisation of Nanostructures Materials

The characterisation of nanostructured materials in the form of thin films, nanoparticles and bulk structures demands special techniques which allow for the structural and chemical analysis with a sufficient lateral resolution. Consequently, special characterisation techniques are required besides the standard techniques available to materials science.

The extremely high surface and interface areas have to be considered. Experimental difficulties such as oxidation/ reaction at surfaces, the disordered structure at the grain boundaries and other internal interfaces and substantial porosity can be present in these materials. The specific surface area of nanopowders with average grain sizes below 10 nm can rise to several hundred m^2/g. That is, two to three grams of nanopowders which fit into a small volume of a few cm^3 can have the same surface area as an entire football field.

Therefore, nanocrystalline powders are considered to be excellent candidates for catalysis and gas sensing devices. The crystallinity even in materials with average particle/grain sizes below 10 nm is very good.

Other standard characterisation techniques were not capable to resolve the thin surface layer with a different composition. It should be pointed out that a change of the synthesis conditions resulted in a homogeneously doped oxide. The knowledge of the detailed elemental distribution is extremely important in order to establish the structure-property relationships and to understand the complex behaviour of nanomaterials. Other frequently used characterisation techniques include nitrogen adsorption for porosity and pore size distribution, small angle neutron scattering (SANS) for particle and pore size determination, [surface analytical techniques such as Xray photoelectron spectroscopy (XPS), ion scattering spectroscopy (ISS), nuclear techniques such as Mössbauer spectroscopy and many more depending on the details of interest.

The interest in nanostructured materials arises from the fact that due to the small size of the building blocks and the high density of interfaces (surfaces, grain and phase boundaries) and other defects such as pores, new physical and chemical effects are expected or known properties can be improved substantially. In addition, the novel processing routes allow a bottom-up approach in materials design. In the following are the several examples of properties which are altered dramatically in the nanometer regime are presented:

Nanoparticles

The main reason for using nanoparticles is the large surface area which will be favourable for gas-solid interactions such as in catalysis and gas sensing. In addition, nanoparticles are the building blocks of bulk nanocrystalline materials, i.e., ceramics, prepared by sintering. In catalysis, alumina with a high specific surface area is used extensively as support material for catalytically active noble metals.

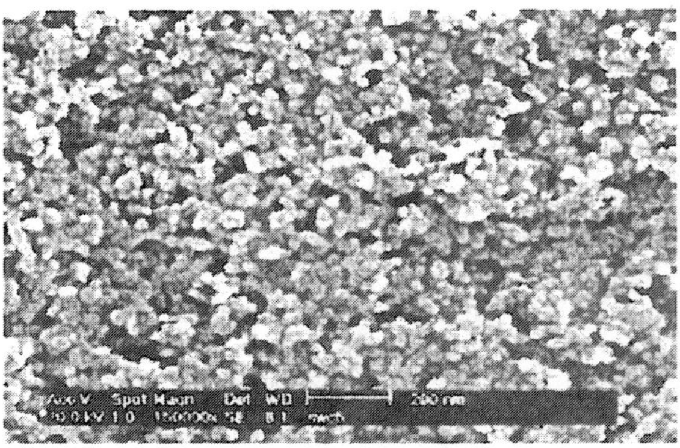

Figure 4. High resolution SEM demonstrating the nanocrystalline structure with nanoporosity of the titania layer prepared by screen printing and sintering.

However, the role of the substrate material was not studied extensively. For several systems it was found that the influence of the substrate material on the catalytic performance in gas reactions, such as complete oxidation of methane, can be quite drastic. Another application of the surface reactivity of nanocrystalline oxides is in gas sensing devices. As an example, nanocrystalline titania prepared by CVS was used for gas sensing.

A typical experimental arrangement consists of an alumina substrate with an interdigitised finger-like metallic structure on one side and a resistive heater on the other side. This allows the deposition of the sensing material and the measurement of the resistivity as a function of the atmosphere. As shown in Figure 4 a nanocrystalline coating was obtained by screen printing a dispersion and a moderate sintering step at 600 °C for one hour.

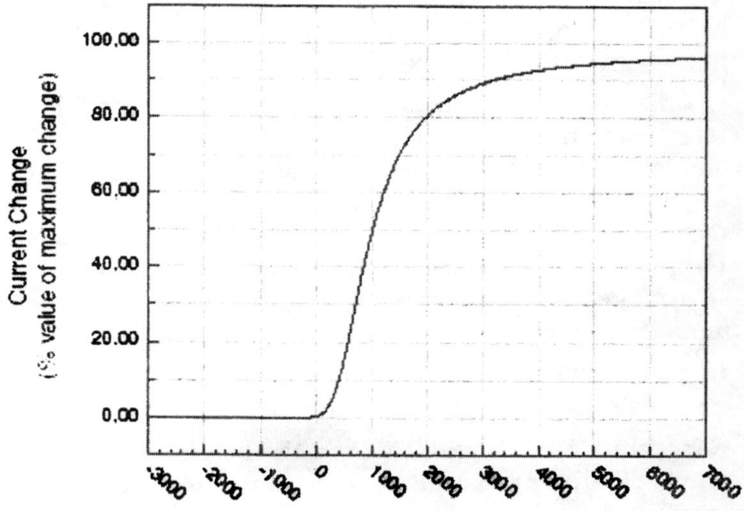

Figure 5. Change of the signal of a sensor made of nanocrystalline titania in response to a change of the oxygen concentration in the atmosphere

The film is highly porous which allows the reactive gases to reach all surfaces of the sensing material in short times. All grains are in good contact to each other and sintering necks with well developed grain boundaries are formed. This is an important prerequisite for the measurement of the resistance of the film.

In Figure 5, the reaction to a change of atmosphere, i.e. exposure to a different concentration of oxygen, is extremely fast, with response times (between 10 and 90 % of the total signal) in the order of less than three seconds. This compares to the response times of several minutes for commercial sensors which are based on dense thin films deposited by physical vapour deposition such as sputtering.

The fast response time is an attractive feature of the nanostructured gas sensors and is a direct consequence of the nanocrystalline and nanoporous structure. Other interesting physical effects are observed in metallic nanoparticles such as FePt prepared by a wet chemical process described by Sun et al.

Fe50Pt50 nanoparticles in the size range from three to seven nanometers can be prepared with an organic coating of oleic acid which prevents the oxidation even when exposing the nanoparticles to air. The organic shell also serves to keep the nanoparticles at a molecular distance. Therefore, the nanoparticles are superparamagnetic and can be arranged on clean surfaces in regular arrays which opens interesting applications for magnetic storage devices.

Nanoceramics

Nanoceramics with grain sizes in the range of 10 to 100 nm are typically prepared by consolidation, i.e., uniaxial compaction, cold isostatic pressing and sintering in air or vacuum. The green density, i.e. the density after initial compaction, reaches values of 40 to 50 % of the theoretical value for CVS nanopowders. The most striking feature in the case of CVS powders is the transparency of the compacted pellet. This is a direct consequence of the narrow size distribution of pores in the material which can only occur if no agglomerates are present in the as prepared powder or are broken up during the consolidation step.

The dependence of the green density with increasing compaction pressure does not show any change in slope which would be an indication of breakage of agglomerates. The size distribution shows only pores smaller than the primary particle size. This feature is a prerequisite for a good sinterability of the CVS powders which has been found to occur in all nanoceramics under investigation (TiO_2, ZrO2, Y_2O_3, Al_2O_3, various doped oxides etc.) at temperatures well below ½ TM.

In the intermediate sintering steps at lower temperatures, the pores disappear but no excessive pore growth is observed. However, in pure ceramics grain growth occurs when the density exceeds 90 % of the theoretical value. This undesirable effect has been reduced by doping, surface doping (core-shell nanoparticles) and composite structures.

In the pure nanocrystalline zirconia extensive grain growth is observed at temperatures and in the fully dense ceramic (100 % TD) sintered at 1000 °C the average grain size is typically above 100 nm. Fully dense ceramics are also obtained for zirconia doped with 3 to 5 mol % alumina at grain sizes in the range of 40 to 50 nm. Further increase of the doping to 15 mol % further reduces the grain growth; however at a sintering temperature of 1000 °C the theoretical density is not reached.

At a higher doping level of 30 mol.-% alumina, the as prepared nanopowders are amorphous, crystallize at the sintering temperatures above 600 °C and show a phase separation. At this doping level the grain growth is suppressed most effectively as the grains grow only up to 30 nm even at 1200 °C. It should be mentioned that the crystallographic structure of as prepared pure zirconia with average grain size below 10 nm is monoclinic and tetragonal, while in the alumina doped samples the tetragonal structure is stabilised.

4

Nanotechnology for Social Transformation

Today most homes get Internet access at 28,000 to 56,000 bits per second. Within a few years a combination of new technologies for compressing information with bigger capacity and entirely new approaches may move household access up to at least six million bits per second, and some believe we may reach the 110 million bits needed for uncompressed motion pictures. An amazing range of opportunities have and will continue to open up as our communications capabilities continue to improve and grow. The application of nanoscience into nanotechnology will introduce disruptive technologies into our lives and, therefore, into the economy.

Large corporations have been very successful at improving a product or service they are already providing. While working to improve existing products, their new science will also create disruptive technologies. It is very hard for corporations to incorporate disruptive technologies. When more research in the area of nanoscience is done, you will not only have a disruption in scientific assumptions that lead to new discoveries, you will see the nanoscience being applied to new economic sectors in ways that cannot be anticipated.

The application of nanoscience into real marketable products will be much more rapid than we saw with the

Internet or other revolutionary technologies. When computing began, we had a remarkably primitive venture capital entrepreneurial system. As nanoscience is translated into nanotechnology it will be entering a very aggressive, very well financed, very experienced entrepreneurial venture world, which will be hungrily looking for the next big deal. So the rate of translation into new startups and new markets should be orders of magnitude faster than it was for computing. Let's turn for a moment away from placing nanoscience in the context of historical trends and look more at the uniqueness of the science itself. Nanoscience is the base of how the world operates.

There may be many layers below the atom, but for practical purposes an atom is an excellent base element. Taking the information nanoscience is teaching us about atoms and their activity and applying it has dramatic implications. Take the environment for example. We can learn to grow products using less energy and with less waste by product. It may mean that if we use dramatically less energy, then the projections and assumptions of current environmental debates, like Kyoto, are totally obsolete. It certainly means in biology that as we get better nano instrumentation and research tools, and if our nanoscale observational capabilities continue to grow, our capacity to deal with the complexities of human biology are going to go up dramatically and may not even be only orders of magnitude, but a different world of capabilities. The potential of nano-level brain wave scanning is a new frontier in mind science. The application towards improving our education techniques alone are enormous. America is certainly not the only country working on advancing the field of nanoscience. The Japanese are working on it. The Europeans are working on it. In a decade you are going to see the Indians and the Chinese with a very major effort in this area because it will become obvious that it is so profoundly important. Technological and social systems shape each other. The same is true on a larger scale.

Technologies, as gunpowder, the printing press, the railroad, the telegraph, and the Internet have shown, shape society in quite profound ways. But equally, social systems, in the form of government, the courts, formal and informal organisations, social movements, professional networks, local communities, market institutions, and so forth, shape, moderate, and redirect the raw power of technologies.

The whole process might best be thought of as one of "co-evolution," with society and technology mutually shaping each other. In considering one, then, it's important to keep the other in mind. Given the crisp edges of technology and the fuzzy ones of society, it certainly isn't easy to grasp the two simultaneously. But grasp both you must, if you want to see where we are all going or design the means to get there. Nanotechnology offers a rather different example of how the future can frighten us. For this, which involves engineering at a molecular level, both the promise and the threat seem unmeasurable. But they are unmeasurable for a good reason.

The technology is still almost wholly on the drawing board. Two of its main proponents, Ralph Merkle and Eric Drexler, worked with us at Xerox PARC. They built powerful nano-CAD tools and then ran simulations of the resulting designs. The simulations showed definitively that nano devices are theoretically feasible. But theoretically feasible and practically feasible are two different things.

And as yet, no-one has laid out in any detail a route from lab-based simulation to practical development. So here the road ahead is unpredictable not because of an unexpected curve, but because the road itself still lacks a blueprint. In the absence of a plan, it's certainly important to ask the right questions.

Can nanotechnology actually fulfil its great potential in tasks ranging from data storage to pollution control? And can it do such things without itself getting out of control? But no one should worry too much about the road's maintenance crew when the road itself has yet to be surveyed. If the lesson of genetic engineering means anything, however, even though useful nano-systems are probably decades away, planners would do well to consult and educate the public early on. Worries about robotics suggest that here, too, the route has been added to our mapbooks long before the road itself has actually been built.

Take for example the much-talked about "bots"—the software equivalent of robots, which search, communicate, negotiate, or act as agents on the Internet. They, it has been claimed, do many human tasks much better than humans and so indeed might come to replace us all. In fact, bots are useful because they are quite different from humans. They are good (and useful) for those tasks that humans do badly. They are often quite inept at tasks that humans do well—tasks that call for judgement, taste, discretion, initiative, or tacit understanding. So bots are probably better thought of as complementary systems, not rivals to humanity. Consequently, though they will undoubtedly get better at what they do, such development will not necessarily make bots more human. They are in effect being driven down a different road.

Certainly, the possibility of a collision needs to be kept in mind. In particular, we need to know who will be held responsible when autonomous bots inadvertently cause collisions—as well they might. But we probably need not look for significant collisions around the next few bends. Are more conventional robots—the villains of science fiction—any greater threat to society? We doubt it. PARC research on self-aware, reconfigurable polybots has pushed at new robotic frontiers. When these are combined with our MEMS (microelectical mechanical systems) research, they point the way to morphing robots whose ability to move and change shape will make them important for such things as search and rescue in conditions where humans cannot or dare not go.

Nonetheless, for all their cutting-edge agility, these robots are a long way from making good free-form dancing partners. In particular, like all robots (but unlike good dancing partners), they lack true conversational skills. The chatty manner of C3-PO still lies well beyond machines. Indeed, what talking robots or computers do, though it may appear similar, is quite different from human talk.

Talking machines travel routes designed specifically to avoid the full complexities of situated human language. True, robots may still seem quite intelligent. Yet such intelligence is profoundly hampered by their inability to learn in any significant way. (This failing has apparently led Toyota, after heavy investment in robotics, to consider replacing robots with humans on many production lines.) And without learning, simple common sense will lie beyond robots for a long time to come. Indeed, despite years of startling advances and innumerable successes like the chess-playing Big Blue, computer science is still almost as far as it ever was from building a machine with the learning abilities, linguistic competence, common sense, or social skills of a five year old.

So, like bots, robots will no doubt become increasingly useful. But, as a result of tunnel design, they will probably also become increasingly frustrating to use. In that regard they may indeed seem anti-social. But they are unlikely to be anti-social in the way of science fiction fantasies, with robot armies exterminating human society. Indeed, the thing that handicaps robots most of all is their lack of a social existence. For it is our social existence as humans that shapes how we speak, learn, think, and develop common sense.

All forms of artificial life (whether bugs or bots) will remain primarily a metaphor for -rather than a threat to— society at least until they manage to enter a debate, form a choir, take a class, survive a committee meeting, join a union, build a lab, pass a law, engineer a cartel, reach an agreement, or summon a constitutional convention. It is these critical social mechanisms that allow society to shape its future. It is through planned, collective action that society forestalls expected consequences (such as Y2K) and responds to unexpected events (such as epidemics). Why does the threat of a cunning, replicating robot society look so close from one perspective, yet from another quite distant?

Other forces are keeping us together despite the availability of great communications technology. So, for example, whether communications technology has killed distance or not, people curiously just can't stay away from the social hotbed of modern communications technology, Silicon Valley. Importantly, the Ds do indicate that the old ties that bound communities, organisations, and institutions are being picked apart by technologies.

A simple, linear reading then suggests that these will now simply fall apart. A more complex reading, taking into account the multiple forces at work, offers a different picture. Undoubtedly some communities, organisations, and institutions will disappear. But others will reconfigure themselves. So, while many nationally powerful corporations have shrivelled to insignificance, some have transformed themselves into far more powerful transnational firms. And while some forms of community may be dying, others bolstered by technology are growing stronger. Two hundred years ago, Thomas Malthus, assuming that human society and agricultural technology developed on separate paths, gloomily predicted that society was growing so fast, it would starve itself to death. A hundred years later, H.G. Wells similarly assumed that society and technology were developing independently. Wells, however, like many today, saw technology outstripping society. So he predicted that technology's relentless juggernaut would unfeelingly crush great swathes of society.

Like Joy, both Malthus and Wells issued important warnings, alerting society to dangers it faced. But by their actions, Malthus and Wells helped prevent the very future they were so certain would come about. These self-unfulfilling prophecies failed see that, once warned, society could wittingly and unwittingly galvanise itself into action. It could develop agricultural technology to increase the food supply dramatically. And it could develop social constraints to temper the exuberance of technology.

Of course, this social action in the face of threats showed that Malthus and Wells were most at fault in their initial assumption. Social and technological systems do not develop independently. The two evolve together in complex feedback loops, wherein each drives, restrains, and accelerates change in the other. Of course, once the social system is factored back into prognostication, the road ahead looks much more convoluted. It is difficult to know what might lie beyond the next bend and which way it is best to turn. But this much can certainly be said.

Communities, organisations, and institutions are indeed the main brake by which society slows the destructive power of technology (and, indeed, accelerates its advantages). As new technologies emerge, old institutional forms inevitably prove inadequate. Consequently, society has to develop new ones. Robert Putnam's new book, Bowling Alone, shows this process in action.

The dawn of the 1900s brought unprecedented technological advances, including the introduction of cars, airplanes, telephones, radio, and domestic power. With these advances came first, unprecedented social disruption, and then a remarkable period of legal, government, business, and societal innovation -stretching from the introduction of anti-trust legislation to the creation of the American Bar Association, the Sierra Club, the American Red Cross, the NAACP, and the YWCA. Society, implicitly and explicitly, took stock of itself and its technologies and acted accordingly. The resulting social innovation has left marks quite as deep as those left by technological innovation.

To deal with recent unprecedented technological change and the disruption it may cause, we will need similarly extensive and unprecedented social reflection and similar organisational and institutional creativity. New social forces, however, take time to develop. And the more people ignore them, the more time development will need. But technological acceleration gives us ever less time. So first the public at large needs to become engaged in these debates and to understand that society and institutions are part of the whole picture—something technological tunnel vision obscures. That way we can all see where the brake lies.

Then we need to consider how an educated public can help construct new social institutions. That way, we can start to apply the brake where necessary. The consequences of economic and informational globalisation, combined with emerging demographic changes, will bring new kinds of threats to national and international security. Individual national security in a world of global collapse will not be tenable. We will have to seek national security in a context of global security. An example of a technology area where we as a nation did not work the entire life cycle problem is that of nuclear power. By not solving the nuclear waste disposal problem adequately as we developed the power generating systems, we left ourselves with a sizeable unresolved societal problem. The analysis of the conditions for global and national security leads us to consider three broad issues. The first revolves around the condition of the planet and its natural resources. We'll refer to this as the "green" issue involving foremost water, energy, and the environment.

The second broad issue, which we call "red," is that of the human condition, with health at its centre. These first two areas are potential sources of conflict that can drive global insecurity if unresolved. If it fulfils its promise, nanotechnology can enable solutions to many problems within these "red" and "green" issues areas.

The third issue—which we call "black"—is military, for example as in the area of bio-warfare. Military advances enabled by nanotechnology, if used wisely in the interests of global security, can help to maintain a just peace. If used for purposes of aggression and domination, they can pose a substantial risk to all.

Natural Resources

There appears to be an increased potential for conflict as a rapidly growing world population tries to sustain itself with limited natural resources. The disparity in wealth between developed and developing nations, in combination with the uneven distribution of natural resources, remains a threat to the stability of states and of the international system. With the advent of modern manufacturing, advanced technologies, and the information age, the importance of natural resources has been reduced for developed nations. But, especially for developing nations, the availability and control of critical resources such as oil, water, and food on an increasingly crowded planet remain among the major sources of long-term insecurity.

It is possible that nanotechnology will contribute to easing resource disparities. Potential areas of impact include new materials, potable water, new energy sources, and sustainable environmental processes. The availability of water resources remains one of the big issues for potential insecurity around the globe.

As the World Commission on Water for the 21st Century has pointed out, What is obvious is that progress, especially in developing countries, is much too slow, and that unless there are drastic changes, water shortages and environmental degradation will become the norm. More people than ever will be added to some of the areas of the planet that are already most vulnerable socially, economically, and environmentally.

Low cost techniques for water purification, self-cleaning, evaporation reduction, and desalination could have tremendous impact by providing adequate supplies of clean water. A major driver for regional conflict might be removed. Adequate water supplies are necessary not only for human health, but also to assure the availability of food for the developing world's growing population. The potential impact of nanotechnology on water supplies is hard to predict at this time, but several areas of significant opportunity come to mind.

Affordable, engineered membranes that incorporated a self-cleaning process to avoid fouling could be used for large-scale desalination, which would go far in solving the water resource problem. While this technology would be a significant leap from current capabilities, the ability to tailor nanoscale membranes in combination with advances in self-assembly processes make it one to watch. In a variation on this concept, the ability to create membranes with molecular receptors that preferentially extract heavy metals and other pollutants is making progress in Department of Energy and other research laboratories.

Another potential means of preserving water resources, particularly for agriculture, may be the control of evaporation through largescale application of nano-engineered films or membranes.

Management of water resources is a good example of where the life cycle systems approach should be taken to assure that the technologies employed do not leave unanticipated environmental problems in their wake. A second "green" issue of growing long-term concern for global security is that of energy resources and their use. Although proven reserves of oil and natural gas are large, heavy energy usage by the developed countries, combined with the demographic and development trends of the third world, will eventually put pressure on the supplies.

In the meantime, the burning of fossil fuels has at least the possibility of substantially degrading the global environment. Nanotechnology may be able to ameliorate energy problems both on the supply side and on the use side. In the near term, new, high-strength nanostructured magnets, nanolubricants, and other improved materials may greatly improve motor efficiency.

In the long term, nanoengineered fuel cells, biocatalysts for crops for food or biomass fuels, or nanostructured photovoltaic films may permit cheaper alternative energy sources. If the efficiency of photovoltaics were improved by a factor of two from the 20 to the 40% range at comparable costs—something that is theoretically possible—the role of solar energy would grow substantially. Likewise, if the oceans could be used for growing biomass fuels or harvesting energy through nano-biotechnology advances, significant increases in global energy supplies would result.

Systems life cycle thinking is particularly important in addressing the energy issue because of the coupling of energy and the environment. For example, if artificially engineered plants that produce ready-to-use energy become possible, at an early stage we will have to address issues akin to those now arising from the field of genetically engineered foods. But, properly designed, systems using such technologies as photovoltaics, engineered photosynthesis, factory process heat reuse, or agricultural fuel production could lead to a world of sustainable energy, agriculture, and climate. Such an "open system biosphere" would clearly have enormous implications for global security.

Nanoscience may also enable new materials and technologies that reduce economic dependence on other kinds of natural resources. The dependence of nations on extraction resources might be altered if common materials could achieve the functions of rarer and more costly materials. We refer to the ability to nanostructure a material for specific desired properties not found in its usual forms as nano-alchemy. In essence one is creating a new material by nanostructuring rather than by merely changing the chemistry.

Common materials in the form of nanoscale clusters have been demonstrated to take on specific chemical catalytic properties, superior to those of more expensive catalysts. At this point we cannot predict whether nano-alchemy will apply broadly, or at what cost, but it is possible to envision large changes in how industries work. Then the relative wealth and power of nations could change, as could some of the contributing sources of international conflict.

Human Condition

The human condition—the "red" issue—also must be considered in an analysis of the potential societal implications of nanotechnology. In the United States the proportion of the population at retirement age is increasing and will continue to grow rapidly over the next several decades, with a corresponding decrease in the available fraction of workers in the society. This trend has been strong in the developed countries where the birth rate has declined significantly, leading to low or even negative population growth, while life expectancy has been increasing. With an aging population, an increasingly large fraction of national and personal resources is being spent on health care. Desirable goals for an aging population include maintaining productivity longer, providing affordable health care, and deploying assistive technologies that maintain independence longer.

Achieving these goals would greatly reduce the burden that an unhealthy, dependent older generation would place on younger citizens. The economic and social benefits to the nation would be great. We consider here just two possible connections to nanoscience and nanotechnology: assistive means to maintain physical independence and tools to support cognitive capability. In the area of assistive devices, the ability to see and to maintain mobility could contribute significantly to maintaining productivity and physical independence.

Advances in micro and nanotechnologies hold promise for contributing to a wide range of assistive solutions, from prosthetic limbs that adjust to the changes in the body, to more biocompatible implants, to artificial retinas or ears. Other opportunities lie in the area of neural prosthesis and the "spinal patch," a device envisioned to repair damage from spinal injuries. In the area of cognition, revolutionary technical advances could have great impact on individual productivity and independence. We do not understand the workings of the brain well enough to predict with any confidence that assistive devices will actually work. However, rapid advances in the intersecting nano-, information science, and biological sciences seem to promise significant surprises.

Possible results include devices that enhance learning, cognition, judgement and decision making. Devices that helped people with dementia—nearly a third of the population over 85—could have great impact. At the same time concerns about the use of artificial or assisted cognition for social control must be addressed. As with the potential benefits of technologies relating to natural resource use, those relating to human health and quality of life also could end up being available only to small segments of the world's population.

Today we talk of the "digital divide"; tomorrow it may be the "nano divide." Only the right combinations of public policy and free enterprise will lead to maximising the societal benefits of the new technologies.

Societal Transformation and Nanotechnology

Technological innovation sustains a fundamental tension of civilisation—the tension between humanity's quest for more control over nature and the future, and our equally strong desire for stability and predictability in the present. Luddites were not against technology per se. They were against losing their jobs, and so they smashed the power looms that had put them out of work.

The change wrought by technological advance continually remakes society, and this transformational process is on the one hand central to the dynamic that is commonly libelled "progress," and yet on the other is a source of continual destabilisation and dislocation as experienced by individuals, communities, institutions, nations, and cultures. In the age of science and technology (S&T), the federal government has increasingly become the prime catalyst for scientific advance and technological innovation.

At the same time, modern government is also continually responding to and managing the transformational power of science and technology. Yet there is little effort to understand the relation between these two critical activities—advancing knowledge and innovation, and responding to their impacts—or to link them in a way that can enhance the value and capability of each. A single technological innovation can remake the world. When the metal stirrup finally migrated from Asia to Western Europe in the 8th century, society was transformed to its very roots. For the first time, the energy of a galloping horse could be directly transmitted to the weapon held by the man in the saddle—a combat innovation of devastating impact.

Because horses and tack were costly, they were possessed almost exclusively by landowners. Battlefield prowess and wealth were thus combined, and from this combination grew not just the traditions of a "warrior aristocracy" but the structure of European feudal society itself. The invention of the cotton gin in the late 18th century allowed a vast expansion of cotton cultivation in the American south—and directly fuelled a commensurate rise in the importation and use of slaves for plantation labour.

One hundred and fifty years later, the mechanical cotton picker suddenly rendered obsolete the jobs of millions of African American share croppers, and catalysed a 30-year migration of five million people out of the rural south and into the cities of the north. While the development of the mechanical cotton picker was no doubt inevitable, its proliferation was consciously accelerated by plantation owners who, fearing the rise of the civil rights movement, sought quickly to find a technological replacement for the existing system of exploitation labour upon which they were economically dependent.

These examples point not only to the power of new technologies to transform society, but to the comprehensive interconnectedness of technological change and the complex social structure of society. The invention of the stirrup as a battlefield tool was in some very intricate way connected to the development and expansion of feudalism in Europe; the evolution of agricultural technology for a single cash crop is indissolubly bound to the ongoing struggle to overcome the U.S. legacy of slavery, segregation, and bigotry.

More familiarly, a single class of technology—nuclear weapons—was a central determinant of geopolitical evolution after the end of World War II. Cars, television, air conditioning, and vaccinations have all stimulated foundational changes in society during the past century. Of course new technologies rarely emerge in isolation. The industrial revolution is not just the story of harnessing steam power to factory production capability, but also the story of technological revolutions in transport, communication, construction, agriculture, resource extraction, and, of course, weapons development. These technological systems penetrated the innermost niches of society—home and family, school, workplace, community—and forced them to change. They also introduced completely new social phenomena, and stimulated the invention of completely new institutions. The industrial revolution created the macroeconomic phenomenon of unemployment.

Prior to the 19th century, even the most economically and politically advanced societies were dominantly agrarian and rural. For the majority of people, work was rooted in the home and the family. Vagaries of weather and transportation imposed irregularities and hardship, but most people and families harbored a di versity of skills that gave them independence from the marketplace and resilience to cope with a variety of challenges.

In hard times, resort to subsistence farming and barter was usually possible. Industrialisation and urbanisation linked workers far more closely to the larger economic market, while removing the need and ability for them to maintain the diverse skills necessary for survival in the pre-industrial world. The traditional connection between manufacturing and agriculture in the home was sundered by new economic organisation and by geography. Labour itself became a commodity, subject to the same fluctuations and influences as other commodities.

During an economic downturn, factories fired people or closed down entirely. For the first time, workers could not easily respond to changing economic conditions by switching to a different type of work or moving to a subsistence mode. As technological innovation interacts with society to create new phenomena, such as unemployment, society also responds by developing new types of institutions and response mechanisms. Today we can recognise the problem of unemployment as central to a diversity of social, political, and economic structures and activities ranging from the organisation of labour to insurance safety nets to educational programmes to immigration policy.

Unemployment rates are a key indicator of economic health, and a key determinant of political behaviour. National and international economic policies focus strongly on managing unemployment, even as theoretical investigations seek to clarify the relation between unemployment rates and other key attributes of modern economies. The general point is that transformational technology represents one variable in a complex assemblage of dynamic, interrelated societal activities.

Decision making processes tend to address each of these activities in isolation from the others, e.g., conduct of research and development (R&D), dissemination of innovation products, development of regulations, reform of institutions. Concerted action occurs when a given innovation stimulates enough transformation to demand a response from other sectors of society. This response then triggers additional changes, which in turn demand further modulation. The process is reactive, discontinuous, disruptive, and sequential—like billiards. The challenge is to move toward a process of technology-supported societal progress where different sectors and activities can continually coevolve in response to knowledge about one another's needs and constraints—like an ecosystem. We are not there yet.

Transforming the Present

A brief consideration of evolution of information technologies helps to bring this look at societal transformation into the present. Gutenberg's perfection of the printing press of course had enormous transformational impact, allowing the broad dissemination of written texts and consequent expansion of information—and literacy—that undermined the Church's hegemony over knowledge and culture, and helped promote the dissolution of medieval social structure.

The implications of the information and communication revolution on democracy itself are far from clear. On the one hand, proliferation of information dissemination networks means greater access by more people to more information—and a greater capacity to communicate one's ideas and preferences in democratic fora. Control of information by authoritarian governments is becoming increasingly futile, and organisation of democratic opposition increasingly enhanced, by new information technologies. But when this same capacity translates into 10,000 identical e-mail messages sent to a Member of Congress in support of a particular bill, one is hard-pressed to suggest that democracy is the beneficiary. Of particular concern is the recent increase in public referenda aimed at bypassing the legislative process.

The barriers to putting referenda on ballots have been enormously reduced by information and communication technologies that can be used to disseminate ideas and organise group action with relatively little effort. While on the one hand this type of direct democracy can be a refreshing antidote to sclerotic legislative process, on the other it is quite often devoid of any serious deliberative process or public discourse, reflecting perhaps the pique of one wellorganised interest group or individual, and the substantiation of a Warholian politics where anyone with access to a decent list-serve can lead a movement for a day. The implications of the information and communications revolution on the distribution of economic benefits in society are also problematic.

Does the troubling increase in wealth concentration that characterises both the U.S. and the global economy derive from the way that advanced technologies diffuse in market economies? Does the synergistic character of information and communication networks mean that disenfranchised populations and nations will find it increasingly difficult to participate in the spectacular economic growth that we have seen in the past decade? In other words, are the benefits of technology becoming increasingly appropriable by particular sectors of society, and is this in part an attribute embodied in new types of technological systems? Society is illprepared to answer such questions, let alone act on them in a knowledgeable manner.

Paradoxically, concerns about appropriability cut both ways. In the information society, the increasing ease of information dissemination may also threaten our system for protecting intellectual property and innovation. From pirated CD's sold on the streets of Shanghai to the advent (and apparent demise) of NAPSTER, the concept of intellectual property seems increasingly vulnerable. Are we looking to a future where such protection is no longer practically possible? Does a world without patents and copyrights seem unimaginable? More unimaginable than, say, the loss of monopoly over the written word would have seemed to the Church in 1450?

At issue here is not the value of change, but the path that change follows. What may look in retrospect like the march of progress may be experienced in real time as wrenching dislocation.

The Dickensian squalor of 19th century London remains a symbol of the human impacts of technological change. Faced with unprecedented societal transformations, the English government (as well as other European states) failed to develop effective policies that could accommodate the rapid transition from rural agrarian to urban industrial society. Today, the plight of many overpopulated developing nations is the post-industrial, global manifestation of the same failure. We see the fingerprints of societally transforming technological systems in the controversy over genetically modified organisms; in the morally reprehensible situation where 24 million HIV-positive sub-Saharan Africans cannot possibly afford AIDS drugs that are widely available in the affluent world; in the existence of 40 million Americans with no medical insurance; in the general inability of our public school systems to create a citizenry able to take advantage of the opportunities of the knowledge economy; in the challenges presented by the aging of our population; in the rising atmospheric carbon dioxide levels that symbolise 150 years of industrial dynamism.

Even the unprecedented rise of civil and ethnic conflict throughout the world in the past decade can be plausibly connected to technological transformation. Approaching this phenomenon from entirely different directions, the political scientists Samuel Huntington and Benjamin Barber each conclude that advanced communication and information technologies have created new fora for expressing ethnic identity and pursuing and strengthening cultural solidarity. Virtual communities, for example, can act to maintain identity over great distance, while also more efficiently garnering resources to support the expression of cultural goals.

The marriage of science and technology beginning in the latter part of the 19th century accelerated the process of innovation, and thus the process of societal transformation as well. If the industrial revolution played itself out in less than 200 years, the electronics revolution seems likely to have a working life of perhaps 75 years, while the biotechnology revolution, although hardly yet on its feet, is already prophesied to be supplanted by the nanotechnology revolution in the first half of the new century.

What type of transformations might this revolution have in store? Our point here is not to predict the future of nanotechnology and its impacts—an impossible goal—but to illustrate the direction and scale of thinking that will be necessary if we are to successfully manage the interaction of new knowledge and innovation with society. Nanotechnology is going to revolutionise manufacturing, health care, travel, energy supply, food supply, and warfare, then it is going, as well, to transform labour and the workplace, the medical system, the transportation and power infrastructure, the agricultural enterprise, and the military. Each one of these technology-dependent sectors is operated by and for human beings, who act within institutions and cultures, according to particular regulations, norms, and heuristics, all of which may reflect decades or even centuries of evolution and tradition. Not one of them will be "revolutionised" without significant difficulty.

The current chaos in our medical system is emblematic of this type of difficulty. In the near term, the current state of knowledge may suggest that the first wave of useful nanotechnologies will lie in the area of detection and sensing. The capacity to detect, precisely identify, and perhaps isolate single molecules, viruses, or other complex, nanoscale structures has broad application in such areas as medical diagnosis, forensics, national defence, and environmental monitoring and control. The potential for direct benefits is obvious; how might this evolving capacity influence society? When detection outpaces response capability—as it usually does—ethical and policy dilemmas inevitably arise. For example, it is already possible to identify genetic predisposition to certain diseases for which there are no known cures, or to diagnose congenital defects in fetuses for which the only cure is abortion. In the environmental realm, new technologies that detect pollutants at extremely low concentrations raise complex questions about risk thresholds and appropriate remediation standards.

The presence of tiny amounts of toxic materials in groundwater may justifiably raise alarm among the public even if the health risk cannot be assessed, and the technological capacity for remediation does not exist. These types of dilemmas may be expected to accelerate and proliferate with the advance of nanodetection technologies. Advances in sensing and detection may transform existing societal mechanisms and institutions that were designed to cope with uncertainty and incomplete or imprecise information.

Medical sensors that can, for example, "detect an array of medically relevant signals at high sensitivity and selectivity" promise to aid diagnosis and treatment of disease, but also to develop predictive health profiles of individuals.

Today, health and life insurance companies often use pre-existing conditions as a basis for denying or restricting coverage. The advent of nanodetection capabilities will considerably expand the information that insurance companies will want to use in making decisions about coverage.

The generation of new information might thus destabilise the risk-spreading approach that allows equitable delivery of social benefits to broad populations. How will society respond? Nanotechnology offers a dizzying range of potential benefits for military application. Recent history suggests that some of the earliest applications of nanotechnology will come in the military realm, where specific needs are well articulated, and a customer—the Department of Defence—already exists.

One area of desired nano-innovation lies in the "increased use of enhanced automation and robotics to offset reductions in military manpower, reduce risks to troops, and improve vehicle performance." How might progress in this realm interact with the current trend toward rising civilian casualties (in absolute terms and relative to military personnel) in armed conflict worldwide? As increased robotic capability is realised in warfare, will we enter an era when it is safer to be a soldier in wartime than a civilian? Such considerations are simple extrapolations of current trends in technological innovation and societal transformation.

More adventurous speculation is tempting but is perhaps best confined to science fiction novels. The question of public response to nanoinnovation, however, should not be avoided, even at this early stage. The ongoing experience of public opposition to old technologies such as nuclear power, new technologies such as genetically modified foods, and prospective technologies such as stem cell therapies, needs to be viewed as integral to the relationship between innovation and societal transformation.

Three observations are particularly relevant here. First, the impact of rapid technological innovation on people's lives is usually not consensual. Second, in the short term at least, the social changes induced by new technologies usually create both winners and losers. Third, rapid technological change can threaten the social structure, economic stability, and spiritual meaning that people strive in their lives to achieve.

As the nanotechnology revolution begins to unfold in all its promise and diversity, such issues are bound to express themselves. They should not be viewed as threats, or as manifestations of intellectual weakness or repugnant ideology. Rather, they need to be recognised as a central part of the human context for technological change. Now nanotechnology had made nearly anything possible, and so the cultural role in deciding what should be done with it had become far more important than imagining what could be done with it. When resources are allocated for R&D

programmes, the implications for complex societal transformation are not considered.

The fundamental assumption underlying the allocation process is that all societal outcomes will be positive, and that technological cause will lead directly to a desired societal effect. The literature promoting the National Nanotechnology Initiative expresses this view. The current policy approach thus addresses two elements:

— Conduct of Science and Technology

— Products of Science and Technology

These elements reflect the internal workings of the R&D enterprise. The fact that societal outcomes are not a serious part of the framework seems to derive from two beliefs: (1) that the science and technology enterprise has to be granted autonomy to chose its own direction of advance and innovation; and (2) that because we cannot predict the future of science or technological innovation, we cannot prepare for it in advance. These are oft-articulated arguments, not straw men. Yet the first is contradicted by reality, and the second is irrelevant. The direction of science and technology is in fact dictated by an enormous number of constraints. And preparation for the future obviously does not require accurate prediction; rather, it requires a foundation of knowledge upon which to base action, a capacity to learn from experience, close attention to what is going on in the present, and healthy and resilient institutions that can effectively respond or adapt to change in a timely manner.

5

Nanoscale Devices

Most research in single electron devices (SED) technology is fundamental and is distributed among universities funded by government agencies. A smaller body of application directed research exists in industrial laboratories; these are mostly in Japan. The field of magnetics has experienced increasing attention since giant magnetoresistance (GMR) in multilayered structures was discovered in 1988. In these structures ferromagnetic layers are quantum mechanically coupled across a 1-3 nm nonmagnetic metallic layer. GMR structures are under intense study for applications in hard disk heads, random access memory (RAM), and sensors. Several laboratories are investigating the physics of the transition of these layers, which are quantum mechanically confined in one dimension, to layered filaments in which there are one- and two-dimensional confinements.

There are numerous experimental process approaches under consideration in fabricating GMR structures are: magnetron or ion beam sputter deposition; epitaxy for layered structures; rubber stamping of nanoscale wire-like patterns; electroplating into nanoscale pores in polymer membranes. In RAM applications, a high ratio of magnetoresistance combined with a small coercive switching field is key to density, speed, and low power. These features are also achieved in magnetic tunnel junctions in which the ferromagnetic layers are quantum mechanically coupled through a thin dielectric layer. Although research in nanoscale magnetics is underway internationally, most of the activities on the practical applications mentioned above are in the United States. Optical devices have already benefited from incorporation of nanostructured materials: commercially available semiconductor lasers incorporate active regions comprised of quantum wells, the presence of which modifies the electronic density of states and the localisation of electrons and holes, resulting in more efficient laser operation.

Extrapolating from those results, even greater improvements are predicted for lasers utilising either quantum wire or quantum dot active layers. Recent advances in the "self-assembled" formation of quantum dot structures have stimulated progress in the fabrication and characterisation of quantum dot lasers in Japan, Europe, and the United States. In late 1991, the first synthesis and characterisation of carbon nanotubes were reported.

The novel material contained a wide variety of multiwalled nanotubes (MWNT) containing 2 to 50 concentric cylindrical graphene sheets with a diameter of a few nm and a length of up to 1 μm. The material was produced at the negative electrode of an arc discharge and appeared to be mixed with a large amount of other forms of carbon. This initial work led many groups throughout the world to produce and purify nanotubes. The theoretical study of their electronic structure followed in the next year. Soon it became clear that nanotubes have unique electronic and mechanical properties that are expected to lead to ground-breaking industrial applications.

Even though the study of single-electron charging effects with granular metallic systems dates back to the 1950s, it was the research of Likharev and coworkers almost 10 years ago that laid much of the groundwork for understanding single-charge transport in nanoscale tunnel junctions. The concept was developed of a Coulomb gap that can be exploited to control the transfer of single charges. Since then, many research groups have made use of the Coulomb blockade effect to develop SED technology. Figures 1 through 11 show some of the myriad approaches to developing SEDs and representative laboratories pursuing the various SED concepts.

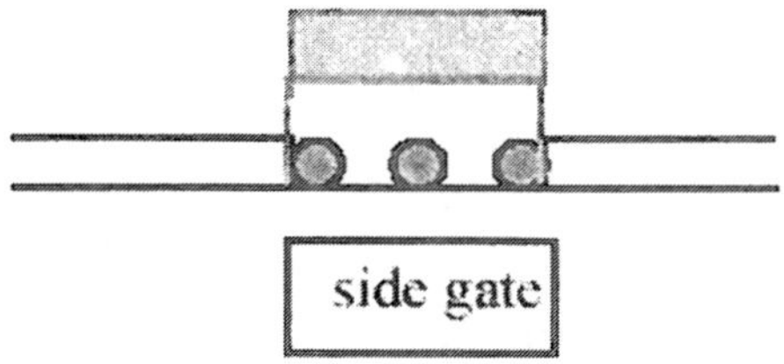

Figure 1. Metal colloids, self-assembled monolayer (SAM) coatings, polysilicon, quantum dots embedded in SiO_2

The group at Hitachi Europe uses a side-gated constriction in a deltadoped GaAs structure to fabricate a magnetic tunnel junction device in which a series of small islands separated by tunnel barriers are formed (for example, Fig. 1). At ~2K, the Coulomb gap voltage oscillates as a function of the side-gate voltage. Using the MTJ device as a building block, both memory and logic (inverter, NOR) functions have been demonstrated.

The fabrication procedure makes use of standard semiconductor processing techniques and does not rely on lithography to define the nanoscale islands, since these are created by disorder in the delta-doped layer. Other groups have utilised fine-line lithography to fabricate SEDs. At IBM, a flash memory SED was demonstrated by fabricating a sub-50 nm Si quantum dot (QD) on top of a MOSFET channel using a silicon-on-insulator (SOI) substrate, with the QD acting as a floating gate. Single-electron charging was observed up to 90 K, while large threshold voltage shifts of up to 0.75 V were measured at 290 K.

The University of Minnesota and Fujitsu have also reported similar structures. To overcome the lithography limitation on the QD size, the Toshiba group used a Si edge quantum wire approach. An inversion layer was formed at the 15 nm high Si sidewall of a SOI structure by growing a gate oxide and depositing a poly-Si gate there. Conductance oscillations were clearly seen at 4.2 K in this edgechannel MOSFET. More recently, the Toshiba group has reverted back to a more planar device configuration, with a 50 nm wide Si quantum wire defined by e-beam lithography and oxidation of the surrounding SiO_2.

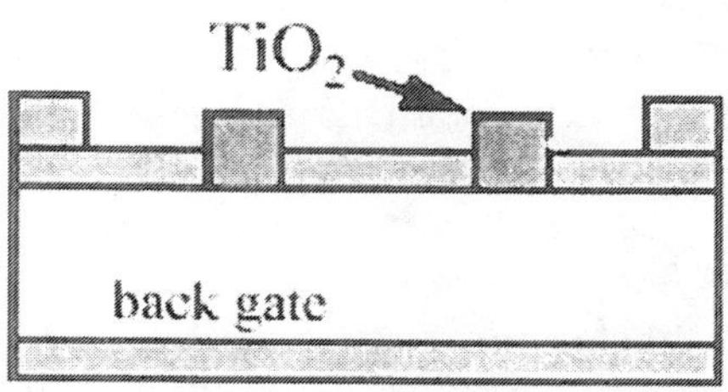

Figure 2. Oxidation of metal or semiconductor with scanning tunnelling microscope (STM) tip (ETL).

One method to form semiconductor QDs without depending on fine-line lithography is to make use of the self-organising nature inherent in the Stranski-Krastanow thin film growth mode. In the initial stages of the heteroepitaxial growth of lattice-mismatched materials, strain-induced coherent relaxation occurs and dislocation-free islands are formed that are in the tens of nanometers range in size.

There has been considerable research in these self-organised quantum dots (SOQDs) in the past few years, though much of the work has been of a fundamental nature. More recently, the University of Tokyo has proposed the embedding of InAs SOQDs in AlGaAs/GaAs heterojunction field effect transistors (HFETs) to form a flash-memory SED.

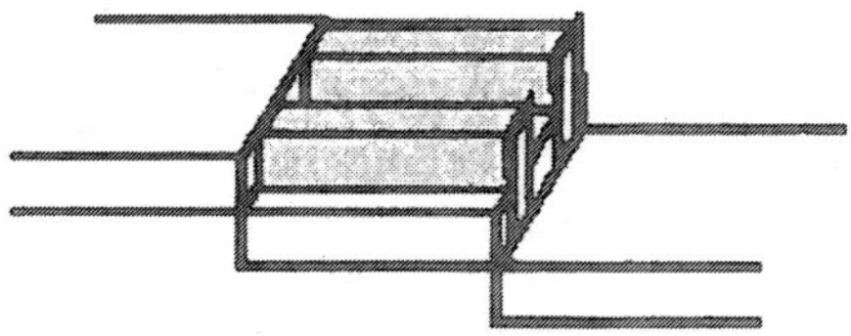

Figure 3. STM probe oxidation of metal on vicinal substrate steps (ETL).

This concept was further demonstrated by the Sony group, which reported observing threshold voltage shifts at 300 K. Fujitsu has also proposed the use of InGaAs QDs in a similar manner. The one difference in thi^ case is that the QDs are formed at the bottom of tetrahedral-shaped recesses formed by substrate patterning. Since SOQDs form in a somewhat random manner on a planar surface, this approach provides positioning control. Of course, QDs can be formed with materials other than semiconductors. In fact, some of the earliest work in single-electron charging was done with metallic tunnel junctions. With modern fabrication tools and techniques, some groups have investigated the formation of nanoscale

Au particles between metallic contacts. The University of Cambridge group used focused ion beam deposition to place Au dots between electrodes spaced 30 - 40 nm apart. At Lund University in Sweden, atomic force microscopy (AFM) is utilised to move a 50 nm Au particle in between contacts formed by e-beam lithography. Researchers observed conductance plateaus stable for several minutes at 300 K. The group at Cambridge University/Hitachi Europe used a colloidal process to form a chain of insulated Au particles between source, drain, and gate electrodes. At 4.2 K, the chain exhibited a Coulomb staircase and periodic conduction oscillations in I-V measurements. For a very different approach, a molecular embodiment of a QD-based system can be realised by connecting a single molecule between metallic contacts. At Yale University a single molecule of benzene-1,4-dithiol was self-assembled from solution onto two electrodes of a mechanically controllable break junction (Fig. 4, left).

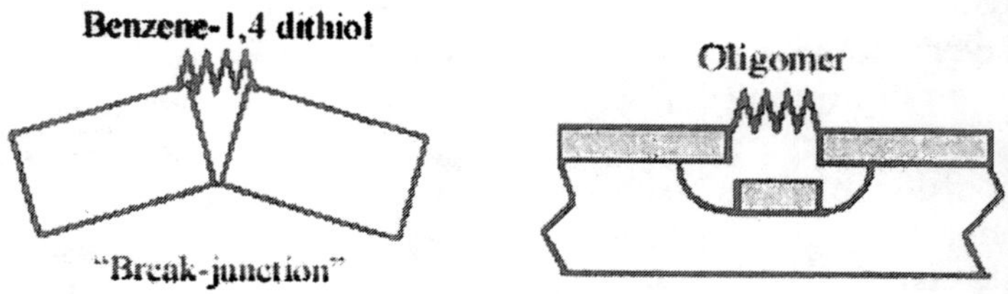

Figure 4. A single molecule connecting metallic contacts

The spacing between the electrodes is ~ 0.8 nm, and I-V measurements at room temperature showed a gap ~ 0.7 V wide, which is attributed to a Coulomb gap. The Delft University of Technology in the Netherlands is also working on transport through oligomers (Fig. 4, right). Concerning the architecture in which SEDs are utilised, a number of approaches have been proposed. One of the more novel ideas is that of quantum cellular automata (QCA), based on some earlier work at Texas Instruments and developed at the University of Notre Dame. The basic QCA cell is made up of a group of capacitively coupled QDs. Each cell holds two electrons, resulting in two polarisation configurations that can represent the logic "0" and "1" states, and each cell interacts via Coulombic forces with neighboring cells.

An array of cells can then be used to transmit binary information, which eliminates the need for physical interconnects between devices and represents a paradigm shift for ultralarge-scale integration (ULSI). Basic Boolean operations (AND, OR, etc.) can be implemented using QCA, and more complex functions have been simulated. Most recently, the Notre Dame group has demonstrated a nonlinear, bistable response of a QCA cell, albeit at a very low temperature of less than 20 mK. The QCA approach is not without its challenges (and critics). Circuit fabrication will be difficult because stringent control in QD positioning is required.

Others have pointed out that bistability is only a necessary but not sufficient condition for the operation of Boolean logic circuits, because isolation is needed between the input and output, while background charge fluctuations will hamper logic implementation. Thus, there is also considerable research in the use of SEDs with more conventional architectures. The group at Hitachi Europe uses its MTJ devices in binary decision diagram logic that is commonly used in large-scale integrated (LSI) circuits.

The Toshiba group is combining its SED with a MOSFET to compensate for the lack of gain in the former, as are, presumably, other groups working on QDbased flash memory SEDs. In short, while significant progress has been made in nanofabrication techniques, the field of single-charge electronics is still limited in scope by the lack of a suitable architecture that fully utilises the unique aspects of single-electron charging.

Current approaches require many SED elements to achieve conventional functions such as adders, exclusive NORs, etc. Simulations of such circuits predict slow operating speed. The field seems to be stuck on applying conventional electronics to SEDs. Either a new architecture will be discovered or SEDs may find a niche home in those applications where measurements of single charges are needed. For the fabrication of nanoscale electronic devices, the self-organising technique appears to be the most promising. The field of self-organised semiconductor QDs is quite active, but aside from optical emitters, very few practical electronic functions have been proposed. Of those, the singleelectron flash memory is attracting attention, but there has been no serious proposal as to how the device could operate under normal integrated circuit performance conditions and reliability specifications. Using the SED as a floating gate to a MOSFET has the same kinds of problems as applying conventional approaches to SED architectures; until someone comes up with a better idea, the future of these approaches remains to be determined.

Magnetics and Nanomagnetics

The discovery in 1988 of GMR in structures of alternating magnetic and nonmagnetic thin layers was the accumulation of several decades of intensive research in thin film magnetism and improvements in epitaxial growth techniques developed mainly in semiconductor materials. Not surprisingly, the first GMR structure was fabricated using molecular beam epitaxy.

The high quality magnetic and nonmagnetic metallic films provide electrons with a mean free path exceeding 100 Å; on the other hand, the epitaxial growth allows for each constituent layer of the structure to be as thin as a few atomic layers. The greatly enhanced spin-dependent scattering in these multilayered structures provides magnetoresistance changes as high as 50%.

Two subsequent major developments from IBM enabled the application of GMR materials to hard disk heads, RAM, and sensors. The first development was the demonstration of equally good or better GMR materials using high throughput and production-worthy magnetron sputtering systems. The other development was the invention of magnetically soft spin-valve structures, which allow low field and low power operation.Industrial R&D efforts on GMR materials initially focused on high density read heads. The major U.S. players are IBM, Seagate, Quantum, ReadRite, and Applied Magnetics. In Japan, all the semiconductor companies are involved, in addition to strong magnetic media powerhouses such as TDK and Yamaha. Korea's Samsung is also actively involved in the GMR race. In 1995, a different class of high magnetoresistive materials was discovered in which the nonmagnetic layer separating the two ferromagnetic layers is made with an ultrathin insulating material, such as an aluminum oxide layer < 20 Å thick.

With the switching of magnetisation of the two magnetic layers between parallel and antiparallel states, the differences in the tunnelling coefficient of the junction and thus the magnetoresistance ratio have been demonstrated to be more than 25%. A distinctive feature of this MTJ class of materials is its high impedance (> 100 kW-μm^2), which allows for large signal outputs. The gradual improvement of GMR and MTJ materials have made them attractive for nonvolatile magnetic random access memory (MRAM) applications.

The potential to make MRAM a high density, high speed, and low power, general purpose memory prompted the Defense Advanced Reseat Projects Agency to fund three MRAM consortia beginning in 1995, led by IBM, Motorola, and Honeywell, respectively. Other companies engaged in MRAM research are Hewlett-Packard, Matsushita, NEC, Fujitsu, Toshiba, Hitachi, and Siemens. The key for a competitive MRAM technology is the fabrication of deep submicron-dimension magnetic cells.

The further development of lithography tools utilising e-beam and deep ultraviolet radiation is essential. Magnetic storage elements as small as 0.25 µm have been demonstrated by both Motorola and IBM. Among the steps of MRAM fabrication that are not yet compatible with semiconductor processing is the ion milling of the magnetic cells. The possibility of dry etching the magnetic materials has, nevertheless, been demonstrated.

Figures 5 through 15 summarise the major directions in memory R&D. Arrows denote ferromagnetic layers. The ability to fabricate submicron magnetic elements has opened a very rich and fascinating area of micromagnetics research. Characterisation techniques having nanoscale resolution have been utilised and improved to measure and image the complex magnetisation patterns in order to understand the magnetisation switching characteristics. Examples of such techniques include the following:

— superconducting quantum interference device (SQUID) magnetometry

— magnetic force microscopy (MFM)

— scanning electron microscopy with polarisation analysis (SEMPA)

— magnetic near-field microscopy

— electron holography

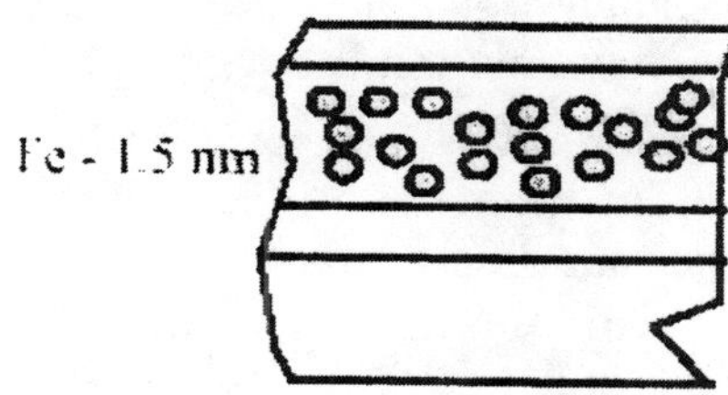

Figure 5. Granular GMR—Co, Fe

Another essential tool is micromagnetics modeling, which is used to predict complex magnetic domain configurations in patterned magnetic elements and to generate transient pictures that demonstrate the process of forming complex domain configurations. By combining MFM, SQUID magnetometry, SEMPA, and micromagnetics modeling, researchers at Motorola have conducted a systematic study of the switching characteristics of single-layer and multilayer submicron magnetic structures.

Figure 6. Ferromagnetic/metal/ferromagnetic: 3 - 60 periods free-standing; plated into pores

Different phases of the magnetisation phase diagram have been identified with regards to material composition, dimension, shape, thickness, and other structural parameters:

(1) the quasi-single domain phase can be well described by the coherent rotation model;

(2) the end-domain phase is dominated by the nonuniform regions of magnetisation at the two ends of the element-the magnetisation switching process can either be rotational or through domain wall nucleation and propagation; and

(3) the trapped magnetisation vortice (TMV) phase, which is characterised by the presence of magnetisation vortices. Nucleation from TMV sites requires lower reversal fields than coherent rotation, but a high field is needed to drive out TMVs in the element. When the driving field is not high enough, TMVs can cause unusually large fluctuations in the switching field. As the size of magnetic elements scales below 20 nm, a superparamagnetic phase emerges in which the room temperature thermal energy overcomes the magnetostatic energy well of the element, resulting in zero hysteresis.

In other words, although the element itself is a single-domain ferromagnet, the ability of an individual magnetic "dot" to store magnetisation orientation information is lost when its dimension is below a threshold. On the other hand, suitably prepared alloys of immiscible ferromagnetic and nonmagnetic metals that contain single-domain ferromagnetic grains in a nonmagnetic matrix have been shown to exhibit GMR characteristics.

The moments of the magnetic grains are aligned at high fields and random at the coercive field, leading to GMR characteristics. In such "granular" metals, GMR has been reported for sputtered alloy films of CoCu, FeCu, NiFe/Ag, and CoAg. GMR values as high as 55% at 4.2 K and 20% at room temperature have been observed. The granular films require magnetic fields of the order of 10 kOe to achieve such a change in electrical resistance.

A very exciting consequence of ultrascaled magnetic particles is quantum tunneling of the magnetisation direction of a collection of spins. There is no simple Schrödinger equation that describes this process, since it is not an elementary particle that is tunneling but a collective coordinate. Below its "blocking temperature," at which thermally assisted hopping between magnetic orientations becomes frozen out, magnetic particles of TbCeFe at sizes around 15 nm have been observed to behave independent of temperature and with no freeze-out magnetic relaxation. Because of the coherent tunneling of the magnetisation orientation between the symmetric double-well potential, a resonance line in the magnetic susceptibility and noise spectra has been observed at temperatures below 200 mK in zero applied magnetic field.

Another interesting type of nanomagnetic structure is nanometer ferromagnetic wires fabricated using conventional nanolithography, nanoimprint lithography, AFM/MFM direct writing, groove deposition, and electrodeposition into pores of template polymer membranes. Such nanowires of either single layer or multilayers may provide new approaches to very small magnetoresistive sensors, ultrahigh-density hard disks, and other extensions of conventional applications.

Another intriguing possibility is the suggestion to use heterostructure nanowires to investigate single electron tunneling. Recently, molecular magnetism has received much attention with the development of a variety of synthesis techniques largely adapted from biology and chemistry. Natural and artificial ferritin proteins are examples of systems obtained using these methods.

The ability to add one magnetic ion at a time has resulted in nanoscale magnets precisely defined by atomic weight. Ferritin consists of a segmented protein shell in the shape of a hollow sphere, with an outer diameter of 12.5 nm and an inner diameter of 7.5 nm. Ir vivo, the inner space is normally filled with a crystal of an iron oxide that is antiferromagnetic below 240 K.

The empty protein shells can also serve as vessels for the synthesis of ferrimagnetic magnetite and maghemite. Thus, there exists a system in which its size as well as the nature of its magnetic interactions can be varied. Another example of molecular magnetism is a cobalt-iron-cyanide-based Prussian blue analog. In the ground state the Fe^{+2} and Co^{+3} ions are low-spin and diamagnetic, and there is no interaction between them.

Red light excitation transfers one electron from an iron site to a cobalt site, resulting in high-spin Fe^{+3} and Co^{+2} ions and magnetic interactions between them. The application of a blue light causes a transition back to the initial state and switches off the Fe^{+3}-Co^{+2} interactions. In addition to this kind of photochemically controllable magnets, electrochemically controllable magnets have also been reported.

Carbon Nanotubes

The first synthesis and characterisation of carbon nanotubes were reported by Iijima from NEC in late 1991. Since then, the fabrication of nanotubes has been improved by several groups, and methods other than arc discharge have been explored.

The main issues are to separate the nanotubes from other forms of carbon also produced in the fabrication process and to increase the yield of singlewalled nanotubes (SWNT) for potential applications. Following Iijima's work, macroscopic quantities of MWNT were produced with an improved arc discharge method by Ebbesen and coworkers at NEC. It was not until 1995 that Smalley and colleagues at Rice University showed that SWNT can be efficiently produced by laser ablation of a graphite rod. In the following year, that same group produced what is considered to be among the best SWNT material generated so far; over 70% of the volume of material was nanotubes bundled together into crystalline ropes of metallic character.

Also in 1996, a group from the Chinese Academy of Science used chemical vapor deposition to produce a 50 mm thick film of nanotubes that were highly aligned perpendicular to the surface. Progress in recent years leads one to predict that it will indeed be possible to produce high quality carbon nanotubes in macroscopic quantities needed for many of the applications outlined below. Nanotube bundles form a low density material and are expected to have high stiffness and axial strength as a result of their seamless cylindrical graphitic structure. It is therefore predicted that they can be used to fabricate a material with better mechanical properties than the present carbon fiber materials. Information about the mechanical properties of nanotubes has been gathered recently by a study of the thermal vibrations of a single SWNT attached to a substrate.

In order to reach a better understanding of the mechanical properties and intrinsic limitations of nanotubes, Bernholc's group from North Carolina State University theoretically studied the behaviour of nanotubes beyond the linear Hooke's law and the nature of the defects leading to dislocations and fractures. Nanotubes are highly polarisable nanoscale straws, a property that confers on them the capacity to ingest inorganic elements by nanocapillarity.

As a result, it has been conjectured that they could be used as minute molds to shape nanometer-sized quantum wires and as miniature test tubes. Finally, external decoration of nanotubes with metal atoms has been demonstrated and is predicted to have applications in catalysis. The primary methods of nanotube fabrication and the institutions engaged in specific methods of nanotube fabrication.

Early theoretical studies already showed that the electronic properties of nanotubes strongly depend on their diameter and their chirality leading to metallic or semiconducting structures. It was conjectured that these properties can be used to construct nanoscale electronic devices. In 1997, two groups, one at Lawrence Berkeley National Laboratory and the second at Delft University in the Netherlands showed that conductivity through nanotubes is controlled by low dimensional effects such as resonant tunneling and single-electron charging effects. Hall effect measurements at the École Polytechnique Fédérale de Lausanne (EPFL) in Switzerland have shown that hole transport is predominant in electronic conductance. Despite these and other very recent and encouraging efforts such as those studying the mean free path of carriers in nanotubes, the conduction mechanism is still only partially understood.

Metallic nanotubes are strongly polarizable in an electric field and thereby lead to field enhancement at their extremity, the strength of which depends on the ratio of the diameter to the length and can be extremely large for routinely produced nanotubes.

For this reason and possibly others related to quantum confinement effects, nanotubes are expected to form outstanding field-emitting materials. In 1995, the Rice University group showed that nanotubes emit electrons very efficiently when immersed in an electric field and irradiated by a laser to remove their cap. They attribute their observation to the unraveling of an atomic wire of carbon atoms. Efficient field emission was also obtained from carefully aligned nanotubes by de Heer and coworkers. at EPFL, whereas Collins and coworkers from the University of California at Berkeley, have used randomly oriented nanotubes with similar results.

Efficient field-emitting material is highly desirable for the production of field-emission displays and microwave tubes. Recently, a group from Mie University in Japan has built a cathode ray tube (CRT) using nanotube field emitters. This fabrication method is presently not compatible with industrial production requirements, and more progress must be made before this effort can be translated into an industrial product.

Nanorobotic Devices

There are many differences between macro and nanoscale robots. These occur mainly in the basic laws that govern their dynamics. Macroscaled robots are essentially in the Newtonian mechanics domain whereas the laws governing nanorobots are in the molecular quantum mechanics domain. Furthermore, uncertainty plays a crucial role in nanorobotic systems.

The fundamental barrier for dealing with uncertainty at the nano scale is imposed by the quantum and the statistical mechanics and thermal excitations. For a certain nanosystem at some particular temperature, there are positional uncertainties, which cannot be modified or further reduced.

The nanorobots are invisible to naked eye, which makes them hard to manipulate and work with. Techniques like scanning electron microscopy (SEM) and atomic force microscopy (AFM) are being employed to establish a visual and haptic interface to enable us to sense the molecular structure of these nanoscaled devices. Virtual reality (VR) techniques are currently being explored in nanoscience and biotechnology research as a way to enhance the operator's perception (vision and haptics) by approaching more or less a state of "full immersion" or "telepresence."

The development of nanorobots or nanomachine components presents difficult fabrication and control challenges. Such devices will operate in microenvironments whose physical properties differ from those encountered by conventional parts. Since these nanoscale devices have not yet been fabricated, evaluating possible designs and control algorithms requires using theoretical estimates and virtual interfaces/environments. Such interfaces/simulations can operate at various levels of detail to trade-off physical accuracy, computational cost, number of components and the time over which the simulation follows the nanoobject behaviours. They can enable nanoscientists to extend their eyes and hands into the nanoworld and also enable new types of exploration and whole new classes of experiments in the biological and physical sciences.

VR simulations can also be used to develop virtual assemblies of nano and bio-nanocomponents into mobile linkages and predict their performance. Nanorobotswith completely artificial components have not been realised yet. The active area of research in this field is focused more on molecular robots, which are thoroughly inspired by nature's way of doing things at nano scale.

Mother Nature has her own set of molecular machines that have been working for centuries, and have been optimised for performance and design over the ages. As our knowledge and understanding of these numerous machines continues to increase, we now see a possibility of using the natural machines, or creating synthetic ones from scratch, using nature's components. The main goal in the field of molecular machines is to use various biological elements-whose function at the cellular level creates motion, force or a signal-as machine components.

These components perform their preprogrammed biological function in response to the specific physiochemical stimuli but in an artificial setting. In this way proteins and DNA could act as motors, mechanical joints, transmission elements, or sensors. If all these different components were assembled together in the proper proportion and orientation they would form nanodevices with multiple degrees of freedom, able to apply forces and manipulate objects in the nanoscale world.

The advantage of using nature's machine components is that they are highly efficient and reliable. Nanorobotics is a field, which calls for collaborative efforts between physicists, chemists, biologists, computer scientists, engineers, and other specialists to work towards this common objective.

Currently this field is still evolving, but several substantial steps have been taken by great researchers all over the world and are contributing to this ever challenging and exciting field. The ability to manipulate matter at the nano scale is one core application for which nanorobots could be the technological solution. A lot has been written in the literature about the significance and motivation behind constructing a nanorobot. The applications range from medical to environmental sensing to space and military applications. Molecular construction of complex devices could be possible by nanorobots of the future. From precise drug delivery to repairing cells and fighting tumor cells, nanorobots are expected to revolutionise the medical industry in the future.

These applications come under the field of nanomedicine, which is a very active area of research in nanotechnology. These molecular machines hence form the basic enablers of future nanoscale applications. A majority of natural molecular machines are protein-based, while the DNA-based molecular machines are mostly synthetic. Nature deploys proteins to perform various cellular tasks—from moving cargo, to catalysing reactions, while it has kept DNA as an information carrier. It is hence understandable that most of the natural machinery is built from proteins.

With the powerful crystallographic techniques available in the modern world, the protein structures are clearer than ever. The ever-increasing computing power makes it possible to dynamically model protein folding processes and predict the conformations and structure of lesser known proteins. All this helps unravel the mysteries associated with the molecular machinery and paves the way for the production and application of these miniature machines in various fields including medicine, space exploration, electronics, and military.

Nanorobotic Devices

The molecular machines into three broad categories:

— protein-based,

— DNA-based, and

— chemical molecular motors.

Protein-Based Molecular Machines

This section focuses on the following main protein-based molecular machines:

1. ATP Synthase
2. The kinesin, myosin, dynein, and flagella molecular motors

"Nano" properties

Reversibility of the ATP Synthase—There are two directions in ATP Synthase system and these two directions correspond to two different functionalities and behaviour. This two-way behaviour is because of the reversible nature of the ATP-ADP cycle and the structure of the ATP Synthase. Let us term the forward direction as when the F_0 drives the γ subunit of F_1 and henceATP synthesis takes place. And the backward direction is when hydrolysis of ATP counter-rotated the γ subunit and hence the F_0 motor and leads to pumping back the protons.

Therefore, the forward direction is powered by the proton motive force and the backward direction is powered by theATP hydrolysis. Which particular direction is being followed depends upon the situation and the environmental factors around the ATP Synthase.

Coupling of Proton Flow (F_0) and the ATP Synthesis and Hydrolysis (in F_1)-Boyer proposed a model which predicted that the F_0 and F_1 motors are connected through the γ subunit. Further he proposed that this connection was mechanical in nature. Figure 7 illustrates the electrostatic surface potential on $\alpha_3\beta_3$ sub-units. The red colour represents a negatively charged surface and blue a positively charged surface. Shown in the Figure 7(a), a predominately neutral hole in the α_3 β_3 subunit through which the γ subunit protrudes. Figure 7(b) shows a γ subunit with a significantly negatively charged region around half across its length. The γ subunit slides through the hole of the $\alpha_3\beta_3$ sub-units.

Boyer's Binding Change Mechanism—Boyer isolated the F_1 part of theATP Synthase complex. It was found that the a and *ß* sub-units alternate in this cylindrical part of the F_1 structure. As per this model each a and *ß* pair forms a catalytic site. The rotation of the γ subunit induces structural conformation in the a3ß3 sub-units. Although the three catalytic units are identical in their chemistry, they are functionally very different at any given point in time. These conformal changes induce a change in the binding affinities of all the three catalytic sites towards the ATPase reactants (ADP, Pi, ATP, etc.).

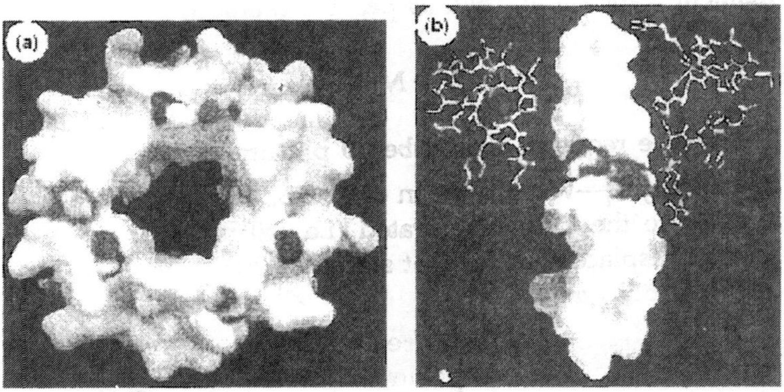

Figure 7. The electrostatic surface potential on the $\alpha_3\beta_3$ and γ sub-units.

F_1-ATPase a True Nanorotary Motor—Till today the exact mechanism of the molecular motor characterised by F_1-ATpase has not been fully determined. What is known till now is that the γ subunit rotates inside the a-ß hexamer, but whether the rotation is continuous or random was not known. Kinosita's lab solved this problem by imaging the F_1-ATPase molecule. The objective of their experiment was to determine the uniqueness of the rotary motion and its characteristics.

Other behaviors of the F_1-ATPase motor

Rotational Rates-Rotational rates were dependent upon the length of the actin filament. Rotational rates were found to be inversely proportional to the filament length. This could be attributed to the fact that the hydrodynamic friction is proportional to the cube of the length of the filament, therefore, longer length implied that the frictional forces were higher and rotational speeds in effect slower. As reported in the principle article, if the filament were to rotate at the speed of 6 rev/sec and the length of the actin filament were 1 μm, then as per the relation:

$$N = \omega\xi$$

The torque required would be 40 pN nm.

Efficiency of F_1—Work done in one step, that is, 120° rotation is equal to the torque generated (i.e., 40 pN nm) times the angular displacement for that step (i.e., $2\pi/3$). This comes to about 80 pN nm.

Here, the standard free energy change per ATP molecule is equal to –50 pNnm at pH 7. The thermal energy at room temperature is equal to 4.1 pN nm. At intracellular conditions, [ATP] and [Pi] is in the order of 10^{-3} M. Therefore, for [ADP] of 50 μM, ΔG is equal to -90.604 pN nm. Comparing this value of the free energy obtained by the hydrolysis of one molecule of ATP with the mechanical work done by the motor (i.e., 80 pN nm), we can deduce that the F_1-ATPase motor works on efficiency close to 100%!

Chemical Synthesis of ATP Powered by Mechanical Energy—In another study, evidence has been provided to justify the claim that the chemical synthesis of ATP occurs when propelled by mechanical energy. This basic nature of the F_1-ATPase was known for quite some time, but it is the first time that it is being experimentally verified. To prove this concept, the F_1 was bound to the glass surface through histidine residues attached at the end of the γ sub-units. A magnetic bead coated with streptavidin was attached to the γ subunit.

Electric magnets were used to rotate this bead attached to the γ subunit. The rotation resulted in appearance of ATP in the medium (which was initially immersed in ADP).

Thus, the connection between the syntheses of ATP as a result of the mechanical energy input is established.

The exact mechanism of the F_1-ATPase rotation is still an active area of research today and many groups are working towards finding it. The key to solving the mechanism is solving the transient conformation of the catalytic sites and the γ subunit when rotation is taking place. What is not clear is the correspondence between the chemical reactions at the catalytic sites and their influence on the rotation of the γ subunit. Which event triggers the rotation and which does not has still to be exactly determined? Many models have been predicted, but they all still elude the reality of the rotational mechanism.

Kinesin, myosin, dynein, and flagella molecular motors

With modern microscopic tools, a cell as a set of many different moving components powered by molecular machines rather than a static environment. Molecular motors that move unidirectionally along protein polymers (actin or microtubules) drive the motions of muscles as well as much smaller intracellular cargoes. In addition to the F_0-F_1-ATPase motors inside the cell, there are linear transport motors present as tiny vehicles known as motor proteins that transport molecular cargoes that also require ATP for functioning. These minute cellular machines exist in three families—the kinesins, the myosins, and the dyneins. The cargoes can be organelles, lipids, or proteins etc. They play an important role in cell division and motility.

There are over 250 kinesin-like proteins, and they are involved in processes as diverse as the movement of chromosomes and the dynamics of cell membranes. The only part they have in common is the catalytic portion known as the motor domain. They have significant differences in their location within cells, their structural organisation, and the movement they generate.

Muscle myosin, whose study dates back to 1864, has served as a model system for understanding motility for decades. Kinesin, however, was discovered rather recently using in vitro motility assays in 1985. Conventional kinesin is a highly processive motor that can take several hundred steps on a microtubule without detaching whereas muscle myosin executes a single "stroke" and then dissociates. A detailed analysis and modelling of these motors has been done. Kinesin and myosin make up for an interesting comparison. Kinesin is microtubule-based; it binds to and carries cargoes along microtubules whereas myosin is actin-based. The motor domain of kinesin weighs one third the size of that of myosin and one tenth of that of dynein. Before the advent of modern microscopic and analytic techniques, it was believed that these two have little in common. However, the crystal structures available today indicate that they probably originated from a common ancestor.

Myosin linear motor

Myosin is a diverse superfamily of motor proteins. Myosin-based molecular machines transport cargoes along actin filaments—the two stranded helical polymers of the protein actin, about 5 to 9 nm in diameter. They do this by hydrolyzing ATP and utilising the energy released. In addition to transport, they are also involved in the process of force generation during muscle contraction, wherein thin actin filaments and thick myosin filaments slide past each other. Not all members of the myosin superfamily have been characterised as of now. However, much is known about the structure and function. Myosin molecules were first sighted through electron microscope protruding out from thick filaments and interacting with the thin actin filaments in late 1950s. Since then it was known that ATP plays a role in myosin related muscle movement along actin. However, the exact mechanism was unknown, which was explained later in 1971 by Lymn and Taylor.

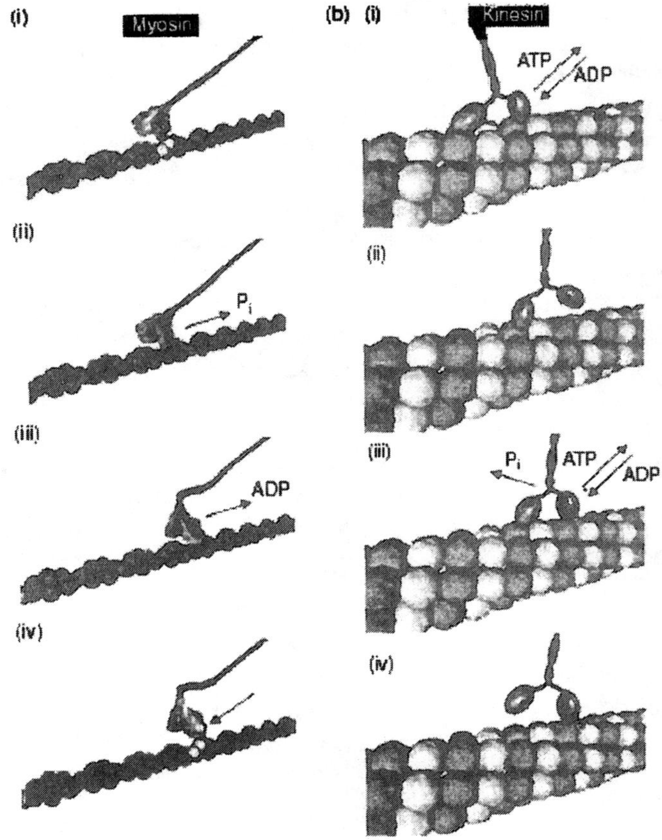

Figure 8. The kinesin–myosin walks: (a) Myosin motor mechanism. (i) Motor head loosely docking to the actin binding site; (ii) The binding becomes tighter along with the release of P_i; (iii) Lever armswings to the left with the release of ADP, and; (iv) replacement of the lost ADP with a fresh ATP molecule results in dissociation of the head; (b) Kinesin heads working in conjunction. (i) Both ADP-carrying heads come near the microtubule and one of them (black neck) binds; (ii) Loss of bound ADP and addition of fresh ATP in the bound head moves the other to the right; (iii) The second head binds to microtubule while losing its ADP, and replacing it with a new ATP molecule while the first head hydrolyses its ATP and loses P_i; (iv) The ADP-carrying black-neck will now be snapped forward, and the cycle will be repeated

A myosin molecule binding to an actin polymer is shown in Figure 8(a). Myosin molecule has a size of about 520 kD including two 220 kD heavy chains and light chains of sizes between 15 and 22 kD. They can be visualised as two identical globular "motor heads," also known as motor domains, each comprising of a catalytic domain (actin, nucleotide as well as light chain binding sites) and about 8 nm long lever arms. The heads, also sometimes referred to as S1 regions (subfragment 1). Both these heads are connected via a coiled coil made of two α-helical coils (gray) to the thick base filament. The light chains have considerable sequence similarity with the protein "calmodulin" and troponin C, and are sometimes referred to as calmodulin-like chains. They act as links to the motor domains and do not play any role in their ATP binding activity but for some exceptions.

The motor domain in itself is sufficient for moving actin filaments. Three-dimensional (3D) structures of myosin head revealed that it is a pear-shaped domain, about 19 nm long and 5 nm in maximum diameter. A crossbridge-cycle model for the action of myosin on actin has been widely accepted since 1957. Since the atomic structures of actin monomer and myosin were resolved, this model has been refined into a "lever-arm model," which is now acceptable. Only one motor head is able to connect to the actin filament at a time, the other head remains passive. Initially, the catalytic domain in the head has ADP and Pi bound to it and as a result, its binding with actin is weak. With the active motor head docking properly to the actinbinding site, the Pi has to be released.

As soon as this happens, the lever arm swings counter-clockwise due to a conformational change. This pushes the actin filament down by about 10 nm along its longitudinal axis. The active motor head now releases its bound ADP and another ATP molecule by way of Brownian motion quickly replaces it, making the binding of the head to the actin filament weak again.

The myosin motor then dissociates from the actin filament, and a new cycle starts. However, nanomanipulation of single S1 molecules (motor domains) show that myosin can take multiple steps per ATP molecule hydrolysed, moving in 5.3 nm steps and resulting in displacements of 11 to 30 nm.

Kinesin linear motor

Kinesin and dynein family of proteins are involved in cellular cargo transport along microtubules as opposed to actin in the case of myosin. Microtubules are 25 nm diameter tubes made of protein tubulin and are present in the cells in an organised manner. Microtubules have polarity; one end being the plus (fast growing) end while the other end is the minus (slow growing) end. Kinesins move from minus end to plus end, while dyneins move from plus end to the minus end of the microtubules. Microtubule arrangement varies in different cell systems. In nerve axons, they are arranged longitudinally in such a manner that their plus ends point away from the cell body and into the axon.

In epithelial cells, their plus end points towards the basement membrane. They deviate radially out of the cell center in fibroblasts and macrophages with the plus end protruding outwards. Like myosin, kinesin is also an ATP-driven motor.

One unique characteristic of kinesin family of proteins is their processivity—they bind to microtubules and literally "walk" on it for many enzymatic cycles before detaching. Also, each of the globular heads/motor domains of kinesin is made of one single polypeptide unlike myosin (heavy and light chains and dynein heavy, intermediate, and light chains). A lot of structural information about kinesin is now available through the crystal structures.

The motor domain contains a folding motif similar to that of myosin and G proteins. The two heads or the motor domains of kinesin are linked via "neck linkers" to a long coiled coil, which extends up to the cargo (Figure 8[b]). They interact with the α and β sub-units of the tubulin hetrodimer along the microtubule protofilament. The heads have the nucleotide and the microtubule binding domains in them. While Kinesin is also a two-headed linear motor, its modus operandi is different from myosin in the sense that both its head work together in a coordinated manner rather than one was being left out. Figure 8(b) shows the kinesin walk.

Each of the motor heads is near the microtubule in the initial state with each motor head carrying an ADP molecule. When one of the heads loosely binds to the microtubule, it looses its ADP molecule to facilitate a stronger binding. Another ATP molecule replaces the ADP, which facilitates a conformational change such that the neck region of the bound head snaps forward and zips on to the head. In the process it pulls the other ADP carrying motor head forward by about 16 nm so that it can bind to the next microtubule-binding site. This results in the net movement of the cargo by about 8 nm. The second head now binds to the microtubule by losing its ADP, which is promptly replaced by another ATP molecule due to Brownian motion. The first head meanwhile hydrolyses theATP and loses the resulting P_i . It is then snapped forward by the second head while it carries its ADP forward.

Hence, coordinated hydrolysis of ATP in the two motor heads is the key to the kinesin processivity. Kinesin is able to take about 100 steps before detaching from the microtubule while moving at 1000 nm/sec and exerting forces of the order of 5 to 6 pN at stall.

Dynein motor

The Dynein superfamily of proteins was introduced in 1965.

Dyneins exist in two isoforms, the cytoplasmic and the axonemal. Cytoplasmic dyneins are involved in cargo movement, while axonemal dyneins are involved in producing bending motions of cilia and flagella. Figure 9 shows a typical cytoplasmic dynein molecule.

The structure consists of two heavy chains in the form of globular heads, three intermediate chains and four light intermediate chains. Recent studies have exposed a linker domain connecting the "stem" region below the heads to the head itself. Also from the top of the heads the microtubule binding domains protrude out. The ends of these stalks have smaller ATP sensitive globular domains, which bind to the microtubules.

Cytoplasmic dynein is associated with a protein complex known as dynactin, which contains ten sub-units. The heavy chains forming the two globular heads contain the ATPase and microtubule motor domains. One striking difference that dynein exhibits compared to kinesins and myosins is that dynein has AAA (ATPases Associated with a variety of cellular Activities) modules, which indicate that its mode of working will be entirely different from kinesins and myosins. This puts dyneins into the AAA superfamily of mechanoenzymes.

The dynein heavy chains contain six tandemly linked AAA modules with the head having a ring-like domain organisation, typical of AAA superfamily. Four of these are nucleotide binding motifs, named P_1-P_4, but only P_1 (AAA1) is able to hydrolyze ATP. Because dynein is larger and more complex structure as compared to other motor proteins, its mode of operation is not as well known. However, very recently, Burgess et al. have used electron microscopy and image processing to show the structure of a flagellar dynein at the start and end of its power stroke, giving some insight into its possible mode of force generation. When the dynein contains bound ADP and Vi (vandate), it is in the prepower stroke conformation.

The state when it has lost the two, known as the apostate is the more compact postpower stroke state. There is a distinct conformational change involving the stem, linker, head, and the stalk that produces about 15 nm of translation onto the microtubule bound to the stalk.

Flagella motors

Unicellular organisms, such as, Escherichia coli have an interesting mode of motility. They have a number of molecular motors, about 45 nm in diameter, that drive their "feet" or the flagella that help the cell to swim. Motility is critical for cells, as they often have to travel from a less favourable to a more favourable environment. The flagella are helical filaments that extend out of the cell into the medium and perform a function analogous to what the oars perform to a boat.

The flagella and the motor assembly are called a flagellum. The flagella motors impart a rotary motion into the flagella. In addition to a rotary mechanism, the flagella machines consist of components such as rate meters, particle counters, and gearboxes. These are necessary to help the cell decide which way to go, depending on the change of concentration of nutrients in the surroundings. The rotary motion imparted to the flagella needs to be modulated to ensure the cell is moving in the proper direction as well as all flagella of the given cell are providing a concerted effort towards it. When the motors rotate the flagella in a counter-clockwise direction as viewed along the flagella filament from outside, the helical flagella create a wave away from the cell body.

Adjacent flagella subsequently intertwine in a propulsive corkscrew manner and propel the bacteria. When the motors rotate clockwise, the flagella fly apart, causing the bacteria to tumble, or change its direction. These reversals occur randomly, giving the bacterium a "random walk," unless of course, there is a preferential direction of motility due to reasons mentioned earlier. The flagella motors allow the bacteria to move at speeds of as much as 25 µm/sec with directional reversals occurring approximately 1 per sec.

A number of bacterial species in addition to E. coli, depend on flagella motors for motility. Some of these are Salmonella enterica serovar Typhimurium (Salmonella), Streptococcus, Vibrio spp., Caulobacter, Leptospira, Aquaspirrilum serpens, and Bacillus. The rotation of flagella motors is stimulated by a flow of ions through them which is a result of a build-up of a transmembrane ion gradient. There is no direct ATPinvolvement, however, the proton gradient needed for the functioning of flagella motors can be produced by ATPase. Newer models of the motor function are still being proposed with an aim to explain observed experimental phenomena . That means that we do not fully understand the functioning of this motor.

A typical flagella motor from E. coli consists of about 20 different proteins, while there are yet more that are involved in the assembly and functioning. There are 14 Flg-type proteins named FlgA to FlgN; 5 Flh-type proteins called FlhA to FlhE; 19 Fli-type proteins named FliA to FliT; MotA and MotB making a total of 40 related proteins.

The name groups Flg, Flh, Fli, and Flg originate from the names of the corresponding genes. Out of these the main structural proteins are FliC or the filament; FliD (filament cap); FliF or the MS-ring; FliG; FliM, and FliN (C-ring); FlgB, FlgC, and FlgF (proximal rod); FlgG (distal rod); FlgH (L-ring); FlgI (P-ring); FlgK and FlgL (hook-filament junction); and MotA-MotB (torque generating units). Earlier it was believed that theMand S are two separate rings and M was named after membrane and S after supramembranous. Now they are jointly called the MS-ring as it has been found that they are two domains of the same protein FliF.

The C-ring is named after cytoplasmic, while the names of the P and L-rings come from "peptidoglycan" and "lipopolysaccharide," respectively. The FlhA, B, FliH, I, O, P, Q, R constitute the "transport apparatus." The hook and filament part of the flagellum is located outside the cell body, while the motor portion is embedded in the cell membrane with parts (the C-ring and the transport apparatus) that are inside the inner membrane in the cytoplasmic region. MotA and MotB are arranged in a circular array embedded in the inner membrane, with the MS-ring at the center.

Connected to the MS-ring is the proximal end of a shaft, to which the P-ring, which is embedded in the peptidoglycan layer, is attached. Moving further outwards, there is the L-ring embedded in the outer cell membrane followed by the distal shaft end that protrudes out of the cell. To this end there is an attachment of the hook and the filament, both of which are polymers of hook-protein and flagellin, respectively.

The flagellar motors in most cases are powered by protons .owing through the cell membrane (protonmotive force, defined earlier) barring exceptions such as certain marine bacteria, for example, the Vibrio spp., which are driven by Na^+ ions. There are about 1200 protons required to rotate the motor by one rotation.

A complete explanation of how this proton flow is able to generate torque is not available as of today. From what is known, the stator units of MotA and MotB play an important role in torque generation. They form a MotA/MotB complex which when oriented properly binds to the peptidoglycan and opens proton channels through which protons can flow. It is believed that there are eight such channels per motor. The protonmotive force is a result of the difference of pH in the outside and the inside of the cell.

The E. coli cells like to maintain a pH of 7.6-7.8 on their inside, hence depending on the pH of the surroundings, the protonmotive force will vary, and hence the speed of rotation of their motors. To test how the speed of rotation depends on the protonmotive force, the motors were powered by external voltage with markers acting as heavy loads attached to them. It was found that the rotation indeed depends directly on the protonmotive force. According to the most widely accepted model, MotA/MotB complex interacts with the rotor via binding sites.

The passage of protons through aMotA/MotB complex (stator or torque generator) moves it so that they bind to the next available binding site on the rotor, thereby stretching their linkage. When the linkage recoils, the rotor assembly has to rotate by one step. Hence, whichever complex receives protons from the flux will rotate the rotor, generating torque. The torque-speed dependence of the motor has been studied in detail and indicates the torque range of about 2700 to 4600 pN nm.

DNA-Based Molecular Machines

DNA mainly as an information carrier. There was no mechanical work assigned to it. Energy conversion, trafficking, sensing, etc., were the tasks assigned mainly to proteins. Probably for this reason, DNA turns out to be a simpler structure - with only four kinds of nucleotide bases adenosine, thiamine, guanine, and cytosine (A, T, G, and C) attached in a linear fashion that take a double helical conformation when paired with a complementary strand. Such structural simplicity vis-à-vis proteins—made of 20 odd amino acids with complex folding patterns—results in a simpler structure and predictable behaviour. There are certain qualities that make DNA an attractive choice for the construction of artificial nanomachines.

In recent years, DNA has found use in not only mechanochemical, but also in nanoelectronic systems as well. A DNA double-helical molecule is about 2 nm in diameter and has 3.4-3.6nm helical pitch no matter what its base composition is; a structural uniformity is not achievable with protein structures if one changes their sequence.

. Furthermore, double-stranded DNA (*ds*-DNA) has a respectable persistence length of about 50 nm which provides it enough rigidity to be a candidate component of molecular machinery. Single stranded DNA (*ss*-DNA) is very flexible and cannot be used where rigidity is required, however, this flexibility allows its application in machine components like hinges or nanoactuators. Its persistence length is about 1 nm nm covering up to three base pairs at 1 M salt concentration.

Other than the above structural features there are two important and exclusive properties that make DNAsuitable for molecular level constructions. These are-molecular recognition and self-assembly. The nucleotide bases A and T on two different *ss*-DNA have affinity towards each other, so do G and C. Effective and stable *ds*-DNA structures are only formed if the base orders of the individual strands are complementary. Hence, if two complementary single strands of DNA are in a solution, they will eventually recognise each other and hybridise or zip-up forming a *ds*-DNA.

This property of molecular recognition and selfassembly has been exploited in a number of ways to build complex molecular structures. In the mechanical perspective, if the free energy released by hybridisation of two complementary DNA strands is used to lift a hypothetical load, a force capacity of 15 pN can be achieved, comparable to that of other molecular machines like kinesin (5 pN). Dr. Nadrian Seeman and colleagues built the first artificial DNA-based structure in the form of a cube in 1991. They then went on to create more complex structures such as knots and Borromean rings. In addition to these individual constructs, 2D arrays with the help of the double-crossover (DX) DNA molecule. This DX molecule gave the structural rigidity required to create a dynamic molecular device, the B-Z switch.

DNA double helices can be of three types - the A, B, or the Z-DNA. The B-DNA is the natural, right-handed helical form of DNA, while the A-DNA is a shrunken, low-humidity form of the B-DNA. Z-DNA can be obtained from certain C-G base repeat sequences occurring in B-DNA that can take a left-handed double helical form. The CG repeated base pair regions can be switched between the left and the right-handed conformations by changing ionic concentration.

The switch was designed in such a way that it had three cyclic strands of DNA, two of them wrapped around a central strand that had the CG-repeat region in the middle. On the two free ends of the side strands fluorescent dyes were attached in order to monitor the conformational change. With the change in ionic concentration the central CG-repeat sequence could alternate between the B and the Z modes bidirectionally which was observed through Förster resonance energy transfer (FRET) spectroscopy.

Protein-Based Motors Under Development

There are two protein-based motors that are at initial developmental stages and yet possess some very original and interesting characteristics.

Viral protein linear motors

The idea of Viral Protein Linear (VPL) motors stems from the fact that families of retroviruses like the influenza virus and the HIV-1 has a typical mechanism of infecting a human cell. When such a virus comes near the cell it is believed that due to the environment surrounding the cell it experiences a drop in pH of its surroundings. This is a kind of a signal to the virus that its future host is near. The drop in pH changes the energetics of the outer (envelope glycoprotein) protein of the viralmembrane in such a way that there is a distinct conformational change in a part of it. A triple stranded coiled coil domain of the membrane protein changes conformation from a loose random structure to a distinctive a-helical conformation.

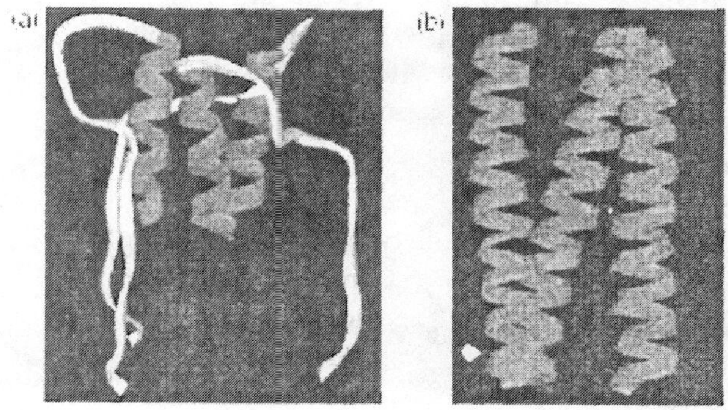

Figure 9. VPL motor at (a) neutral and (b) acidic pH

It is proposed to isolate this domain from the virus and trigger the conformational change by variation of pH in vitro. Once this is realised, attachments can be added to the N or C (or both) terminals of the peptide and a reversible linear motion can be achieved. Figure 9 shows a triple stranded coiled coil structure at a pH of 7.0; the inverted hairpin-like coils shown in the front view in Figure 9(a) and top view in Figure 9(b) change conformation into extended helical coils as seen in Figure 9(b).

Synthetic contractile polymers

In a recent development, large plant proteins that can change conformation when stimulated by positively charged ions were separated from their natural environment and shown to exert forces in orthogonal directions. Proteins from sieve elements of higher plants that are a part of the microfluidics system of the plant were chosen to build a new protein molecular machine element.

These elements change conformations in the presence of Ca^{2+} ions and organise themselves inside the tubes so as to stop the fluid flow in case there is a rupture downstream. This is a natural defence mechanism seen in such plants. The change in conformation is akin to a balloon inflating and extending in its lateral as well as longitudinal directions.

These elements, designated as "forisomes" adhered on to glass tubes were shown to reversibly swell in the presence of Ca^{2+} ions and shrink in their absence, hence performing a pulling/pushing action in both directions.

Artificially prepared protein bodies like the forisomes could be a useful molecular machine component in a future molecular assembly, producing forces of the order of micronewtons. Unlike the ATP-dependant motors discussed previously, these machine elements are more robust because they can perform in the absence of their natural environment as well.

Future Trends of Bio-nanorobotics

The development of bionanorobotic systems and their components present difficult fabrication and control challenges. Such devices will operate in biological environments whose physical properties differ from those encountered by conventional parts.

The idea is to use molecular motors as the actuators of such nanorobots, where the structural elements are carbon nanotubes, while the joints are formed by appropriately designed protein and/or DNA elements. Development of a complete database of different biomolecular machine components, the ability to interface or assemble different machine components and the development of accurate models are some of the challenges to be faced in a near future. The application of advanced virtual reality techniques (VR) in bio-nanotechnology allowed to study, simulate, visualise and interact with molecular biology, genomics, proteomics, structural and computational biology.

As far we know, only basic molecular elements have been studied until now. As a perspective of these developments, VR-based technology could be used for the biomolecular robot design. VR refers to computer-generated, interactive, 3-D environments into which people are immersed. It provides a way for people to visualise, manipulate, and interact with simulated environments through the use of computers and extremely complex data.

Emerging VR applications such as manipulation of molecules for development of molecular machines will enhance the operator's perception (vision and haptics) by approaching more or less a state of 'full immersion' or 'telepresence'. They will enable the designer of molecular machines to extend his / her eyes and hands into the molecular-world and also enable new types of exploration and whole new classes of experiments in the biological and physical sciences.

Although many of the described technologies have been developed into more or less mature products for robots acting in the macro-world, the nano-size of the molecular robots poses extreme challenges and requires a complete rethinking of the visual and haptic perception of nanoworld. Using simulated biological nanoenviroments in VR, the operator can design and characterise through physical simulation the behaviour of bio-nanorobots.

Adding haptic interaction, the operator can explore and prevent the problems of bio-nanorobots in their native environment. These immersive VR techniques allows the 3D visualisation of scientific data and for modelling and animating complex nanoengineering systems. This article review some of the emerging applications of VR currently underway in the field of bio-nanotechnology with envisioned applications to molecular robotics.

Structural Biological Macromolecules

Structural information on biological macromolecules is an essential requirement for our understanding of biological functions. From the very beginning of structural biology, visualisation was essential for determining and understanding structures.

The initial work in this area was the use of Visualisation and Virtual Reality for Bioinformatics, especially for the 3D structural analysis of biomolecular system.

Surface and volume based visualisation provide three-dimensional concepts of bio-molecular structure. Virtual Reality offers a channel to reach-into the molecular space in an immersive and interactive environment. Progress in the X-ray and nuclear magnetic resonance (NMR) instrumentation and computer and software technology has led to an increasing rate of accumulation of new biological structures such as proteins and DNA.

The Protein Data Bank has a database of coordinate entries of 21,248 proteins. Proteins are complex biological structures made up of several hundred atoms. The usual approach to visualise such a molecule is to retrieve the coordinate files from the database and then use one of the molecular graphics software packages.

These packages largely provide mono representations of molecular images without any interactivity. Use of Virtual Reality Modelling Language (VRML) can provide a 3D and immersive environment with provision for stereo representations of the molecules. This not only helps in better understanding the molecular structure but also provides insight into the chemical and biochemical properties of the molecule such as number of hydrogen bonds.

The bio-systems are made up of atoms and since atoms cannot be observed directly. Commonly available physical models provide an intuitive representation of structural molecular biology. When applied to large molecules, such as proteins and the molecular assemblies found in cells, computer graphics simulation can be used to accurately portray various molecular computational models, with their varying complexities.

Electrostatic field data around the molecules of interest, interatomic forces, laws of quantum mechanics, and so on represents the variety of bio-molecular nanointeractions. However, these methods lack the beneficial tactile and kinaesthetic attributes of real physical models. By coupling an accurate molecular dynamics simulation code to an immersive virtual reality display with interactive capabilities and manual force feedback, "immersive" visualisation of molecular atoms could be improved.

In order to create multimodality enhancements of such tangible models, VR-based technology is an interesting tool. By superimposing additional graphical information on top of fabricated models, e.g. augmented reality, by incorporating support for voice commands and by providing haptic interface for sensing the electrostatic charges and interatomic collisions, the user would be able to interact with these virtual enhancements haptically while manipulating the physical model.

6

Modelling and Simulation

Molecular modelling is one of the key technologies that the chemical industry needs to revolutionise its ability to design and optimise chemicals and the processes to manufacture them. Molecular modelling already plays a major role in the chemical, materials, and pharmaceutical industries in the design of new products, the design and optimisation of manufacturing processes, and the troubleshooting of existing processes. However, the exquisite dependence on details of molecular composition and structures at the nanoscale means that attempting to understand nanoscale systems and control the processes to produce them based solely on experimental characterisation is out of the question. The field of nanoscience is quite broad and encompasses a wide range of yet-to-beunderstood phenomena and structures.

Rational fabrication and integration of nanoscale materials and devices offers the promise of revolutionising science and technology, provided that principles underlying their unique dynamics and properties can be discovered, understood, and fully exploited. However, functional nanoscale structures often involve quite dissimilar materials (for example, organic or biological in contact with inorganic), are frequently difficult to characterise experimentally, and must ultimately be assembled, controlled, and utilised by manipulating quantities (e.g., temperature, pressure, stress) at the macroscale. This combination of features puts unprecedented demands on theory, modelling, and simulation: for example, due to nanoscale dimensionality, quantum effects are often important, and the usual theories valid either for bulk systems or for small molecules break down.

Qualitatively new theories are needed for this state of matter intermediate between the atomic scale and a large-enough scale for collective behaviour to take over, as well as methods for connecting the nanoscale with finer and coarser scales. Theory, modelling, and simulation in nanoscale science considered three broad classes of nanosystems:

— The first class consisted of nano building blocks (such as nanotubes, quantum dots, clusters, and nanoparticles), some of which can be synthesised quite reproducibly and well characterised experimentally.

— The second class consisted of complex nanostructures and nano-interfaces, reflecting the importance of nanointerfaces in a wide variety of nanoscale systems. This session was specifically asked to consider steady-state properties of complex nanostructures and nanointerfaces.

— The focus of the third session was dynamics, assembly, and growth of nanostructures, and so was concerned with the dynamical aspects of complex nanostructures.

Hence, transport properties of complex nanostructures, as well as the dynamic processes leading to their creation, particularly self-assembly, were central to this session. Given the ostensibly different charges presented to each group, there is remarkable unanimity in their conclusions with respect to the outstanding theory, modelling, and simulation needs and opportunities. Among the common themes are:

— the need for fundamental theory of dynamical electron structure and transport

— algorithmic advances and conceptual understanding leading to efficient electronic structure calculations of large numbers of atoms

— new theoretical treatments to describe nano-interfaces and assembly of nanostructures

— fundamentally sound methods for bridging length and time scales and their integration into seamless modelling environments

— commitment to an infrastructure for community-based open-source codes.

Nano Building Blocks

Well characterised building blocks for nanoscience need to be created and quantitatively understood for a number of crucial reasons. A key aspect of construction, whether at the macroscopic or microscopic scale, is the notion of a "building block." Office buildings are often made from bricks and girders, molecular components from atoms. Just as knowledge of the atom allows us to make and manipulate molecular species, knowledge of bricks and mortar allows us to construct high-rise buildings. Well-characterised nano building blocks will be the centerpiece of new functional nanomechanical, nanoelectronic, and nanomagnetic devices. A quantitative understanding of the transport, dynamics, electronic, magnetic, thermodynamic, and mechanical properties is crucial to building at the nanoscale. As an example, current theoretical approaches to nanoelectronics often cannot accurately predict I-V curves for the simplest molecular systems. Without a coherent and accurate theoretical description of this most fundamental aspect of devices, progress in this area will necessarily be limited.

Theoretical studies for these systems will necessarily have to be based on approximate methods; the systems are simply too large and too complex to be handled purely by ab initio methods. Even if the problems are tractable, we will make much greater progress with well-validated approximate models.

Thus a variety of benchmarking methodologies and validation testing are needed to establish the accuracy and effectiveness of new models and approximate theory. At the nanoscale, what are the nano building blocks that would play an analogous role to macro building blocks? Several units come to mind which range from clusters less than 1 nm in size to nanoparticles, such as aerosols and aerogels much larger than 100 nm. However, we believe the bestcharacterised and most appropriate building blocks are:

— clusters and molecular nanostructures

— nanotubes and related systems

— quantum wells, wires, films and dots.

These blocks are well defined by experiment and frequently tractable using contemporary theory. Moreover, they have been demonstrated to hold promise in existing technology.

Electronic Devices

Any electronic device needs to control and manipulate current. At the nanoscale, new phenomena come into play. Classical descriptions become inoperable compared to quantum phenomena such as tunneling, fluctuations, confined dimensionality, and the discreteness of the electric charge. At these dimensions, the system will be dominated entirely by surfaces. This presents further complications for electronic materials, which often undergo strong and complex reconstructions.

Defining accurate structure at the interface will be difficult. However, without an accurate surface structure, it will be even more difficult to compute any transport properties. Moreover, current-induced changes within the structure may occur. This situation will require the complexity, but not intractable approach, of a careful self-consistent solution in a nonequilibrium environment.

At confined dimensions, optical properties of matter are often dramatically altered. For example, silicon is the dominant electronic material, but it has poor optical properties for optoelectronic devices such as solar cells or lasers. However, at small dimensions the properties of silicon can be dramatically altered; the band gap in silicon can be blueshifted from the infrared to the optical region. One of the first manifestations of this effect occurs in porous silicon, which exhibits remarkable room temperature luminescence. To properly capitalise on such phenomena, a deeper quantitative understanding of the optical properties of matter will be required. Optical excitations are especially challenging because most commonly used methods for structural energies, such as density functional theory, are not well suited for excited state properties. The problem is exacerbated for nanoscale systems, where the many-body effects are enhanced by the physical confinement of the excitation.

While silicon dominates electronic devices, there is a fundamental limit to this technology. As the size of a transistor is reduced each year, eventually one will approach the new size regimes where traditional electronics must be viewed in different terms. The approach to this regime will happen in the not too distant future. Current lithographic techniques can create semiconductor chips with characteristic lengths of only a few hundred nanometers; quantum effects are likely to dominate at tens of nanometers. At this latter length scale, transistor technology will be solidly in the regime of quantum phenomena.

Components will eventually function solely through quantum effects, for which we will need the capability to accurately simulate or predict in order to control. It has been suggested that new computers can be devised at nanoscales that will function by using the creation of coherent quantum states. By creating and maintaining such coherent states, it should be possible to store enormous amounts of information with unprecedented security. In order to construct such new quantum computers, new fabrication methods will need to be found and guided by theory. Current technology is far removed from the routine generation of quantum logic gates and quantum networks. Without a better quantitative description of the science at the nanoscale, the emergence of quantum computing will not happen.

Nanotechnology has the potential to make great advances in medical technology and biosecurity. The technologies for controlling and processing materials for semiconductor devices can be used to make types of nanointerfaces. Nanostructure synthesis and joining of biological or soft matter with traditional semiconductors like silicon would offer new pathways to the construction of novel devices. For example, one could gain the ability to develop new types of sensors directly integrated into current device technology. A number of clear applications such as biosensors for national security, drug delivery and monitoring, and disease detection are plausible.

However, numerous complex and difficult issues must be addressed. These include quantitative descriptions of nanofluids, reaction kinetics, and a selectivity to particular biological agents. Perhaps no systems are as complex at the nanoscale as these, because they require the understanding of the details of interactions between quite diverse systems, i.e., soft, biological materials inter-faced with semiconductors or other in organic solids.

Spintronics centers on controlling the spin of electrons in addition to controlling other transport properties. For example, dilute magnetic semiconductors have attracted considerable attention, because they hold the promise of using electron spin, in addition to charge, for creating a new class of spintronic semiconductor devices with unprecedented functionality.

Suggested applications include spin field effect transistors, which could allow for software reprogramming of the microprocessor hardware during run time; semiconductor-based spin valves, which would result in high-density, non-volatile semiconductor memory chips; and even spin qubits, to be used as the basic building block for quantum computing. At the nanoscale, spintronic devices offer special challenges owing to the enhanced exchange terms arising from quantum confinement. Few quantitative studies exist on magnetic properties of quantum dots and the evolution of ferromagnetic properties with size.

Theory and Modelling

These five areas of research offer great promise but will require new theories (approximate models) and computationally intensive studies. Current algorithms must be made more efficient and sometimes more accurate, or new algorithms must emerge in order to address the challenges highlighted above.

Ab initio methods can address systems with hundreds of atoms, and empirical methods can handle tens of thousands of atoms. To fully exploit these approaches, algorithms need to be made scalable and take full advantage of current computer technology, i.e., highly parallel environments. Fully ab initio methods are especially useful in providing benchmarks for these building blocks, where experimental data is lacking or is unreliable due to unknown variability or uncontrolled critical function characteristics. Embedding methods whereby one can take the best features of a particular approach will be crucial. Algorithms for particular aspects of nanoscale systems need to be developed. For example, ab initio methods for optical properties such as GW and Bethe-Salpeter methods are known to be accurate and robust, yet these systems are limited in their applicability to rather small systems, e.g., to systems of less than 50 atoms. The essential physical features of these methods need to be adapted to address much larger systems.

Nonequilibrium and quantum dynamics present special problems. These systems often lack clear prescriptions for obtaining reliable results. Some recent attempts to match experiments on electron transport through molecular systems often get the correct transport trends, but not quantitative numbers. A number of entanglements exist: Is the experimental data reliable owing to problems with contacts? Or is there some fundamental component missing from our understanding?

New experiments will need to be designed to ensure reproducibility and the validity of the measurements. New theories will need to be constructed and crosschecked by resorting to the fundamental building blocks. A chronic and continuing challenge arising in most nanosystems concerns a lack of understanding of structural relationships. Often nanosystems have numerous degrees of freedom that are not conducive to simple structural minimisations. Simulated annealing, genetic algorithms, and related techniques can be used for some systems, but in general it will require new optimisation techniques in order to obtain a quantitative description of the structure of nanoscale systems.

While great strides have been made in simulation methods, a number of fundamental issues remain. The diversity of time and length scales remains a great challenge at the nanoscale. Rare event simulation methods will be essential in describing a number of phenomena such as crystal growth, surface morphologies, and diffusion. Of course, the transcription of quantum force fields to classical interatomic potentials is a difficult task. Intrinsic quantum attributes like hybridisation and charge transfer remain a challenge to incorporate into classical descriptions. At best, current classical-like descriptions can be used for targeted applications.

Complex Nano-Interfaces

Central to nanoscience is the assembly and manipulation of fundamental building blocks on the nanoscale to create functional structures, materials, and devices. Unlike traditional materials, nanostructured materials that will enable the nanotechnology revolution will be highly complex and heterogeneous in shape and substance, composed of dissimilar materials, and dominated by nano-interfaces (Figure 1). These characteristics require that new theoretical approaches and computational tools be developed to provide a fundamental understanding of complexity at the nanoscale, the physics and chemistry of nano-interfaces, and how interfaces and complexity at the nanoscale control properties and behaviour at larger scales.

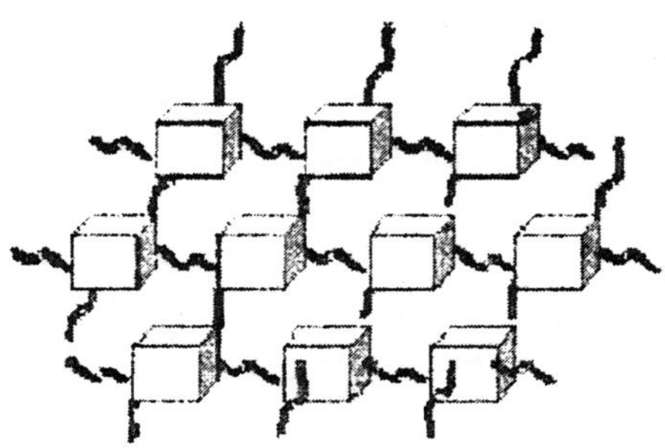

Figure 1. Schematic of an assembled structure of nanoscopic building blocks tethered by organic "linkers." The structure is dominated by interfacial connections

Nano-interfaces and complexity at the nanoscale play a central role in nearly all aspects of nanoscience and nanotechnology. For example, in molecular electronic devices, DNA and other biomolecules such as proteins are being explored both as assemblers of molecular components like carbon nanotubes and semiconductor quantum dots (Figure 2), and as active components themselves. In such devices, soft biomolecular matter and hard matter will come together at complex nanointerfaces across which transport of charge may occur, or which may provide structural stability.

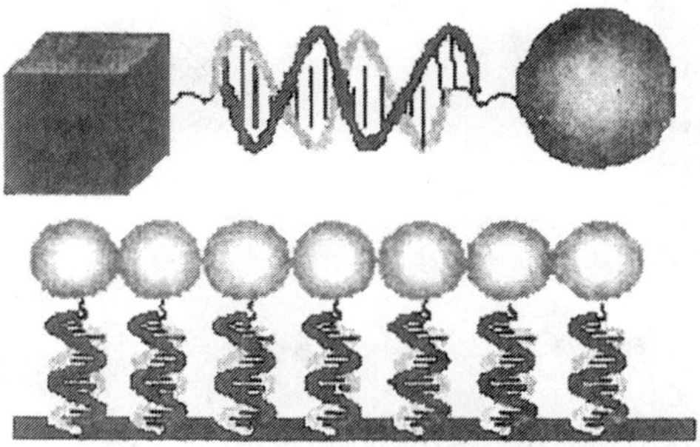

Figure 2. Top: Schematic of nanoscale building blocks tethered by DNA

In new spintronic devices, the nano-interfaces between ferromagnetic and antiferromagnetic domains may control the speed of switching needed for faster computers. In polymer nanocomposites, where nanoscopic particles are added to a polymer, interactions at the polymer/particle nanointerface can have profound effects on bulk properties, leading to stronger yet lighterweight structural and other materials. The manipulation of interfaces in soft matter systems at the nanoscale provides a wealth of opportunities to design functional, nanostructured materials for templating, scaffolds for catalysis or tissue growth, photonic devices, and structural materials.

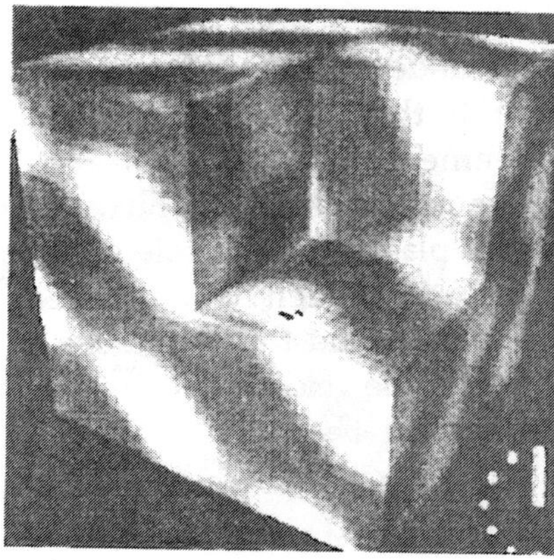

Figure 3. Simulation of nanostructured domains in a polymer blend where the interfaces are controlled at the nanoscale

The high surface-to-volume ratio resulting from the prevalence of nano-interfaces, combined with the complexity of these nano-interfaces and of nanostructures, provides much of the challenge in developing predictive theories in nanoscience. In this respect, materials designed at the nanoscale are distinctly different from traditional bulk materials. One of the largest driving forces behind the need for new theory and simulation in nanoscience is the fact that there are few experimental techniques capable of directly imaging or probing nano-interfaces. Typically, those techniques having atomicscale resolution require extensive theory to produce more than qualitative information. Indeed, it is likely that the fundamental interfacial and spatial information required to predict the behaviour and performance of nanostructures will come from simulation and theory in many cases.

Focused theory and simulation at a wide range of scales is needed to develop a quantitative understanding of nano-interfaces and their consequent influence on properties and emergent behaviour of nanoscale materials and devices. Breakthroughs in theory and simulation will also be necessary in order to describe and predict the complexity of nanostructures and the relationship between structural complexity and emergent properties and behaviour. A major challenge for nanoscience in which theory, modelling, and simulation will play a pivotal role lies in the definition of the nano-interface, which is nontrivial because the definition may depend upon the properties or behaviour of interest. For example, the relevant nano-interface leading to a particular mechanical behaviour may be different than that for transport properties, such as electrical transport.

Strategies for addressing nano-interfaces will also be needed. With an appropriate definition of nanointerfaces, new approaches can be developed that characterise relevant nano-interfaces in order to construct quantitatively predictive theories that relate the nano-interfaces to interesting nanoscale properties and behaviour. To develop theories and quantitative understanding of nano-interfaces, it will be necessary to obtain information on the organisation of matter at nano-interfaces, that is, the arrangement, composition, conformation, and orientation of matter at hard-hard, hard-soft, and soft-soft nano-interfaces.

Much of this information may only be accessible by simulation, at least for the foreseeable future. The geometry and topology of nano-interfaces, bonding at nanointerfaces, structure and dynamics at or near a nano-interface, transport across nanointerfaces, confinement at nano-interfaces, deformation of nano-interfaces, activity and reactivity at nano-interfaces, etc. must all be investigated by simulation. Such information is needed before very accurate theories relating all of these to material and device operations and behaviour will be fully formulated and validated. For example, to properly design, optimise and fabricate molecular electronic devices and components, we must quantitatively understand transport across soft/hard contacts, which in turn will likely depend on the arrangement of components on the surface and the complexity of structures that can be assembled in one, two, and three dimensions.

Comprehending transport will likely require a quantitative understanding of the nature of nano-interfaces between biological matter and hard matter, between synthetic organic matter and hard matter, and between biological matter and synthetic organic matter. It will also require optimisation of structures and tailoring of nanointerfaces, which in turn will require a quantitative understanding of the stability of nano-interfaces. As we move towards the goal of firstprinciples-based fully theoretical prediction of the properties of nanoscale systems, there is an urgent need to critically examine the application of bulk thermodynamic and statistical mechanical theories to nanostructures and nano-interfaces, where violations of the second law of thermodynamics have been predicted and observed, and where mechanical behaviour is not described by continuum theories. Theories are required that abstract from behaviour at a specific nano-interface to predict the behaviour of extended structures or material that is comprised of primarily nanointerfaces.

Additionally, when describing nanostructures that are collections of a countable number of fundamental building blocks, one must question whether the concept of temperature has the same meaning as in a bulk system. An important task for theoreticians and simulationists will be to identify what can be brought to nanoscience from traditional methods of investigation and description, and then determine what new theories or approaches must be invoked at the nanoscale. When materials or devices are dominated by nano-interfaces, new physics is likely to result. Examples of nano-interfacedominated physics include the electric field at surfaces, luminescence of rare-earth orthosilicates, surface-enhanced Raman scattering, and deformation of nanocrystalline materials. Nanocomposites and nanoassemblies are just two examples of nanostructures where nano-interfaces are prevalent and may dominate behaviour at larger scales.

The high surface-to-volume ratio of complex nanostructures may also lead to novel collective or emergent phenomena, which would require new theory and simulation efforts to address and understand. Because of the present lack of theories to fully describe nano-interfaces at the nanoscale and the ramifications of nanointerfaces on larger scales, and the lack of experimental data on nano-interfaces, simulations will play a pivotal role in advancing knowledge in this area.

Ab initio calculations in particular will be required, but the present state of the art limits the number of atoms to numbers too small to obtain meaningful data in many instances. Consequently, breakthroughs in methodologies will be required to push ab initio simulations to larger scales. Ab initio simulations containing of the order of 10,000 atoms would enable, for example, the study of spin structure at antiferromagnetic-ferromagnetic nano-interfaces. New or improved computational methods are needed to simulate also the dynamics of nano-interfaces from first principles.

Such simulations will be needed to predict, for example, electronic transport across nano-interfaces, as well as to provide validation or benchmarks for coarser-grained theoretical descriptions of nano-interfaces in which electronic structure is not explicitly considered. For molecular dynamics methods and other classical, particle-based methods, new (for many purposes reactive) force fields capable of describing nano-interfaces between dissimilar materials are urgently needed. For some problems, further coarsegraining will be required to capture complexity on all relevant length and time scales, and thus new mesoscale theories and computational methods will be needed. To connect the properties and behaviour of complex nanostructures and/or nano-interfaces to properties and behaviour at the macroscale, it may be necessary to develop new constitutive laws (and ask if it is even appropriate to talk about constitutive laws in systems where properties and behaviour are dominated by nano-interfaces) and then develop and integrate theories at different levels.

Time and Length Scales

Most phenomena of interest in nanoscience and nanotechnology, like many phenomena throughout science and engineering, demand that multiple scales be represented for meaningful modelling. However, phenomena of interest at the nanoscale may be extreme in this regard because of the lower end of the scale range.

Many phenomena of importance have an interaction with their environment at macro space and time scales, but must be modeled in any first-principles sense at atomistic scales. The time scale required to resolve quantum mechanical oscillations may be as small as a femtosecond (10^{-15} s), whereas protein folding requires microseconds (a range of 10^{9}), and engineered nanosystems may require still longer simulation periods, e.g., creep of materials relevant to reliability considerations may be measured in years.

Counting trials in probabilistic analyses contributes another time-like factor to the computational complexity, although this latter factor comes with welcome, nearly complete algorithmic concurrency, unlike evolutionary time. Meanwhile, spatial scales may span from angstroms to centimeters (a range of 10^{8}). The cube of this would be characteristic of a three-dimensional continuum-based analysis. Counting atoms or molecules in a single physical ensemble easily leads to the same range; Avogadro's number is about 10^{24}.

Exploiting the concurrency available with multiple independent ensembles multiplies storage requirements. Space-time resource requirements are staggering for many simulation scenarios. Therefore, nanoscience poses unprecedented challenges to the mathematics of multiscale representation and analysis and to the mathematics of synthesising models that operate at different scales. Existing techniques may certainly yield some fruit, but we are undoubtedly in need of fundamental breakthroughs in the form of new techniques.

Faced with similar types of challenges in macroscopic continuum problems, applied mathematicians have devised a wide variety of adaptive schemes (adaptation in mesh, adaptation in discretisation order, adaptation in model fidelity, etc.). Bringing these schemes to a "science" has required decades, and is not complete in the sense of predictable error control for a given investment, e.g., for some hyperbolic problems. Probably the greatest range of scales resolved purely by mesh adaptivity to date is about 10 decades in cosmological gravitation problems.

Of course, this range is practical only when the portion of the domain demanding refinement is small compared to the domain size required to include all of the objects of interest or, what is often the more demanding requirement, to graft on to reliably posed boundary conditions in the far field. Migrating such adaptive schemes into production software lags their scientific development by at least an academic generation and usually more. The challenge for nanoscience is therefore not only great, but also urgent. Applied mathematicians being trained today can acquire a doctoral degree without ever having been exposed to nanoscale phenomena.

The mathematical models and algorithms of nanoscience cover the gamut of continuous and discrete, deterministic and random. Ultimately, all simulations are executed by deterministic programmes on discrete data. The most capable computer platforms of 2002 (costing in excess of $100M) execute at most tens of teraflop/s (10^{13} floating point operations per second) and store in fast memory at most tens of terabytes and in disk farms at most hundreds of terabytes. Moreover, these machines do not perform efficiently for models at these capability extremes.

A typical extreme problem in computational science today encompasses only billions of discrete degrees of freedom (filling storage larger than this with auxiliary data, including geometry, physical constitutive data, and linear algebra workspaces) and runs for days at tens to hundreds of gigaflop/s. Routine problems encompass only millions of degrees of freedom and run for hours at around 1 gigaflop/ s.

The wildest extrapolations of Moore's Law for silicon cannot sate the appetite for cycles and memory in nanoscience modelling. It is clear that a brute force, firstprinciples approach to nanoscale phenomena will not succeed in bridging scales-or perhaps, given the promise of nanotechnology, we should say that it can only succeed through some "spiral" process, whereby nanotechnology yields superior computers, which yield superior nanoscale models, leading to improved nanotechnology and better computers, and so forth. Mathematical homogenisation (or "upscaling") whereby reliable coarse-scale results are derived from systems with unresolvable scales, without the need to generate the (out of reach) fine scale results as intermediates -is a success story with extensive theory (dating at least to the 1930s) and applications.

The trade-off between accuracy and efficiency is well understood. It is particularly fruitful, for instance, in simulating flows through inhomogeneous porous media or wave propagation through inhomogeneous transmissive media with multiple scatterers. One begins by considering just two scales. Given a 2 × 2 matrix of interactions: "coarse-coarse," "coarse-fine," "finecoarse," and "fine-fine," where the first member denotes the scale of an output behaviour and the second member the scale of the input that drives the behaviour, one can formally solve to eliminate the "fine-fine" block. (If the interactions are all linear, for instance, this can be done with block Gaussian elimination.)

This leaves a Schur complement system for the "coarse-coarse" block, where the interaction matrix is the original "coarse-coarse" block and a triple product term with the "fine-fine" inverse in the middle. The effect of the triple-product term can often be reliably approximated, yielding a model for coarse scales that incorporates the dynamics of both scales.

In principle, this process can be repeated recursively. The standard theory succeeds when there is good separation of scales between the inhomogeneous structure to be "homogenised" and the scales of interest in the solution. When there is significant interaction across length scales (when the "coarse-fine" and the "fine-coarse" interactions are large), the computation of effective properties at the coarse scales becomes more difficult. Work continues on such concepts as "multilevel renormalisation," and homogenisation should certainly be studied for fruitful approaches to nanoscale science. Another successful and now quotidian means of bridging scales in modelling is the concept of "space sharing" of different models, with different resolution requirements.

For instance, crack propagation in a solid can be effectively modeled with adaptive finite elements for linear elasticity in the mid and far fields, grafted onto molecular dynamics models at and immediately surrounding the crack tip and the newly exposed surface. As another example, the Richtmyer-Meshkov instability in fluid mechanics has been studied with a conventional computational fluid dynamics analysis for Navier-Stokes in the mid and far fields and direct simulation Monte Carlo on "lumped" fluid particles at the mixing interface. Atmospheric reentry problems have similarly been successfully modeled with sparse continuum models away from the body and Boltzmann models in the boundary layer at the body surface. Very significant scientific and engineering progress can be made with such models on today's high-end computers with such two-physics scale bridging.

Less dramatically, one can also cite a multitude of successful dual-continuum model approaches with different asymptotic forms of the governing equations in different regimes, e.g., classical boundary layer theory, in which viscosity terms are computed only in regions of steep gradients. In all of these examples, it is important that the dual models have a regime of overlap, where their solutions can be simultaneously represented and joined. In this sense, these approaches are somewhat complementary to that of homogenisation. An even less dramatic example, still, is the scenario in which the physical model remains the same throughout the domain, but the mathematical representation of it changes for computational efficiency.

The classic example of this is a combination of finite elements to resolve the geometry around a complex object (e.g., scatterer) in a differential equation approach and boundary elements to resolve the far field in an integral equation approach. These space-sharing approaches sometimes lack the mathematical rigor of adaptive approaches within a single physical and mathematical formulation, but with care to monitor and enforce conservation properties at the interface, they are practical and possibly to be emulated in nanoscale phenomena. A somewhat more trivial instance of bridging scales is what we might call "time sharing" of models, in analogy to "space sharing."

In such cases, different dynamically relevant physics "turns on" at different points in the simulation, so that it is acceptable to step over fast scales during one period, but necessary to resolve them in another. Modelling ignition in a combustion system provides one industrially important example. Cosmology enters again here with vastly different physics relevant in the very early universe (e.g., first three minutes) than in the long-term evolution. It is conceivable, with good software engineering, to marry the concepts of space sharing and time sharing of multiple physics models in a large and complex system, so that each region of space-time adaptively chooses the most cost-effective model and advancement algorithm.

One concept in the continuum modelling of multirate systems whose applicability to nanoscale multirate systems should be explored is that of im-plicit integration methods to "step over" fast time scales that are not dynamically relevant to the result, even though they are timestep limiting, due to stability considerations, in explicit integration. Examples abound, including acoustic waves in aerodynamics, gravity waves in climate modelling, Alfven waves in magnetohydrodynamics, and fast reactions between intermediate species in detailed kinetics of combustion. In these and many other cases, acceptably accurate results on slower (dynamically relevant) time scales can be achieved by making some equilibrium assumption about the fine dynamics in order to filter out the fast scales, enabling the integration to take place in coarse timesteps.

The price for this transformation of the equations to be integrated is usually an implicit solve, where a mathematical balance is enforced on each timestep. The algorithmic cost of an implicit integrator is much higher per step than that of an explicit integrator, but one can take many fewer steps to get to a desired point in simulation time. Whether this trade-off is a winning one for the overall simulation depends upon the cost of the implicit solve. As a rule of thumb in large-scale partial differential equations (PDEs), if the fast scales are two orders of magnitude or more faster than the dynamical scales of interest, implicit methods usually pay off.

If the ratio of scales is 10 or less, they likely do not. It may be that many ranges of time scales required by nanoscientists (e.g., integration intervals lasting billions of quantum mechanical oscillation periods) can be condensed by implicit algorithmics without loss of any relevant physics, following some statistical or equilibrium assumptions. Retreating further into simple, but often adequate, scale-bridging scenarios, there are many examples of one-way cascades of models, whereby a fine-scale problem is solved off-line to develop constitutive laws or material properties for a coarser-scale problem. It is increasingly practical, for instance, to simulate properties of novel alloys or explosives -materials with simple structure compared to fiber composites or nanotube networks-and then to employ these properties as proxies for experimental data in continuum simulations.

Sometimes the properties are quite ad hoc, for instance, eddy models in turbulence, to account for mixing at larger scales than molecular by an enhancement of the molecular viscosity in turbulent regimes. Large-eddy simulation, a fairly rigorous approximation, is emerging as very popular, and its practitioners may have fresh ideas when faced with nanoscale phenomena.

Source terms in turbulent reacting flows attempt to account for additional reaction intensity along fractally wrinkled flame fronts by parameterising smoother, resolvable flame front area. Both deterministic and probabilistic tools have proved fruitful in tuning to experiments and linking up with the fundamental conservation principles. This is a very applicationspecific technology, as will be, undoubtedly, many of those appropriate for bridging nanoscales. Although it is not a modelling technique but a solution technique, one should also mention multigrid as a paradigm.

Multigrid has already found success in molecular dynamics and in electronic structure algorithms and is likely to be embraced across a wider range of nanoscale applications. Multigrid has the beautiful property of conquering numerical ill conditioning (essentially caused by the presence of too many scales in view of the numerics all at once) by treating each scale on its own terms. This improves linear conditioning and nonlinear robustness of the solution method, and often leads to physical insight as well. For instance, problems in geometric design are often best approached by resolving largewavelength geometric parameters on coarse grids, and small-wavelength geometric parameters on finer ones.

Multigrid depends on a (usually purely mathematical) decomposition into ranges of scales, and on the ability to construct intergrid transfer operators and coarsened versions of the fundamental fine-scale operator on coarser scales. Another mathematical paradigm that may prove to have a resonance with the nanoscale community is the method known variously as proper orthogonal decomposition or principal component analysis. In both linear and nonlinear problems, it is often possible to represent the underlying dynamics of interest with a relatively small number of dynamical coefficients representing the weight of complex, system-dependent modes.

The challenge is to discover the modes of interest, which are almost never as numerous as the number of characteristic basis functions in the finest grid. The finely resolved setting may be required to determine the principal modes, but once found, production computing can be done in a reduced basis. Some degree of stochasticity is intrinsic at atomistic scales; hence, a Monte Carlo simulation will yield a fluctuation with statistics that must be carried to larger length scales.

The numerical analysis of stochastic partial differential equations could enter here, the goal being a coarse solution with the right statistics. The theory of large deviation for stochastic PDEs allows the designing of sampling methods for so-called "rare events." The long time integrations that are burdensome to the accuracy of deterministic models may actually be a benefit to the accuracy of statistical models. It is axiomatic to a mathematician that there are better ways than brute-force propagation of fine scales to attack a multiscale problem. A mathematician would argue that anyone requiring a billion degrees of freedom for a week of wall clock execution time is running the wrong algorithm. Indeed, the nanoscale community must learn to compute "smarter" and not just "harder." Part of this will come from optimal algorithmics (e.g., linear scaling in DFT), but a larger and yet unknown portion of it will come from intrinsically multiscale models, created collaboratively with mathematical scientists.

It is easy to construct scenarios in which such modelling is attractive, and probably necessary. We mention here an example that appears to demand vast bridging of scales for unified scientific understanding, the operation of a biosensor to detect trace quantities of a biologically active molecule.

— At the smallest scale, a molecule can be sensed by the luminescence characteristic of an optical energy gap. Quantum Monte Carlo could be used for a highaccuracy comparison with experiment.

— At the next scale, where one needs to gain a quantitative understanding of surface structure and interface bonding, DFT and first-principles molecular dynamics could be employed.

— At the next higher scale, one would need to gain a quantitative understanding of the atomistic coupling of the molecule to be detected with the solvent that transports it to the sensor.

— Finally, at the macroscale, the solvent itself could be characterised with a continuous model, based on finite elements.

Each phenomenon depends upon the phenomenon at the scale above and the scale below, which means that there is two-way coupling between mathematically different models at different scales.

The Holy Grail of nanoscale modelling is a seamless bridging of scales with tight bidirectional coupling between every scaleadjacent pair of a sequence of models, from nano through micro and meso to macro. This bridging necessarily must involve scaleappropriate algorithmics at each scale, with well-understood error dependence on the computational resolution in each model, and with error control for information transfer between scales. For optimality, algorithms should be prudent in their use of fine-scale information-using the coarsest scale suitable for obtaining the requisite error in each result.

Algorithmic advancement

Due to the inherent complexity of nanostructures, theoretical models will generally need to be instantiated as computational simulations. Many such simulations will involve intensive computation, requiring sophisticated algorithms and software running on state-of-the-art parallel computers. Algorithmic advances can be a critical enabling component for progress in nanoscience modelling. New and more efficient algorithms advance scientific frontiers in several ways:

— Larger simulations can be performed. For example, more atoms or basis functions can be included in a model, increasing fidelity and accuracy. Or dynamical models of the same size can be run for longer physical times. Enabling larger simulations is particularly important in the nanosciences to allow methods at one time or length scale to extend into the range of applicability of other, more coarse-grained methodologies in order to validate or pass information to the coarser-grained methodologies.

— Physical models with more detailed science can be simulated, increasing accuracy and reliability and hence confidence that simulation results represent reality.

— With faster kernel computations, new types of analysis become tractable. For instance, fast linear solvers enable the solution of nonlinear systems. Efficient modelling of forward problems allows for the solution of inverse problems. Hence, faster kernel computations enable a sufficient number of simulations to be performed in order to improve the statistical sampling.

The potential benefits from new capabilities in modelling in the nanosciences require continuous advances in the key algorithms that underlie nanoscale computations. This progress may come about in any number of ways. Many of the key algorithms (fast transforms, eigensolvers, etc.) have applications in other settings, but their impact in the nanosciences alone could justify continued development.

Entirely new approaches for some of these problems are difficult to anticipate but could have tremendous impact on not only the feasibility of the computations, but also what will be learned from the computations. For example, wavelets or other new bases might be able to reduce the complexity of some nanoscience calculations and may expose features of the science in new ways.

An alternative approach for making progress is to specialise a general algorithm to the precise needs of an application. This approach is the most common way to advance the application of algorithms and often allows for dramatic im-provements in performance. Recent progress in linear scaling methods for electronic structure provides one such example. Developments in electronic structure calculations provide a particularly telling illustration of the enabling power of algorithmic advances. First-principles DFT methods for this problem traditionally scale as the cube of the system size, N. This rapid growth with system size limits applications of these powerful techniques to systems containing a few hundred atoms on traditional computers.

More efficient cubic algorithms and parallel implementations have allowed larger systems to be simulated, but substantial progress is still limited by the N_3 complexity. Recent algorithmic progress is removing this barrier. For system sizes of up to a thousand electrons, ab initio plane wave electronic structure codes using fast Fourier transforms now effectively scale as N_2logN. Developments using local representations are close to achieving linear scaling for very large systems, at least in some application domains.A second important example comes from molecular dynamics simulations, where advances in fast multipole methods have reduced the time for computing Coulombic or other long-range forces from N_2 to NlogN or N.

Recent innovations in time integration for molecular dynamics are enabling simulations for much longer physical times. Continued developments and advances will be needed to enable the necessary simulations for complex nanoscale dynamics. These types of advances generate new challenges. The asymptotically more efficient algorithms are generally more complex than their antecedents, and in order to have high fidelity and enough accuracy, some may only be more efficient for very large problems.

High-quality implementations are a significant undertaking, and parallel versions will likely require additional algorithmic advances. Modern software practices and open-source parallel libraries can have an enormous impact in easing the development of new functionality and then delivering that new capability to scientists in a timely and efficient manner. More generally, the asymptotic complexity of an algorithm is only one of several aspects relevant to an algorithm's potential impact in nanoscience.

Algorithmic researchers must also consider ease of implementation, parallelizability, memory locality, and robustness. In an area as diverse as nanoscience, an enormous range of computational techniques and algorithms have a role to play, and the workshop was able to touch on only a subset of them. The following areas were identified as particularly important.

Many of them are generally applicable for a wide range of applications; however, they will be particularly important to enabling discoveries and quantitative understanding in the nanosciences.

Visualisation and exploration of data interactivity

Large simulations can generate copious quantities of data. A physical scientist is often interested in exploring these large datasets for interesting features. This process is difficult to automate, since often the most important features are unexpected and they tend to be very application specific. Such explorations are valuable because they generally reveal deficiencies in the simulation itself or unanticipated and interesting aspects of the physics. This kind of datadriven exploring requires rich and easy-touse environments for visualisation and data interactivity. Good tools will hide the complexity of the data management from the user and will respond in real time to user interactivity, even though the data analysis may be occurring on a distant parallel machine. Although there is considerable research activity in this general area, there will be significant benefit from customisation to effectively impact the research of specific nanoscientists.

On the other extreme, strategies for deriving maximal information from a limited data environment are needed, since experiments may be difficult or expensive to conduct. This will be critical, for example, in getting a handle on management of uncertainty. In both these contexts, strategies that include experiments for the purpose of supporting the theoretical objective are needed, in contrast, say, to modelling for the purpose of explaining experiments.

Optimisation and predictability

In virtually every branch of science, there is a need for calculations to estimate the parameters of a system, to find the extremum of an objective function such as minimum energy or maximum entropy states of a system, and to design and control systems. Since mathematical models are often used to guide experimentation and to predict or adapt to behaviours, there is an equally strong need to understand the errors in these models and to be able to make mathematically sound and precise statements regarding the accuracy and precision of the predictions.

Since all of these needs pervade science, it is natural to ask in what way nanoscience is special. The payoff to developing a new set of computational models and tools would be better understanding, prediction, design, optimisation, and control of complex nanosystems with confidence in the reliability of the results. Successes in this field would almost certainly have impact on other fields that share the complexity of a large range of complex behaviour on nonseparable temporal and spatial scales. Many of the problems mentioned above rely on formulating and solving optimisation problems. For example, in order to gain a quantitative understanding of nanosystems at a fundamental level, it is essential to have the capability to calculate the ground state of the system.

This can be formulated as a minimum energy problem where the solution gives the configuration of the particles of the system at the lowest energy, given an energy functional. Complicated nanosystems of interest can have millions to billions of particles, resulting in huge optimisation problems characterised by an equally huge number of local minima with energy levels close to the ground state. There is no hope of solving this problem with brute force methods. To make any headway on such problems requires careful formulation of the objective function and the constraints. For example, progress in the protein-folding problem has been achieved by understanding that certain sequences of amino acids in the unfolded molecule almost always end up in a standard form, e.g., an alpha helix.

By inducing the optimisation path towards this conformation, better results have been attained. Constraints, based on additional knowledge, can also be formulated to further reduce the search space. Optimisation methods that exploit physical insight could have a dramatic impact on efficiency. But other stochastic or deterministic optimisation methods can also be accelerated by domain knowledge. For example, when trying to simulate a novel material, knowledge about the structural properties and energetics of related materials could be used to preferentially steer the computation towards promising regions of the state space. Such methods are likely to be much more efficient than general optimisation strategies, but quite limited in their applicability.Self-assembly is a central feature of nanoscience. Understanding, predicting, and controlling this process is crucial for the design and manufacture of viable nanosystems.

Clearly the subsystems involved in this process are assembling themselves according to some minimum energy principle. Once an understanding of the underlying physics is attained, optimisation problems can be formulated to predict the final configurations. Since these systems are also huge and likely to have many local minima, a careful development of the models, the constraints, and the algorithms will also be required here.

Given the necessity to create models that incorporate many scales, it has been suggested that a hierarchy of models be created to span this range, i.e., a connected set of models that capture the quantum effects through the micromorphic effects. In this case, the parameters at a given level should be attainable from the next lowest level using parameter-determining techniques.

Optimisation formulations for such parameter estimation problems are ubiquitous, but constructing the correct error models and the associated optimisation problem is not obvious. Simply using least squares may not be appropriate; more general maximumlikelihood estimators will likely be required. As alluded to above, the design and control of nanosystems is vital to the eventual manufacture of products. The problem here is to optimise the design to achieve a desired characteristic or to control the process so that a given state is reached. In these cases, the constraints of the optimisation problem contain the hierarchy of models describing these systems.

In particular, the constraints contain coupled systems of partial differential equations (PDE). There is considerable interest in such problems in other fields, e.g., aerodynamics, and some efficient algorithms have been created, but the number of levels involved in nanoscience is far higher than in other fields. Progress has been made by understanding that these coupled systems of PDEs do not have to be satisfied at each step of the optimisation process, but only need to be satisfied in the limit. This has resulted in an optimised solution in a modest multiple of the time required for one nonlinear solve.

Such approaches, however, require that the formulation of the optimisation problem incorporate some or all of the state variables in addition to the control variables. Effective optimisation methods in these cases must have more control over the PDE software than is typically the case, e.g., gradients and/or adjoints must be computed along with other quantities. Thus, the formulation of the models, the algorithms, and the software with the ultimate goal of design and optimisation is crucial. One can easily envision optimisation problems arising in many other aspects of nanoscience. For example, methods for shape optimisation for determining the optimal geometry of both tools and products, non-smooth optimisation due to derivative discontinuities between the models at adjoining levels, and discrete optimisation for particles restricted to discrete locations will be needed.

All of the developments in these areas, as with those mentioned above, should be done collaboratively between optimisers and nanoscientists. Although part of the predictability problem can be addressed using optimisation techniques (e.g., maximum likelihood), other statistical methodologies will be necessary to develop a final statement of confidence in the answers. First, however, it is important to recognise all of the possible sources of errors in the process. This starts with the recognition that none of our models is exact.

And, since most of the models are based on PDEs, these equations cannot be solved exactly. There will be a combination of discretisation errors in the formation of the algebraic systems that the computer sees and roundoff errors in the actual computation. There are errors associated with the physical models and errors related to parameters and initial conditions that define these models. Some of these errors are observational, related to field or laboratory data, and some are numerical or modelling errors, related to simulation data.

These two types of errors are actually of a similar form, as laboratory errors are often the result of a simulation needed to interpret the experiment. Furthermore, errors at one scale will be propagated to other scales in ways that will be difficult to track and manage. It is important to develop methods for determining comprehensive and inclusive bounds on the final errors. Such methods include sampling technologies for developing sensitivities to parameters, analytic techniques for propagation of errors, and probability models for numerical or modelling errors in simulations.

The predictions of science are not a simple forward map of an input to an output in a simulation. Parameters and input values needed in the forward simulation are determined as an inverse problem through statistical inference based on measurements of outputs. Thus propagation of errors and uncertainty is mapped both ways, from input to output in direct simulation and from output to input in parameter determination. Statistical inference is the tool that connects the two. This inference can be conveniently formulated in a Bayesian framework, so that the inverse problem acquires a probabilistic expression, and disparate data collected from different sources can then be used to reduce uncertainty and to aid in the predictions.

The ultimate goal of such an approach is the determination of error bars or confidence intervals associated with a prediction, based on all sources (data and simulation) on which the prediction is based. A necessary intermediate goal is the association of error bars or other measures of quantified uncertainty with simulations.

7

Biomolecular Machines

A nanometer is a billionth of a meter, that is, about 1/80,000 of the diameter of a human hair, or ten times the diameter of a hydrogen atom. The size-related challenge is the ability to measure, manipulate, and assemble matter with features on the scale of 1 to 100 nm. In order to achieve cost-effectiveness in nanotechnology, it will be necessary to automate molecular manufacturing.

The engineering of molecular products needs to be carried out by robotic devices, which have been termed nanorobots. A nanorobot is essentially a controllable machine at the nanometer or molecular scale that is composed of nano-scale components and algorithmically responds to input forces and information. The field of nanorobotics studies the design, manufacturing, programming, and control of the nanoscale robots. Nanorobots would constitute any active structure (nano-scale) capable of actuation, sensing, signalling, information processing, intelligence, and swarm behaviour at nano-scale.

These functionalities could be illustrated individually or in combinations by a nanorobot (swarm intelligence and cooperative behaviour). So, there could be a whole genre of actuation and sensing or information processing nanorobots having ability to interact and influence matter at the nano-scale. Some of the characteristic abilities that are desirable for a nanorobot to function may include:

(i) Swarm intelligence—decentralisation and distributive intelligence;

(ii) Self-assembly and replication—assemblage at nano-scale and "nano-maintenance";

(iii) Nano-information processing and programmability—for programming and controlling nanorobots (autonomous nanorobots);

(iv) Nano- to macro-world interface architecture—an architecture enabling instant access to the nanorobots and its control and maintenance;

There are many differences between macro-and nano-scale robots. However, they occur mainly in the basic laws that govern their dynamics. Macro-scaled robots are essentially in the Newtonian mechanics domain whereas the laws governing nanorobots are in the molecular quantum mechanics domain. Furthermore, uncertainty plays a crucial role in nanorobotic systems. The fundamental barrier for dealing with uncertainty at the nano-scale is imposed by the quantum and the statistical mechanics and thermal excitations. For a certain nanosystem at some particular temperature, there are positional uncertainties that cannot be modified or further reduced.

The nanorobots are invisible to the naked eye, which makes them hard to manipulate and work with. Techniques like scanning electron microscopy (SEM) and atomic force microscopy (AFM) are being employed to establish a visual and haptic interface to enable us to sense the molecular structure of these nano-scaled devices.

Virtual reality (VR) techniques are currently being explored in nano-science and biotechnology research as a way to enhance the operator's perception (vision and haptics) by approaching more or less a state of "full immersion" or "telepresence." The development of nanorobots or nanomachine components presents difficult fabrication and control challenges. Such devices will operate in microenvironments whose physical properties differ from those encountered by conventional parts. Since these nano-scale devices have not yet been fabricated, evaluating possible designs and control algorithms requires using theoretical estimates and virtual interfaces or environments.

Such interfaces or simulations can operate at various levels of detail to trade-off physical accuracy, computational cost, number of components, and the time over which the simulation follows the nano-object behaviours. They can enable nano-scientists to extend their eyes and hands into the nano-world, and they also enable new types of exploration and whole new classes of experiments in the biological and physical sciences.

VR simulations can also be used to develop virtual assemblies of nano and bio-nano components into mobile linkages and to predict their performance. Nanorobots with completely artificial components have not been realised yet. The active area of research in this field is focused more on molecular machines, which are thoroughly inspired by nature's way of doing things at nano-scale.

Mother Nature has her own set of molecular machines that have been working for millions of years, and have been optimised for performance and design over the ages. As our knowledge and understanding of these numerous machines continues to increase, we now see a possibility of using the natural machines or creating synthetic ones from scratch using nature's components. The main goal in the field of molecular machines is to use various biological elements - whose function at the cellular level creates motion, force, or a signal—as machine components.

These components perform their preprogrammed biological function in response to the specific physiochemical stimuli but in an artificial setting. In this way proteins and DNA could act as motors, mechanical joints, transmission elements, or sensors. If all these different components were assembled together in the proper proportion and orientation, they would form nanodevices with multiple degrees of freedom, able to apply forces and manipulate objects in the nano-scale world.

The advantage of using nature's machine components is that they are highly efficient and reliable. Nanorobotics is a field which calls for collaborative efforts between physicists, chemists, biologists, computer scientists, engineers, and other specialists to work towards this common objective.

The ability to manipulate matter at the nano-scale is one core application for which nanorobots could be the technological solution. A lot has been written in the literature about the significance and motivation behind constructing a nanorobot. The applications range from medical to environmental sensing to space and military applications.

Molecular construction of complex devices could be possible by nanorobots of the future. From precise drug delivery to repairing cells and fighting tumour cells, nanorobots are expected to revolutionise the medical industry in the future. These applications come under the field of nanomedicine, which is a very active area of research in nanotechnology. These molecular machines hence form the basic enablers of future applications.

A majority of natural molecular machines are protein-based which involve using the exact replica of nature's mechanism, while the DNA-based molecular machines use the basic properties of DNA to design various synthetic mechanisms (which might not be present in the nature). Nature deploys proteins to perform various cellular tasks-from moving cargo to catalysing reactions, while it has kept DNA as an information carrier. It is hence understandable that most of the natural machinery is built from proteins. With the powerful crystallographic techniques available in the modern world, the protein structures are clearer than ever.

The ever increasing computing power makes it possible to dynamically model protein folding processes and predict the conformations and structure of lesser known proteins. All this helps unravel the mysteries associated with the molecular machinery and paves the way for the production and application of these miniature machines in various fields including medicine, space exploration, electronics, and military.

Importance of Biomolecular Machines

The recent explosion of research in nanotechnology, combined with important discoveries in molecular biology have created a new interest in biomolecular machines and robots. The main goal in the field of biomolecular machines is to use various biological elements—whose function at the cellular level creates motion, force, or a signal, or stores information—as machine components. These components perform their preprogrammed biological function in response to the specific physiochemical stimuli but in an artificial setting.

In this way proteins and DNA could act as motors, mechanical joints, transmission elements, or sensors. If all these different components were assembled together in the proper proportion and orientation, they would form nanodevices with multiple degrees of freedom, able to apply forces, and manipulate objects in the nanoscale world. The advantage of using nature's machine components is that they are highly efficient and reliable. Just as conventional macro-machines are used to generate forces and motions to accomplish specific tasks, bionanomachines can be used to manipulate nano-objects to assemble and fabricate other machines or products and to perform maintenance, repair, and inspection operations. Such bio-nano robotic devices will hopefully be part of the arsenal of future medical devices and instruments that will:

1) perform operations, inspections, and treatments of diseases inside the body, and
2) achieve ultra-high accuracy and localisation in drug delivery, thus minimising side effects.

The bio-nanorobot will be able to attach to the infected cell alone and deliver a therapeutic drug that can treat or destroy only the infected cell, sparing the surrounding healthy cells.

Development of robotic components composed of simple biological molecules is the first step in the development of future biomedical nanodevices. Since the planned complex systems and devices will be driven by these components, we must first develop a detailed understanding of their operation.

From the simple elements such as structural links to more advanced concepts as motors, each part must be carefully studied and manipulated to understand its functions and limits.

Figure 1 shows one such concept of a nano-organism, with its "feet" made of helical peptides and its body using carbon nanotubes while the power unit is a biomolecular motor. For this phase to be successful, a library of biological elements of every category must be available. At that point, conventional robotics can be used as a guide for fabrication of bio-nanorobots that function in the same manner.

There will be systems that have mobile characteristics to transport themselves, as well as other objects, to desired locations. Some bio-nanorobots can be conceived as able to manufacture additional elements and various structures. There may also be robots that not only perform physical labour, but also sense the environment and react accordingly. There is no doubt that biomedical applications will be both a driving force and a beneficiary of these developments.

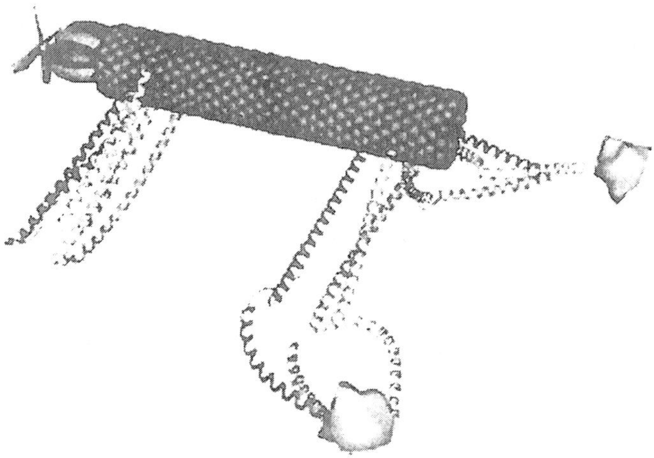

Figure 1. The biological elements will be used to fabricate robotic systems

In the macroscopic world, what we understand by a 'motor' is a machine capable of imparting motion associated by the conversion of energy. Biomolecular motors have attracted a lot of attention recently because: (1) they operate at high efficiency, (2) some could be self-replicating and hence cheaper in mass usage, and (3) they are readily available in nature. A number of enzymes function as nano-scale biological motors, such as kinesin, RNA polymerase, myosin, and adenosine triphosphate (ATP) synthase, function as nano-scale biological motors.

ATPase Motor

One of the most abundant rotary motors found in life forms is F0F1 ATP synthase, commonly known as the "ATPase motor." Motor proteins are tiny vehicles that transport molecular cargoes within cells. These minute cellular machines exist in three families: the kinesins, the myosins, and the dyneins. Conventional kinesin was found to be a highly processive motor that could take several hundred steps on a microtubule without detaching, whereas muscle myosin has been shown to execute a single "stroke" and then dissociate.

Escherichia coli and similar organisms are equipped with a set of rotary motors only 45 nm in diameter. Each motor drives a long, thin, helical filament that extends several cell body lengths out into the external medium. In addition to rotary engines and propellers, E. coli's standard accessories include particle counters, rate meters, and gearboxes and thus has been described as a nanotechnologist's dream in Berg's research.

Berg developed one of the earliest models for the rotary motor. Flagella motor analysis coupled to real-time computer assisted analysis of motion has also been performed. Researchers in Japan have applied crystallographic studies in order to understand the molecular structure of flagella motors as well as that of kinesin. Since motor proteins are a thousand times smaller than any man-made motor, they aim to utilise them in a synthetic environment as engines powering the nanotrains.

Motors and mechanisms

In addition to work on naturally existing motors, considerable effort is also being applied to develop synthetic molecular motors. The structure of the ATP synthase, a rod rotating inside a static wheel, suggests the use of rotaxanes as potential artificial models for natural motors. Rotaxanes are organic compounds consisting of a dumbbell-shaped component that incorporates one or more recognition sites in its rod section and is terminated by bulky "stoppers", encircled by one or more ring components. The possibility of manufacturing specific forms of rotaxane and creating molecular motors capable of guided rotary motion and the possibility of fuelling such a motor by light, electrons, and chemical energy has been proposed. Schemes for using pseudorotaxanes, rotaxanes, and catenanes as molecular switches to perform chemical, electrochemical, and photochemical switching and controllable molecular shuttles have also been proposed recently. Molecular shuttles have been reported using a-cyclodextrin—a parent of rotaxanes and catenanes.

A light-driven monodirectional rotor made of helical alkene, with rotation around a central carbon-carbon covalent bond due to chirality has been reported. Another simple way to convert chemical energy into mechanical motion in a controlled fashion is by using a metal ion which can be translocated reversibly between two organic compartments with the change of its ionisation state, controllable by redox reaction or pH change.

Motility. of unicellular organisms like vortecellids reminds us of energy storage and release by mechanical springs on a macromolecular scale. Spring-like action has been observed in sperm cells of certain marine invertebrates during fertilisation. Springs and supramolecular ratchets by actin polymerisation have yet to be built in vitro, but they theoretically can be generalised, as recently demonstrated.

Molecular Nanomachines

Several researchers are exploring the use of DNA in nano-scale mechanisms. DNA is small, relatively simple, and homogeneous and its structure and function is well understood. The predictable self-assembling nature of the double helix makes it an attractive candidate for engineered nanostructures. This property has been exploited to build several complex geometric structures, including knots, cubes, and various polyhedra. Mathematical analyses of the elastic structure of DNA using energy minimisation methods have been performed to examine its molecular stability, wherein short DNA strands were treated as an elastic rod. Initial experiments on DNA visualisation and manipulation using mechanical, electrical, and chemical means have been underway for a decade. A dynamic device providing atomic displacements of 2-6 nm was proposed in Mao et al., wherein the chemically induced transition between the B and Z DNA morphologies acts as a moving nano-scale device.

A method for localised element-specific motion control was seen in the reversible transition between four stranded topoisomeric DNA motifs (PX and JX2) thereby producing rotary motion. A very important, though simple DNA machine that resembles a pair of tweezers has been successfully created, whose actuation (opening and closing) is also fuelled by adding additional DNA fuel strands.

Technology of Nanosensoring

The technology of nanosensing is also under development. For example, silicon probes with single walled carbon nanotube (CNT) tips are being developed. For sensing certain analytes, genetically engineered versions of pore-forming proteins like Staphylococcus aureus alpha-hemolysin are also being studied. Efforts to detect biological warfare agents like cholera toxins by utilising their ability to bind to a bilayer membrane in the presence of gangliosides is another example. Light sensors could be made using certain photoreceptive polypeptides containing azobenzene or spyropyran units as they respond to light or dark environmental conditions by undergoing conformational change, for example, transition from random coil to a a-helix. An optical DNA biosensor platform has been reported using etched optical fibre bundles filled with oligonucleotidefunctionalised microsphere probes. Finally, work is in progress to develop sensors for brain implantation, which would foretell the development of a stroke and be useful for perioperative online monitoring during coronary by-pass surgery.

In addition to many of the examples mentioned above which generally correspond to one degree of freedom (DOF) rotary actuators, there are many other machine elements, the functional capabilities of which have not yet been represented by biomolecular elements. In addition, the assembly of different molecules in a multi-degree of freedom machine or the formation of hybrid systems composed of biomolecules and synthetic nonorganic elements has not yet been explored.

Design for the Bio-Nano Robotic Systems

(a) *Modular organisation*: Modular organisation defines the fundamental rule and hierarchy for constructing a bio-nano robotic system. Such construction is performed through stable integration (energetically in the most stable state) of the individual 'bio-modules or components', which constitute the bio-nanorobot. For example, if the entity ABCD, defines a bio-nanorobot having some functional specificity then A, B, C, and D are said to be the basic bio-modules defining it. The basic construction will be based on the techniques of molecular modelling with emphasis on principles such as energy minimisation on the hypersurfaces of the bio-modules, hybrid quantum-mechanical and molecular mechanical methods, empirical force field methods, and maximum entropy production in least time.

Modular organisation also enables the bio-nanorobots with capabilities, such as organising into swarms, a feature, which is extremely desirable for various applications. Figure 11A and Figure 11B show the conceptual representation of modular organisation. Figure 11C shows a more realistic scenario in which all the modules are defined in some particular spatial arrangements based on their functionality and structure. A particular module could consist of other group of modules, just like a fractal structure.

The concept of bionanocode has been devised, which basically describes the unique functionality of a bio-nano component in terms of alphabetic codes. Each bionanocode represents a particular module defining the structure of the bio-nanorobot. For instance, a code like E-M-S will describe a bio-nanorobot having capabilities of energy storage, mechanical actuation, and signalling at the nano-scale. Such representations will help in general classifications and representative mathematics of bio-nanorobots and their swarms.

(b) *The Universal Template—BioNano STEM System*: The modular construction concept involves designing a universal template for bionanosystems, which could be 'programmed and grown' into any possible bionanocoded system. This concept mimics the embryonic stem cells found in the human beings, that are a kind of primitive human cells which give rise to all other specialised tissues found in a human foetus and ultimately to all the three trillion cells in an adult human body. BioNano STEM system will act in a similar way. This universal growth template will be constituted of some basic bionanocodes, which will define the BioNano STEM system. This STEM system will be designed in a manner that could enable it to be programmed at runtime to any other required bio-module.

Self-replication—Mimetics of Living Systems

Mimetics of self-replication, as exhibited by nature, would influence any nano-level application. We would need an army of nanorobots (or living systems), mass-produced via techniques of self-replication (or life), to carry out many meaningful tasks at the nano-scale. These applications involving nanorobots demand that these machines are manufactured in millions or billions and in a time-frame reasonable for a particular application. One of nature's noblest properties is that of life. It is how nature progresses through its environment ever adapting and evolving. Although philosophically what life means and what constitutes it is not very clear, what is clear is how nature propagates itself with time and survives, every day and every moment! This is one attribute of nature which is of prime importance to us as researchers of science and engineering, and which, if understood, would bring a unique revolution that in a way would change the course of our lives. The concept of self-replicating mechanisms (SRM) or mimetics of life is not new. There are perfect examples of these kinds of systems. We are wounded and our internal mechanisms heal it with some differences in some cases. Taking the example of the wound and its healing process, we move ahead and try to analyse how we can achieve such behaviours in the mechanisms that we design.

At the core of the concept of self-replication lies the basic material (DNA/RNA) which undergoes such activity. Though we hardly know why these materials behave in this fashion, what we do know is how they behave and this provides the stepping stone for us to move ahead.

Ways for applications

Consider that the application depends upon a particular part -mechanical or electrical, or any other physical, biological, or chemical element—which fails or starts developing problems. We need self-rectifying mechanisms within the application to detect the problem and rectify it. We can think of many applications where we would desire such behaviour. Given some initial material feedstock, it would be desired that the self-replicating mechanisms would rectify the problems. We can classify the self-replicating mechanisms in to following types:.

— Mechanical self-replicating mechanisms;

— Electrical self-replicating mechanisms;

— Chemical or biological self-replicating mechanisms.

There could be other classifications as well and numerous other examples following the lines of our wound example, can be thought of. It just depends on our imagination. For example, suppose that we build some SRM which mimics the living system.

Its function is to detect the crucial defect in a mechanical element and then mend that defect. If we are able to devise such an application, it could significantly enhance the life and performance of the system. The system in this example would be designed and constructed to work at nano-scale, and therefore it would have an ability to detect the slightest of defects and start working towards rectifying it.

Remote Applications would also benefit from SRM systems. Maintaining remote applications requires constant human interaction. If these systems mimic the coded logic and goals of the living system, then it would be able to performance optimally with minimal human interventions. For example, deep space explorations would require circuits, machines, and equipments to adjust and adapt with time and as per the conditions they would be subjected to.

Applications at the nano-scale. This category of applications would be most influenced by our bio mimetic systems because they could lay the foundations of nanodevices that have the capability of manipulating molecular matter. The design of life-mimetic systems requires new innovative materials to be designed that behave in the same fashion as that designed by nature. These new materials are termed "intrinsic materials", these are follows:

Intrinsic material

The unique arrangement of the constituent atoms of intrinsic materials would give rise to:

— unique potential field surface around them;

— unique charge distribution;

— unique internal energy gradients.

It is through these internal energy gradients that two particular intrinsic materials would interact with each other. Hence the behaviour of the intrinsic material would be a direct function of its internal energy gradients.

Interaction laws

The final objective of any interacting intrinsic materials would be to achieve the intrinsic balance of the resulting system (termed self-balancing). This would translate to achieving minimum energy gradients in all directions for all interacting materials. The final system would then be defined by its new achieved internal energy gradients. These intrinsic energy gradients would also be influenced by the external fields.

Self-balancing

It implies that the materials considered would tend to align with its intrinsic energy gradients and would try to minimise the formed unbalance. The classical instance self-replication via energy-minimised self-assembly was first demonstrated in the late 1950s. The canonical example of this approach is called the Penrose Blocks. The unbalance and the property of self-balancing are similar in essence to what is postulated by the law of entropy. This concept of self-balancing is motivated from the law of maximum entropy production according to which a system follows a path which minimises the potential or maximises entropy at the maximum rate.

Limitation of reproductive growth

An intrinsic material would have a property of growth (an important variable for replication). This property of growth only occurs when the system is provided with some energy maybe in the form of additional intrinsic material or external gradients. Growth cannot happen in isolation. This implies that in the process of self-balancing, it is possible that the particular configuration of the intrinsic material is stable up to a particular level. This level would be governed by the strength of the potential gradients for that intrinsic material and the extrinsic gradients.

Therefore, the growth implies that the intrinsic material can achieve higher state by not disturbing its self-balance or increasing it further. But this growth can only be achieved to a particular extent; beyond it, it tends to disintegrate by following the paths defined by the laws of maximum entropy production. And this particular limit of growth is termed Reproductive Limit.

Self-filtering and self-healing

The concept of replication further demands that the materials thus designed should exhibit the property of self-filtering and self-healing. Self-filtering implies that the material involved in the systems exhibiting self-replication will not allow any kind of growth pattern but only a particular one. This particular growth pattern (which inherently depends on the interactions of the components) will determine which material it binds to and to which it doesn't. Hence such systems will only interact with certain intrinsic materials. In the process of this growth, a realignment of the intrinsic material occurs.

As the addition of further intrinsic material takes place, the whole system tries to realign itself towards the most stable state and in the fastest possible time. This realignment goes on with the self-filtering process. If at any incremental stage system doesn't find the kind and type of material it is looking for, it doesn't realign and rejects that particular material and doesn't grow. By rejection, it might imply that either the system doesn't align with the material or marks it as an unstable configuration and seeks for the opportunity to replace it immediately. Hence it acts as a self-healer.

Designing a Self-Replicating Systems

Following are the various design parameters that need to be considered while designing a self-replicating system.

Selection of intrinsic materials

This is, of course, the most important parameter in designing the desired system. The obvious choices would be biomaterials and chemicals found in the human body, which have exhibited self-replication. Their choice is mainly because of their availability and the fact that they themselves are the materials resulting from a replicative process. This does not limit the selection of other replicative materials. Also a lot of data on nature's biomaterials is available from the experiments performed in the field of biology and genetic engineering. The field of nanotechnology is the biggest area where the concept of self-replication system would be a success and the biomaterials could be managed at that scale.

External gradient parameters

It is extremely important to define the external gradient parameters within which the system needs to perform. Our choice of the intrinsic materials would be greatly impacted by their behaviour. Also their sensitivities to these external gradients need to be calculated so as to fine-tune the system.

Selection of the appropriate intrinsic materials for our system implies that we need to also select the appropriate internal gradient functions and the alignment generated by these intrinsic materials. We need to calculate the most stable configuration for our system at no external gradient level and then fine tune our alignment as it is applied.

Application of these external gradients could generate a situation where no stable configuration is possible within our operating conditions. This calls for adding some further intrinsic materials to the system, which would help us to get to the stable configuration. This variation of the intrinsic gradient in this manner is termed as intrinsic variational gradients to distinguish it from the inherent intrinsic gradients generated due to the intrinsic materials.

8

Veterinary Applications

Nanotechnology holds out the possibility that 'smart' treatment delivery systems could be activated long before macro-symptoms appear. For example, a 'smart' treatment delivery system could be a miniature device implanted in an animal that samples saliva on a regular basis. Long before a fever develops, the integrated sensing, monitoring and controlling system could detect the presence of disease and notify the farmer and veterinarian to activate a targeted treatment delivery system.

Smart treatment delivery systems are envisioned for biology and bioactive systems such as drugs, nutrients, probiotics, nutraceuticals and implantable cell bioreactors. In agriculture, the fundamental life processes are explored through research in molecular and cellular biology. New tools for molecular and cellular biology are needed that are specifically designed to separate, identify and quantify individual molecules. This is possible with nanotechnology and could permit a wide range of advances in agricultural research, such as developments in reproductive science and technology, conversion of agricultural and food wastes to energy and other useful by-products through enzymatic nanobioprocessing, and disease prevention and treatment in animals.

Nanotechnology is an exciting and rapidly emerging technology allowing us to work at the molecular level, often atom by atom, to create and manipulate tools, materials and functional structures that have nanometre dimensions. Nature has been performing 'nanotechnological feats' for millions of years. Through the arrangement of atoms and molecules, biological systems combine wet chemistry and electro-chemistry in a single living system. 'Nano' usually refers to a size scale between 1 nanometre (nm) and 100 nm. For comparison, the wavelength of visible light is between 400 nm and 700 nm. A living cell has dimensions of microns (thousands of nanometres).

Microfluidics

On the microscopic scale, fluids in microchannels appear to take on viscous properties and move more like molasses than water. When two or more microfluidic channels are converged into a single stream, the converging streams do not mix easily. Laminar or creep flow at microfluidic level cause living cells to become aligned in single-file order, thus allowing new levels of precision science in cell biology.

Other microfluidic applications have the potential for precision 'point-of-care' diagnostics, drug screening and deoxyribonucleic acid (DNA) manipulation. Microfluidics is used today in animal science to significantly simplify traditional in vitro fertilisation procedures used in animal breeding. Microfluidics is also an integral part of today's precision miniaturised 'Lab-on-a-Chip' technology, which allows for the analysis and chemical manipulation of small samples.

Microfluidics is a science which deals with largerscale measurements than does nanotechnology, but the merger of the 'dry' world of nanotechnology with the 'wet' world of biology involves the use of microfluidic techniques.

Methods of making micro-sized machines or microelectromechanical systems (MEMS) are already established. Fully functional pumps, rotors, sensors and levers exist at the microscale. Moving from the micro to the nano scale, nano-electromechanical systems (NEMS) devices will present new engineering challenges. However, as with microfluidics, the integration of existing MEMS technology with biological systems has yielded a new class of machines, 'BioMEMS', that can perform functions at the nanoscale or on nanoparticles. Biochips that are smaller than a postage stamp exist today. These biochips contain sealed channels and wells, electrodes for detection, connectors and fluidic input/output ports. BioMEMS provide the interface between the macro and nano worlds, as well as the interface between the biological and electromechanical worlds of technology.

Many of the nanotechnology devices of today have been fabricated from pieces of silicon or other material, through etching, much like sculpting away portions of the beginning material block to obtain the final structure. Nucleic acid bioengineering approaches manufacture from the opposite end—a 'bottom-up' approach. Nucleic acid engineering utilises DNA molecules as building blocks, and forms specifically shaped particles that can be used to build larger units. Nanowires and nanomembranes from these basic building blocks are envisioned.

On the macro-scale, delivery systems such as postal services, accept items for delivery that are sealed in a package and have address instructions written on the outside of the package; both motorised and human carriers transport the package from one location to another. The development of 'smart' treatment delivery systems on the nanoscale uses similar concepts applied at the molecular level. For example, 'smart' drug delivery systems in animals would most likely contain small, sealed packages of the drug to be delivered. The packages would not be opened until they reach the desired location in the animal, e.g. the site of infection. This would allow judicious use of smaller quantities of antibiotics than would otherwise be possible. A molecular-coded 'address label' in the package could allow the package to be delivered to the correct site in the body.

Nano- and microscale mechanical systems would serve as the 'carriers' in such a system. Smart delivery systems could also contain on-board chemical detection and decision-making capability for selfregulation that could deliver drug or nutrient treatments as needed. The remote activation and monitoring of intelligent delivery systems will assist livestock producers of the future to minimise antibiotic use.

Nanosensors

Detection of very small amounts of a chemical contaminant, virus, or bacteria in agricultural and food systems is envisioned from the integration of chemical, physical and biological devices working together as an integrated sensor at the nanoscale. Bioanalytical nanosensors are devices or systems with devices that measure or detect a chemical with the use of a biological material or tissue.

Surfaces are the environment and location on which most chemical and biological interactions occur. A bioselective surface has either an enhanced or reduced ability to bind or hold specific organisms or molecules. Bioselective surfaces are important to the development of biosensors, detectors, catalysts and the ability to separate or purify mixtures of biomolecules.

Nanomaterials

Nanomaterials are materials (either newly created through nanotechnology or that exist in nature) that provide the potential to manipulate structures or other particles at the nanoscale and to control and catalyse chemical reactions. Materials are generally composed of particles of many sizes. The shape, structure and aggregation of particles at the nanoscale influence the properties of the material at the macro-level. Specific examples of nanomaterials are buckeyballs, dendrimers, nanoshells, nanotubes and quantum dots, each of which is described in more detail in the following sections.

—   *Buckeyballs:* A buckeyball is a novel collection of carbon atoms in a spheroid shape in which each carbon atom is bonded to three of its neighbours. Scientists have discovered how to make the metal-filled buckeyballs soluble, bringing them a step closer to biological applications, such as the delivery of medicine or radioactive material to a disease site. The idea of using the 60-atom to 80-atom hollow carbon molecules for drug delivery is what gives added biological functionality to a buckeyball. The aim is to attach water-soluble groups of peptides or hydrophilic chains to get these molecules into the blood stream.

—   *Nanotubes:* Nanotubes are essentially buckeyballs that have been opened on two sides with additional atom groups added in the characteristic hexagon shape to form a hollow carbon tube (cylinder). They can be thought of as a sheet of graphite (a hexagonal lattice of carbon) rolled into a cylinder.

—   *Dendrimers* : Dendrimers (polymers) are a new class of threedimensional, man-made molecules produced by an unusual synthetic nanofabrication route that incorporates repetitive branching sequences to create a unique novel architecture. Exceptional features of the dendritic architecture include a high degree of structural symmetry, a density gradient displaying an intra-molecular minimum value and a well-defined number of terminal groups, which may be chemically different from the interior. These features create an environment within the dendrimer molecule to facilitate an avenue for reliable and economical fabrication and manufacturing of functional nanoscale materials that can have unique properties that can be the basis of new nanoscale technology and devices. Dendrimers can be designed to aggregate to form cylinders or spheres depending upon the nature of the fundamental building unit.

Quantum Dots

Quantum dots are nanometre-scale crystals that were originally developed in the mid-1980s for optoelectronic applications. They are created with nanometre precision during chemical synthesis and are composed of hundreds or thousands of atoms of an inorganic semiconductor material, which gives them intriguing optical properties. When a quantum dot is excited with a beam of light, they re-emit light (fluoresce) with a narrow and symmetric emission spectrum that depends directly on the size of the crystal.

This means that quantum dots can be fine-tuned to emit light at a variety of wavelengths simply by altering the size of the core, and they therefore constitute a set of multicoloured molecular beacons for use in imaging. A 3 nm particle made from cadmium selenide, for example, radiates green light at 520 nm, while a slightly larger 5.5 nm particle of the same material radiates red light at 630 nm. The core of the quantum dot is usually contained within a protective inorganic shell such as zinc sulphite, which has a higher electronic band gap than the core.

This increases the intensity of the fluorescence. However, until recently the hydrophobic nature of this outer shell prevented quantum dots from being used in aqueous biological environments, but some scientists have produced new, biocompatible quantum dots. There is considerable debate among biological scientists whether the technology for coating quantum dots adequately alleviates toxicity issues.

Nanoshells

Nanoshells are a new type of optically tunable nanoparticle

composed of a dielectric (for example, silica) core coated with an ultra-thin metallic (for example, gold) layer. Gold nanoshells possess physical properties similar to those of gold colloid, in particular a strong optical absorption due to the collective electronic response of the metal to light.

The optical response of gold nanoshells depends dramatically on the relative sizes of the nanoparticle core and the thickness of the gold shell. By varying the relative core and shell thicknesses, the colour of gold nanoshells can be varied across a broad range of the optical spectrum that spans the visible and the near-infrared spectral regions.

Gold nanoshells can be made to either absorb light or to scatter it preferentially by varying the size of the particle relative to the wavelength of the light. Scientists can create nanoshells that carry molecular conjugates to the antigens that are expressed on cancer cells or in the tumour microenvironment. This second degree of specificity preferentially links the nanoshells to the tumour and not to neighbouring healthy cells. It is then possible to externally supply energy to these cells.

The specific properties of nanoshells allow for the absorption of this directed energy, creating an intense heat that selectively kills tumour cells. The external energy can be mechanical, radio frequency or optical - the therapeutic action is the same.

Nanotechnology in Veterinary Medicine

Animal health is an increasingly important issue, both for animal agriculture and pet owners. Feneque, a veterinarian, writes that nanotechnology has the potential to significantly affect the way veterinarians practice veterinary medicine. Food security and safety and an increasingly aged pet population, along with heightened costs for medication and veterinary care create a need for new solutions. Nanotechnology has the potential to provide these solutions, since the possible applications of the technology in medical and veterinary applications are almost mind-boggling. Although much research and major company developments are necessary before nanotechnology is common place in veterinary medicine, there are numerous glimpses of the future in applications for drug delivery, disease diagnosis and treatment, breeding and identity preservation (IP). Following are the some applications:

'Smart' drug delivery

Today, antibiotics, probiotics and pharmaceuticals are delivered to animals primarily through feed or injection systems. Delivery of medicines is either provided as a preventative measure or as a treatment once the disease organism has multiplied and symptoms are evident. Nanoscale devices are envisioned that will have the capability to detect and treat an infection, nutrient deficiency, or other health problem, long before symptoms are evident at the macro-scale. This type of treatment could be targeted to the affected area. 'Smart' delivery systems can have multifunctional characteristics to avoid biological barriers to successful targeting and they may also be:

— time-controlled
— spatially targeted
— self-regulated
— remotely regulated
— pre-programmed.

Smart delivery systems can also have the capacity to monitor the effects of the delivery of pharmaceuticals, nutraceuticals, nutrients, food supplements, bioactive compounds, probiotics, chemicals and vaccines. Thus, in the future, further technological advances will make it possible to:

— develop delivery systems for biological and bioactive systems for targeted site delivery capability
— develop integrated sensing, monitoring and controlling capabilities, including the ability to be self-regulating
— develop large animal health monitoring and therapeutic intervention
— develop small animal health monitoring and therapeutic intervention
— develop nucleic acid (e.g. DNA) delivery systems through a bottom-up approach using DNA molecules to build nanowires and nanotubes for assisted reproduction, animal vaccines and animal control agents.

The nanotechnologies described above will only reach their full potential through integration. Thus, 'smart systems integration' is similar to designing and building the logic of a 'nervous system' that will allow the individual parts to work together. Integration of the nanotechnologies into a working control system will require electronic communication between several technologies, including the sensing systems, reporting systems, localisation systems and control systems. The logic to control the subsystems must be developed and eventually translated into a computer language. Research needs to be undertaken to:

— integrate NEMS with remote receive/transmit systems
— develop integrated sensing, monitoring and controlling capabilities including self-regulation and remote activation
— design and develop automated integrated networks for the monitoring and control of animal systems and food safety and security
— develop a 'smart herd system' that detects, identifies, reports and treats the illness of a single infected animal in a herd prior to the onset of symptoms.

Diagnosis and treatment

Imagine the possibility of injecting nanoparticles into an animal and then a week or so later being able to run a light over the animal's body to activate cancer-killing agents to destroy the tumour. Researchers at Rice University are doing just this by using nanoshells injected into the animal's bloodstream with targeted agents applied to the nanoshells to seek out and attach to the surface receptors of cancer cells. Illumination of the body with infrared light raises the cell temperature to about 55°C, which 'burns' and kills the tumour.

Others have been experimenting with 'smart' superparamagnetic nanoparticles. These nanoparticles when injected in the bloodstream target tumour receptor cells. These nanoparticles are made from iron oxides that when subjected to a magnetic field enhance the ability of the nanoparticles to locate tumour cells. At the site of the tumour the nanoparticles emit an attached drug to kill the cancer cells. Quantum dots may also be injected into the bloodstream of animals and they may detect cells that are malfunctioning.

Because quantum dots respond to light it may be possible to illuminate the body with light and stimulate the quantum dot to heat up enough to kill the cancerous cell. Nucleic acid engineering-based probes and methods offer powerful new ways to deliver therapeutic or preventative treatment for particular diseases.

The greatest challenge is to develop a nonviral DNA delivery system that has high levels of efficiency and specificity but low toxicity and cost. Therefore, future DNA delivery may depend on a hybrid system that combines the benefits of both viral and nonviral components.

Identity Preservation (IP) system

An identity preservation (IP) system is a system that creates increased value by providing consumers with information about the practices and activities used to produce an agricultural product. Today, through IP it is possible to provide stakeholders and consumers with access to information, records and supplier protocols regarding the farm of origin, environmental practices used in production, food safety and security, and information regarding animal welfare issues.

Each day shipments of livestock and other agricultural products are moved all over the world. Currently, a lack of finances limits the number of inspectors that can be employed at critical control points of the production, shipment and storage processes. Quality assurance of the safety and security of agricultural products could be significantly improved through IP at the nanoscale.

Nanoscale IP has the potential to continuously track and record the history of a particular agricultural product. We envision nanoscale monitors linked to recording and tracking devices to improve the IP of food and agricultural products.

The keys are biodegradable sensors for temperature and other stored data containing the history of stored food for both physical and biological parameters. The future of the meat industry may well depend on an ability to track all stages in the life of the product, including the birth of the animal, its medical history, and its movements between the ranch, the slaughterhouse and the meat-packing plant, right through to the consumer's table.

Management of breeding

Management of breeding is an expensive and timeconsuming problem for dairy and swine farmers. One solution that is currently being studied is a nanotube implanted under the skin to provide real time measurement of changes in the level of estradiol in the blood. The nanotubes are used as a means of tracking oestrus in animals because these tubes have the capacity to bind and detect the estradiol antibody at the time of oestrus by near infrared fluorescence. The signal from this sensor will be incorporated as a part of a central monitoring and control system to actuate breeding.

Future Development

Nanotechnology is a part of the future of animal health. Clearly, this technology has a high potential to benefit animal agriculture and food systems. However, as with any new technology, we have an ethical responsibility to apply it wisely and to recognise that there are potential unforeseen risks that may come with the tremendous positive potential. Nanotechnology and nanomaterials have the potential to play a significant role in risk reduction for animal agriculture and food systems' security.

Of major importance to the development of nanotechnologies will be a thoughtful, thorough and balanced assessment of the benefits and risks of nanotechnologies. The public should be educated through television, the internet, and point-ofsale informative bulletins that explain the added value and increased safety and food security that the application of nanotechnology provides. In addition to improving contaminant detection and the security of tracking systems, the use of nanotechnology can increase the efficiency of animal agriculture and food systems processes and help to reduce the use of antibiotics, thus increasing food safety for the consumer.

Nanomedicine

Nanomedicine is the science and technology of diagnosing, treating and preventing disease and traumatic injury, of relieving pain, and of preserving and improving human health, using molecular tools and molecular knowledge of the human body. It embraces five main sub-disciplines which are in many ways overlapping and are underpinned by common technical issues.

The aim of Nanomedicine may be broadly defined as the comprehensive monitoring, control, construction, repair, defence and improvement of all human biological systems, working from the molecular level using engineered devices and nanostructures, ultimately to achieve medical benefit.

Nanoscale should be taken to include active components or objects in the size range from one nanometre to hundreds of nanometres. They may be included in a micro-device or a biological environment. The focus, however, is always on nanointeractions within a framework of a larger device or biologically a sub-cellular system. The highest causes of mortality in Europe are cardiovascular disease and cancer. In addition demographic changes are producing an ageing population. This in itself is leading to new healthcare challenges.

There is rising prevalence in diseases of the central nervous system, such as senile dementia, Alzheimer's disease, Parkinson's disease, and diseases associated with ageing, for example arthritis and ocular diseases. Whilst much progress was made in the 20th century in respect of the therapies for infectious diseases, emergence of resistance, HIV/AIDS and other new infectious diseases, for example SARS, present new challenges.

Nevertheless, as the 21st century begins, we are witnessing a paradigm shift in medical practice. Nanomedicine is expected to contribute significantly to the overall healthcare portfolio. Genomics and proteomics research is already rapidly elucidating the molecular basis of many diseases. This has brought new opportunities to develop powerful diagnostic tools able to identify geneti predisposition to diseases.

In the future, point-of-care diagnostics will be routinely used to identify those patients requiring preventative medication, to select the most appropriate medication for individual patients, and to monitor response to treatment. Nanotechnology has a vital role to play in realising cost-effective diagnostic tools. There are increasing challenges within the pharmaceutical industry to locate drugs more efficiently to their disease targets.

As the search for improved medicines for life-threatening and debilitating diseases continues, two distinct approaches are being taken to achieve this aim. The first is within drug discovery and builds on identification of new molecular targets which are being used to design 'perfect fit' drug molecules with more specific therapeutic activity. These efforts continue via: screening of natural product molecules to identify candidates with pharmacological activity; preparation of carefully tailored synthetic low molecular weight drugs via traditional medicinal or combinatorial chemistry;

— nanofluidics for targeted synthesis;
— nanodetection for target identification; and
— discovery of natural macromolecules, including antibodies, proteins and genes that have inherent biological activity.

The second, and a complementary approach, is the creation of drug delivery systems that can act as a vehicle to carry and guide more precisely the above mentioned agents to their desired site of action. In 2002 and 2003, more biotechnology products and drug delivery systems were approved by the US Food and Drug Administration as marketed products than new low molecular weight drugs. Nanosized hybrid therapeutics (e.g. polymerprotein conjugates) and drug delivery systems (liposomes and nanoparticles) have already been approved for routine use as medicines.

The drug delivery systems entering the market have been designed to achieve disease-specific targeting, to control the release of the drug so that a therapeutic concentration is maintained over a prolonged period of time, or to provide more convenient routes of administration and reach locations in the body that are traditionally difficult to access, such as the brain. Via the use of coatings, ever more sophisticated devices are emerging that allow localised controlled release of biologically active agents. Complex supramolecular assemblies, nanoparticles and polymeric materials in many different forms are already playing an important role in the construction of nanopharmaceuticals.

It is clear that the contribution of nanotechnology will continue to grow in the future, and it is widely believed that effective delivery gene therapy and other macromolecular therapeutics will be realised only with the aid of multicomponent, nanosized delivery vectors.

Non-invasive patient imaging using techniques such as gamma camera imaging, magnetic resonance imaging, X rays and ultrasound are important established tools used to assist diagnosis and monitor response to treatment. Molecular level imaging using techniques such as positron emission tomography (PET) can also provide information on drug targeting, drug metabolism and disease response to therapy.

Several nanoparticle-based magnetic resonance imaging (MRI) agents have already been approved for routine clinical use, and it is recognised that future application of nanotechnology has an enormous potential in this field.

Complex supramolecular assemblies are already being explored in research and development to yield agents for molecular imaging in the context of MRI, ultrasound, optical imaging, and X-ray imaging. Moreover, in the longer term, the combination of imaging technologies and drug delivery systems has the potential to yield theranostics devices.

Nanomedicine Research

Analytical techniques and diagnostic tools

There is considerable anticipation that miniaturisation via the application of nanotechnology and new nanotools will lead to novel surgical and analytical tools and diagnostics for use ex vivo. It is envisaged that such techniques will increase our ability to identify predisposition to disease, monitor disease progression and identify the most relevant patient treatments.

Moreover, a new generation of surgical tools is predicted that will be able to assist diagnosis and deliver therapy at a cellular level. In the context of larger ex vivo diagnostic devices, the focus of this research lies on nanointeractions. Europe has a relatively strong position in basic research in this field but failure to exploit its inventions is a continuing problem.

DNA and protein chips are already widely used as research tools and are helping to provide a better understanding of the molecular basis of diseases and identify new molecular targets for therapy. It is perceived that many nanotechnology-derived tools will, in the future, be routinely used in diagnosis of many diseases long before they will be approved as treatments. In the case of these devices, nanoscale objects were defined as molecules or devices within a size range of one to hundreds of nanometres that are the active component or object, even within the framework of a larger micro-size device or at a macrointerface.

In the area of nanoanalytical techniques and diagnostic tools that will find application in the sectors of diagnostics, medical devices and pharmaceutical drug discovery, a wide range of technologies are being developed for both in vitro (diagnostics and sensors) and in vivo use (in line sensors, implantables and surgical tools) with a range of biological targets including cells, DNA and proteins.

Research and development in this field is extremely multidisciplinary and there is considerable synergy with the 'nanoimaging and manipulation' and the 'nanomaterials and nanodevices'.Analytical and point-of-care diagnostic product design is already supported by the use of nanoparticles and nanodevices. For example, biosensor technology based on nanotechnology represents a huge opportunity to revolutionise diagnostics in the healthcare environment.

Healthcare professionals in primary care and hospital clinics are shortly expecting to be able to use low-cost tests able to aid the diagnosis by simultaneous measurement of multiple parameters using a simple test strip without having to measure each parameter individually. Such test strips must be disposable and cost effective. There is an opportunity to focus on technically more mature developments that are more likely to be successful, and also to address niche markets that have better prospects for exploitation. Moreover, techniques and tools developed for analysis and diagnostics in the medical field have the potential for wider application, for example, in the context of environmental monitoring, control of food hygiene etc.

An ideal near-patient diagnostic system

—	Fast	Minimise consultation time (<1 minute)
—	Simple	Lay person (nurse's aid) can use
—	Portable	Take the test to the patient
—	Storage	Room temperature for consumables
—	Painless	Minimally invasive blood sampling
—	Single step	One sample, one strip, many analytes
—	Platform	One instrument, many diseases

While there is no lack of innovation in Europe, there was agreement that in many areas Europe is lagging behind. The

DNA array market, for example, is dominated by Affimetrix, an American company. While DNA chips are being widely used in research, their difficulties in securing quality assurance and regulatory approval, their production flexibility and speed to result are well known.

Although other more technically complex chips are available, so far they are substantially more expensive. Underlying research was seen as a further European strength, particularly in relation to the identification of medical targets. Current genomics and proteomics techniques give a limited insight into cellular function. In the future, the combination of these techniques with imaging methods such as TOF-SIMS analysis, and raster electron microscopy by atomic force microscopy of living cells will give more information on individual protein function and cell signalling.

Imaging is becoming an ever more important tool in the diagnosis of human diseases. Both the development of imaging agents based on micro- or nanoparticles, organic dyes etc., and the development of highly sophisticated instruments supported by powerful computation (2D, 3D reconstruction) have already given rise to a significant move from invasive to less invasive clinical imaging. This is allowing an ever more sophisticated imaging-based diagnosis, particularly in cancer, neurological and heart diseases. Nanotechnology has an important role to play in further developing this field. Earlier diagnosis with a non-invasive tool can allow earlier treatment and this treatment approach can be much less expensive and often more effective. In addition, economists consider living healthier, longer lives to be economically beneficial.

There are potential risks and side-effects from new imaging agents based on nanomaterials, but risk-benefit analyses will be/are being conducted at an early stage. One of the greatest problems in the transfer of these approaches into routine clinical use lies in the slow approval process of new materials for human use by regulatory agencies. Imaging at cellular, and even sub-cellular and molecular level, is still largely a domain of basic research. However, it is anticipated that these techniques will find their way into routine clinical use.

Atomic force microscopy (AFM) and AFM-related techniques have become sophisticated tools, not only to image surfaces of molecules or sub-cellular compartments, but also to measure molecular forces between molecules. This is substantially increasing our knowledge of molecular interactions. Because of its interdisciplinary nature, the field of Nanoimaging and Manipulation is also identified as having a considerable overlap with the other disciplines, particularly in relation to nanomaterials (nanoparticles will play an ever more important role as imaging agents), and clinical, regulatory and toxicological issues.

The field termed here 'Nanoimaging' overlaps with the field already called 'Molecular Imaging'. In this case the target to be imaged will have a spatial resolution in the order of 1-100 nanometres, and preferably a time resolution for imaging in the order of milliseconds. The opportunities for improvements and breakthroughs with the assistance of nanotechnology were seen in terms of both existing and emerging technologies.

Europe has a number of leading academic groups and several leading companies who are pioneers in the development of imaging techniques and innovative contrast agent production. Basic research has already developed the first methods to monitor in vitro the assembly of multicomponent biological complexes, protein trafficking and the interactions between single molecules.

There is a recognised opportunity to use nanotechnology to improve these molecular imaging techniques, and to construct real-time intracellular tomography. Objective methods for assessment of image quality are also needed in vitro and in vivo.

Tools are currently under development that allow in vitro evaluation of basic mechanisms, but it was felt that these could quickly be developed towards real ex vivo and clinical applications. In the context of in vivo and clinical imaging, the development of novel techniques for macromolecular imaging was seen as a particular priority. Europe has been at the forefront of the development of polymeric gamma camera imaging agents and dendrimer-based MRI imaging agents. Improved image analysis is a particular goal.

There is a need to improve 3D reconstruction and quantitative data analysis. Improved visualisation techniques are needed also for stereo-imaging, virtual and augmented reality imaging, and image-guided manipulation. Opportunities exist for both invasive and noninvasive clinical imaging, e.g. endoscopy for targeted imaging, use of optical catheters and development of nanosized systems allowing manipulation, target selection, local stimulation and potentially local modification.

Development of more sophisticated imaging equipment requires an integrated approach. Underpinning research must involve all aspects of the process. Parallel to the development of the analytical equipment, research and clinical development is ongoing to provide a new generation of nanoimaging agents. These include both synthetic nanoparticles and biological nanoparticles. In the future it is likely that these imaging tools will become ever more complex, multicomponent systems combining contrast agents and tracking probes (e.g. quantum dots, magnetic and super-paramagnetic beads, nano-shells and nano-colloids) with new targeting ligands.

For targeted systems, carriers can be used which may require additional surface modification, and linkers that bring additional challenges for physico-chemical characterisation and safety evaluation. In some cases combination of a range of signal modalities (e.g. organic dyes) is also used. Imaging and contrast agent design has a considerable overlap with nanomaterials and drug delivery system development. Historically, radio-labelled antibodies have already been transferred to market as diagnostic tools in cancer, and in the form of radio-labelled antibodies and antibody conjugates as a therapeutic agent. It can be argued that the radio-labelled therapeutic antibody is the first nanosized theranostic.

Nanomaterials and Nanodevices

All aspects of Nanomedicine rely on progress in nanomaterials research, and the nano-engineering needed to create devices to realise their goals. Materials science is being employed to generate probes and techniques that are helping to understand basic biological mechanisms.

On the other hand, emergence of more sophisticated nanomaterials and nanodevices is required to develop diagnostic and surgical tools, drug delivery systems and in vivo diagnostics into routine clinical practice. Moreover, nanoscale assemblies for ligand display are already emerging as multicomponent 3D architectures able to assist tissue engineering and promote tissue repair. Nanopharmaceuticals (drugs and drug delivery systems) are nanoscale assemblies, which can be relatively simple; for example, nano-emulsions, nanoparticles or polymer conjugates (of proteins or drugs), or complex mutlicomponent systems containing drugs, proteins or genes, and an array of targeting ligands and signal systems to enable in vitro or in vivo detection.

The nanomaterials and nanodevices that are being developed have scales from molecule to assembly-to functional device in the nano-metresize range. This field is rapidly moving from the development of individual building blocks to multifunctional, often biomimetic and bio-responsive systems.

The combined knowledge and expertise of synthetic and physical chemistry as well as biological chemistry are required for the development of effective nanomaterials and nanodevices that are efficient and safe in the biological environment. Most importantly, it was noted that the research in nanomaterials and nanodevices must strive for biological and medical relevance with this in mind.

The potential timescale for development of practical-to-use systems could be relatively short. As nano-diagnostics, e.g. a dendrimer-MRI agent, are already in clinical development, it can be predicted that those nano-diagnostics under in vitro development today should be available for clinical evaluation within the next few years.

Over the next few decades, considerable growth in the routine clinical use of in vivo nano-diagnostics as well as nanotherapy was predicted. Europe is particularly strong in physical and multifunctional chemical assembly of nanostructures (supramolecular chemistry), and colloid and polymer science including development of micro-electro-electro-mechanical systems (MEMS), nanoparticles, and polymer therapeutics. There are also considerable strengths in engineering materials to control and direct cellular function for biomedical applications, and the materials science relating to tissue engineering and regenerative medicine, bioactive materials and the related stem cells as sources. The overall Nanomedicine-related goals for the research and development in nanomaterials and nanodevices were identified as the development of technologies to satisfy the following applications:

Biological applications

Definition of target and pathway and network identification

— Via multiple, co-assembled biomolecules

Definition of mechanisms of signalling and signal transduction

— Via artificial assemblies in vitro

Clinical use, regulatory and toxicology issues

As for any other conventional medicine, the entire life cycle of nanopharmaceuticals includes production, distribution, clinical administration, consumer safety, and waste disposal. While the clinical applications usually concern only the selected stages of the life cycle, toxicological effects may exist in all the stages. Both clinical applications and toxicology of nanopharmaceuticals must be studied and examined comprehensively. When designing a clinical protocol for a nanopharmaceutical there are new challenges. Clinical trials and epidemiology studies may be significantly different from those for conventional diagnostic and therapeutic agents. Early dialogue and collaboration between scientists, clinicians, toxicologists and regulatory authorities are increasingly recognised as one of the important issues to ensure rapid clinical uses of safe nanopharmaceuticals.

Nanoscale objects, typically but not exclusively with dimensions smaller than 100 nm, smaller than 200 nm for ultrafiltrable range and smaller than 1,000 nm for dendrimers, exhibit fundamentally different physical, chemical and biological properties from those of the corresponding mass materials. These distinctive properties, together with the nanoscale size which is in the same scale of the naturally occurring biomolecules, promise revolutionary potential applications in clinical practice.

Nanomedicines or nanopharmaceuticals may therefore be defined as nanoscale material to be used for clinical diagnosis, treatment, and prevention of human disorders. Nanomedicine application depends on the structures and mechanisms which are functional only on nanoscale-mediated macro-molecular and supra-molecular assemblies. In particular, the following areas were considered:

There are very strict regulations and approval processes for any medicine (via regulatory agencies such as FDA, EMEA etc.) or any material proposed for human use.

It must undergo rigorous toxicology studies as part of the regulatory approval process. However, the special properties of nano-objects that are only exhibited at the nanoscale suggest that nanopharmaceuticals may also require a new array of toxicological and safety tests. It was agreed that new strategies in toxicology for Nanomedicine must go hand-in-hand with the development of nanopharmaceuticals in order to ensure the safe yet swift introduction of nanomedicines to clinical use.

Although the nanopharmaceuticals that have already entered routine clinical use have been rigorously tested with regard to safety, there have been comparatively few toxicological studies published on nanopharmaceuticals. However, this issue needs to be explored, based on the large literature in the toxicology field describing the effects of nanoparticles, either present in the environment as pollutants or made as a result of the industrial production of non-medical and non-biological materials. Europe has considerable experience in the clinical development of nanopharmaceuticals (particularly in cancer).

Pre-clinical toxicology to 'good laboratory practice' (GLP) has assessed antibodydrug conjugates, polymer-drug conjugates and nanoparticle-based chemotherapy. During the development of novel anticancer treatments there is always a careful evaluation of risk-benefit. Since Europe has particular strengths in the research areas of toxicology of inhaled ambient or occupational fine and ultrafine particles there is an excellent opportunity to redress the current mismatch between studies on toxicology of nanomaterials and those involved in research and development of Nanomedicine-related technologies.

As there seems to be enormous prospects for the application of nanotechnology in medicine, the European Nanomedicine research community should act proactively to seize the opportunity to clearly define the ground rules for the related toxicological research, and the related clinical and industrial development of these important technologies. As yet there are no regulatory authority guidelines specific to Nanomedicine.

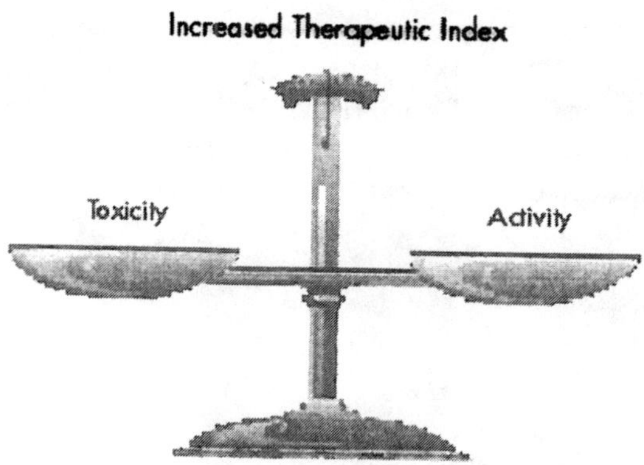

Cancer Chemotherapy and Drug Targeting

As the number of nanopharmaceuticals increases there is a need to review and define appropriate regulatory authority guidelines directed towards each new class of Nanomedicine. It would be timely to produce 'Good Clinical Practice' (GCP) guidelines that may be applied to the clinical development of specific families of drug delivery systems or therapeutics.

Some examples of well-established categories of pharmaceuticals involving nano-objects are polymerprotein, polymer-drug conjugates and nanoparticle associated chemotherapy. There may be specific clinical end points that are unique to these nanomedicines, and there may also be specific issues relating to good manufacturing practice (GMP) compliance. Second generation nanopharmaceuticals are already being, or will be, developed based on first generation systems. An integrated strategy will be the key for toxicological evaluation of new nanomaterials that are emerging.

There is a need for pre-clinical and clinical test standardisation and an evaluation of the environmental impact of these systems in the context of academic research and industrial development. On a case by case basis there is a need to define toxicokinetics, toxicogenomics, and toxicoproteomics. This field might be defined as 'Toxiconanomics'. This research effort should be conducted by virtual networks of basic and applied scientists using existing expertise as a starting point. Industrial collaboration should be used to establish standard reference materials.

9

Nanoscience in Biology

Systems biology analyses biological systems by measuring the steady-state and dynamic relationships of the elements in the system in response to genetic or environmental perturbations across their developmental or physiological time dimensions. Systems biology is concerned with defining the protein biomodules (e.g., groups of proteins that execute a particular phenotypic function such as galactose and glucose metabolism or protein synthesis) and the protein networks of life (e.g., the skeletal framework of cells and their signal transduction pathways).

Systems biology is also concerned with delineating the gene regulatory networks that govern the expression patterns of proteins across developmental or physiological time spans. It is also concerned with delineating the cells effective integration of the protein and gene regulatory networks. Systems biology must capture global sets of biological information from as many hierarchical levels of information as possible (DNA, RNA, protein, protein interactions, biomodules, protein and gene regulatory networks, cells, organs, individuals, populations, ecologies) and integrate them. This is the start point for the formulation of detailed graphicalor mathematical models of biological systems, which are then refined by hypothesis-driven, iterative systems perturbations and data integration. The key is that phenotypic features of the system must be tied directly to the behaviour of the protein and gene regulatory networks. Ultimately, these models will explain the systems or emergent properties of the biological system of interest.

First, variant forms of human genes predispose to certain diseases. For example, when a woman has a single bad copy of the breast cancer 1 gene, she has a 70% possibility of getting breast cancer by the time she is 60 years of age. In the next 10 to 15 years, we will be able to sequence individual human genomes rapidly and economically and, accordingly, provide each individual with a probabilistic future health history. Second, during this same time span, we will be able to use hand-held microfluidics devices to analyse tens of thousands of blood elements (e.g., mRNAs, proteins, metabolites) and distinguish health and disease states specifically. This analysis will detect the consequences of both disease predisposing genes and pathologic environmental signals (e.g., infections) and each of these pathologies will have unique molecular signatures.

Preventive medicine will use the tools of systems biology to define the protein and/or gene regulatory networks within which pathologic environmental cues or defective genes operate. It will also provide the methods for circumventing the consequences of these pathogenic signals by re-engineering the behaviour of these malfunctioning networks through drugs, proteins, genes, or cellular therapies. It is now well known that virtually all cancers are genetic in origin, and that any class of cancer (breast cancer, for example) stratifies into a variety of diseases, each with their own molecularly distinct signatures of gene expression and protein translation.

These signatures arise from different combinations of genetic mutations, but lead to the common clinical presentation of, for example, an unexpected tumour mass in the breast. The sequenced human genome has provided a genetic parts list, which is serving as a powerful database against which disease mRNA or protein signatures can be catalogued. However, it could also be argued that this genetic parts list has had very little impact on either the drug discovery process, or on the clinical practice of medicine to date. As the fundamental knowledge of the genetic signatures of disease grows, the application of systems approaches to disease will revolutionise medicine.

The approach of systems biology is to take as an input the many molecular signatures of gene and protein expression, as well as other, more phenomenological information. Network platform programmes where the nodes are mRNAs (or proteins) and the edges are properties that interrelate the nodes (e.g., interactions) will be employed to understand the systems basis of disease. As more types of interrelationships are integrated, the structure of the networks will be refined and clarified. The assembled networks constitute a hypothesis of how the system works at the molecular scale. This hypothesis may be represented graphically in the form of interacting clusters, or modules of proteins, and each module is typically assigned primary responsibility for some biological function, such as respiration or reproduction.

This hypothesis is then tested by designing and performing a systematic series of topdown and bottom-up perturbations on the system. For example, a top-down perturbation might be to expose the system to a particular molecule to, for example, inhibit a protein node in a cell circuit. A bottom-up perturbation might be a genetic knock-out to, for example, alter the transcription and translation of proteins that are necessary for a signal transduction pathway in a cell. In practice, hundreds or even thousands of such systematic perturbations can be carried out in parallel. The various molecular and phenomenological signatures are again measured, and the hypothesis is appropriately modified to account for these new results.

This modified hypothesis is again tested, and so on, until the hypothesis becomes fully predictive. In principle, with a sufficient number of measurements, a complete molecular description of the system is possible.

Such a description contains within it not just the molecular signatures useful for identifying the nature and progression of disease, but also the critical molecular nodes of disease that can serve as drug targets. In fact, the topdown molecular perturbations to the system may be viewed also as a pharmaceutical screening procedure. However, instead of screening molecules against a particular molecular (protein) target, for example, the molecules are screened against a particular system function. In order to gauge the response of the system to the molecular perturbation, it may well be necessary to monitor the responses of tens of thousands of molecular signatures.

A fully realised systems biology approach might appear to be an overly ambitious and unwieldy method for either drug discovery or for disease diagnosis. In fact, within the context of current biotechnologies, it is. For example, just the process of cell sorting, polymerase chain reaction (PCR) amplification, DNA arrays, etc., can take a few days, and this is just for a relatively simple analysis of gene expression patterns.

A proteomic analysis would require significantly larger cell populations and more time and, of course, many of the proteins (perhaps the majority) would still not be detected. At the very least, a systems biology approach on even the simplest of systems today would constitute a major and expensive research project. An emerging set of molecular and nanotechnologies that are being developed and integrated into a systems biology laboratory. The point is that the needs of systems biology will drive the nature of the tools developed.

Also, there will be an attempt to integrate the ability to make multiple interrelated measurements on one nanochip.

These are technologies that can potentially analyse many products of gene and protein expression, in real time, and at the level of a single cell or small cell population—i.e., without the need for PCR amplification.

When these nanotechnology-based laboratories (nanolabs) are combined with appropriate informatics routines, the resulting output can be a visualisation of the molecular signatures of disease and disease progression, resolved at the level of a single cell. The potential for real-time, multivariable analysis implies that the various molecular signals that are recorded can be utilised to predict new experiments in a direct feedback fashion.

Coupling these nanolab and informatics platforms with molecular imaging techniques brings about the potential for identifying the critical molecular nodes of disease, and then directly translating that knowledge to the mouse and patient. The end-goal is to carry out a full systems analysis of a biological organism, and then to utilise that knowledge to regulate, through molecular intervention, critical molecular nodes within a disease cycle, with direct applications to mouse models of disease and patients. Between the extremes, the systems biology models must on one hand be consistent with in vitro findings in the expression of DNA and its translation into proteins and at the other end of the spectrum must be consistent with findings in the mouse and most importantly, the patient.

Single Cells

A biological system has many layers of diversity, each building upon the previous. These layers traverse from genes to proteins and from there to protein modules, cells, organs, organisms, and so on up to ecosystems. From the aspect of molecular diagnostics and therapeutics, the cell is the fundamental building block.

Experimental measurements on particular cellular processes are typically performed on large cell populations. Such experiments lead necessarily to measurements of an inhomogeneous distribution of responses. For example, consider an experiment in which the cell-cycle is to be investigated on a population of cells.

All of the cells can be arrested at the initial (G1) phase of the cell cycle, and will remain at that starting point until they are exposed to some specific extracellular signal, such as a mitogen. Let us say that at time = 0 we introduce this signaling molecule, and so initiate the cell cycle process. If we check back in a few hours, we will find that some of the cells have not yet moved beyond their initial stage, while others are variously distributed in the later (S, G2, M) phases of the cycle.

In other words, no matter when we stop this experiment-whether after minutes, hours, or days, we will always find an inhomogeneous distribution of cells. It is clearly interesting, from both fundamental and applied perspectives, to understand both the cells that are not dividing as well as those that have accelerated through the cycle. However, unless these processes are resolved at the level of a single cell, it is not possible to elucidate some of the most interesting and critical details of the system.

Similar arguments can be made for immunological processes, such as the interactions between bacterial pathogens and cells of the innate immune system, such as macrophages. Once again, we can set a t = 0 for this experiment by introducing the pathogens into a colony of macrophages. After a given time period, some macrophages will be highly mobile, others will be consuming and destroying pathogens, and still others will be transferring information about the pathogens to T-cells.It is of course attractive to be able to carry out at least some of the systems biology perturbations on populations of similar or diverse cells. However, the systems analysis is best done at the single cell level. By carrying out our systems biology experiments on enough single cells, and then by combining this series of homogeneous measurements we will be able to reconstruct the heterogeneous distribution of responses. The systems biology approach outlined here requires the simultaneous measurement of many signatures of gene and protein expression in real time across the dynamically changing landscape of developmental or degenerative progression or physiological responses.

There are three issues that require nanotechnology solutions large-scale multiparameter analysis, high sensitivity, and temporal resolution. The most sensitive standard molecular detection method is provided for by the single-photon counting capabilities of fluorescence detection. For the past few years there have been research reports of chemical sensors based on single-walled carbon nanotubes (SWNTs) or semiconductor nanowires.

For these sensors, the chemical event changes the conductivity of the nanotube or nanowire, and so the event may be electronically transduced, hereby avoiding the problem of photo-bleaching. It also implies that the number of different molecules that can be sensed is only limited by the number of electrically addressable nanowire sensors that can be fabricated, allowing large-scale multi-parameter analysis, with the caveat that each nanowire has to be encoded with a different molecular probe.

A standard transistor consists of a semiconductor wire, connected at eitherend to metal electrodes (the source and drain). A third, noncontacting electrode, called the gate, raises or lowers the conductivity of the nanowire (opens or closes the switch) via the application of an electric field. There are alternative ways in which this gating electric field may be applied. Changing the chemical environment surrounding the nanowire changes the local chemical potential. This also amounts to changing the local electric field and can gate the nanowire conductivity, thereby providing a basis for chemical sensing. If a single strand DNA is bound to a nanowire as a linker, the binding of the complimentary mRNA will cause a signal to be generated, thereby indicating a specific hybridisation has occurred. This sensing mechanism is called chemically gated nanowire sensing.

A completely different mechanism for nanowire sensing involves a nanomechanical signal transduction mechanism. In this case, the nanowires are piesoresistive wires and are fabricated so that the central part of the nanowire is suspended, but with source and drain electrodes connected at either end, as before. The nanowires are again coated with an appropriate molecular linker for the molecule to be detected.

When a molecular target (protein or mRNA) binds to the nanowire, the result is that the mechanical coupling (Brownian motion) of the nanowire to the surrounding solution is increased, thereby increasing the piezoresistive electrical noise of the nanowire. Such a sensing mechanism (called mechanically gated) has the advantage that it is completely immune to phenomena such as the charge screening by electrolyte solution of the chemical potential surrounding the nanowire (i.e., the detection mechanism of chemically gated nanowires). The fabrication challenges for mechanically gated nanowire sensors are, however, more severe.

One important characteristic of nanowires is that they have a very high surface to volume ratio, and this means that the smaller the nanowire, the larger the relative interaction area between the molecular environment surrounding the nanowire and the electrically conducting core of the nanowire. It turns out that the best chemically gated nanowire sensors are about 5-10 nm in diameter. If they are much smaller, the measured response is too noisy, and if they are much bigger, the sensitivity is reduced.

A large number of nanowire sensors, each chemically encoded with a probe molecule to sense a particular signature of gene or protein expression, can therefore serve as a key part of our systems biology nanolab.

Chemically encoding (biopassivating) each nanowire does represent a significant challenge, although there are literature methods based on scanning probe techniques (dip-pen lithography)or electrochemical methods, that can be (and have been) applied to this problem. Another key aspect of the nanolab that is uniquely addressed by employing nanofabrication methods is the concept of real-time systems biology.

Certainly there are many molecular processes that can take place within the time scales of 10^{-14} to 10^{-3} seconds, such as the making and breaking of chemical bonds, the folding of proteins, etc. However, we are more interested in the rates of molecular signaling. Given that molecules are heavily screened from each other within the electrolyte solution of an intracellular environment, the limiting timescale for signaling processes within a cell is molecular diffusion.

The time it takes for a molecule to diffuse through a typical 10 micrometer diameter cell is approximately 0.1 seconds, and so we take this as our critical time scale unit. If we wish to retain this level of time-resolution, then we need to not only place our sensor suite within a few micrometers of the cell we are interrogating, but we would also need to have the entire sensor circuit, containing a thousand or more nanowires sensors, to occupy a footprint of only about 10×10 micrometers squared. This provides a significant challenge.

The highest resolution lithographic technique, called electron-beam lithography, cannot pattern semiconducting nanowires at either the diameters or circuit densities that are required. However, a recently developed method, called Superlattice Nanowire Pattern Transfer, or SNAP, does generate the appropriate circuits (Figure 3). Other issues, such as how one goes about electrically addressing each of the nanowires when they are placed together at such high densities, also provide for significant nanofabrication challenges, but are solvable.

Microfluidics

Imagine the following experiments aimed at investigating the cell cycle. First, we stipulate a molecular-based model for the cell cycle that is constructed from existing genomic and proteomic analyses. We test this model by starting with a population of cells that we have arrested at the start of the G1 phase of the cycle. We have transfected these cells with various reporter genes such that as the cells enter each of the four stages of the cycle, they will fluoresce at a different colour. We then initiate the cell cycle with some signaling molecule, and we wait some period of time until we can tell, using fluorescence imaging, that there are cells that have progressed into the G1 and the S-phases of the cycle. We then extract several cells from our culture medium, sort them according to their progression through the cycle, and place them into separate nanolab compartments, each containing a suite of electronic (nanowire) sensors.

We have separate chemical control over each of the individual nanolab compartments. This enables us to inject small molecules designed to perturb the cells, or introduce nonionic surfactants so that we can investigate cytoplasmic proteins. We can also add ionic surfactants to dissolve the nucleus walls and release the mRNA so that we can measure the signatures of gene expression.

At the completion of these experiments, we have carried out a multivariable analysis of approximately 100 cells, with between a few hundred and a few thousand measurements per cell, we have fed those results back into our informatics algorithm, and the initial hypothesis has been modified accordingly. We are now ready to re-test our model by again similarly interrogating and perturbing the cells remaining within our original population.

In fact, not only can it be automated, but the entire suite of experiments, from cell culture to cell sorting to cell lysing, etc., can all be incorporated into a single chip-based platform. The key technology for integrating the biology with the nanolab in a highly parallel fashion is a unique and flexible class of microfluidics technologies developed by Steve Quake's group at Caltechand illustrated in Figure 4. They have developed largescale integrated microfluidic circuitrythat is based on multilayer soft-lithography to fabricate micromolded (poly(dimethylsiloxane), or PDMS) elastomer valves, channels, chambers, and pumps. These microfluidics platforms have been demonstrated for cell-sorting applications, (PCR-based) gene-expression profiling at the single cell level, and much more.

Molecular Imaging

Imaging in general implies a technology that can open up a wide aperture to collect signals and generate a picture of structures and/or processes within the fieldof-view. The nanolab, when coupled with bioinformatics algorithms, will eventually turn into an imaging tool that efficiently collects, processes and displays a molecular-based picture of the biological system being investigated.

By contrast, microscopy and molecular imaging tools begin by presenting the picture. The information content of that picture is nominally based upon the fundamental physical quantity being imaged (i.e., optical fluorescence, surface topography, proton density, radioactive decay, etc.) that are translated into information about biological structures and functions. When coupled with mathematically based data analysis and image reconstruction techniques, imaging methods can be engineered into powerful tools for visualising key aspects of the biological system under investigation. A systems biology-derived picture of an organism may be drawn at multiple levels, but has at its origin a molecular basis that connects back to a digital code (the genome) and the molecular machinery that executes that code (the proteome).

Thus, if an imaging tool, such as fluorescence microscopy, positron emission tomography imaging (PET), magnetic resonance imaging (MRI), etc., is going to provide a direct connection to a systems biology picture, then that imaging tool, at its most fundamental level, must provide a direct correlation to the molecular basis of the systems biology description. This is, at a minimum, what defines molecular imaging. However, the true benefit of molecular imaging is not that it provides redundant information of the molecular description of the system, but that it can also provide the critical link from the cellular based environment of the nanolab and the in vivo environment of the living organism. The nanolab will eventually evolve into a platform for discovering the molecular probes that can perturb and test the hypothesis of the biological system. The most effective of those probes for molecular imaging diagnostics and therapeutics from cells and mice to patients using various molecular imaging technologies along this pathway that best serve the purpose.

Nanolab

The nanolab is an automated experimental environment based upon large-scale integrated microfluidics interfaced to a variety of nanotechnologies. Within this lab there exists a large array of addressable locations and controllable operations in fluid space. Many types of coupled operations and experimental conditions can be laid out within such an interconnected biochemical environment. It is instructive to understand how these various functions can be employed within the context of identifying therapeutic targets and developing both pharmaceutical candidates and molecular imaging probes. The initial goal of the nanolab is to perform large-scale multi-parameter analysis of the molecular basis of systems biology in cells or collections of cells. The second goal is to then reduce this large-scale systems biology problem to a small set of variables that can be used for in vivo molecular diagnostics and therapeutics. This reduction in information dimensionality is one of the major challenges of molecular medicine. It is through meeting this goal that we seek to establish the connection between the systems biology experiments and the mouse and patient.

In order to meet this second goal, nanolab capabilities that extend beyond what has already been described are needed. It turns out that many of the engineering problems that are solved by bringing together biology with nanofabrication and microfluidics are general for a host of other applications that are of direct relevance to this goal. For example, additional chips can be devoted to storing molecular libraries, carrying out molecular synthesis, performing protein crystallisation, quantifying protein-protein interactions (using nanomechanical devices), etc.

In fact, most of these tasks have already been reported in the literature, although many of these applications, such as the carrying out of molecular synthesis within a microfluidic environment, are very poorly developed. The manner in which these various platforms will be coordinated will certainly vary widely, perhaps limited only by the numbers of practitioners. Those nodes are drug targets, and exposure of the system to a candidate pharmaceutical aimed at those proteins, followed by a multivariable analysis of the response of the system, may provide a compelling pathway for drug testing. It may be necessary to screen many molecules, to chemically modify some of the best initial candidates to optimise the system response, to crystallise the protein in order to assess the nature of the drug candidate-binding, or even to screen the drug candidates against the protein to assess and chemically optimise the interaction forces.

The nanolab will allow for these types of large-scaleand rapid multiparameter analyses that are only possible in vitro. However, a good drug candidate or an analog of it, perhaps discovered as described above, may also serve as an excellent molecular imaging probe for diagnostically interrogating the state of the disease in the living organism. Thus, the nanolab becomes a molecular probe (diagnostic and therapeutic) discovery platform as well.

There are various types of molecular and structural imaging techniques that have been and continue to be developed to link in vitro imaging to in vivo imaging. These include various optical imaging modalities, PET, MRI, single photon emission computed tomography (SPECT), computed tomography (CT) and ultrasound. Figure 6 illustrates a pathway from in vitro studies of cells to in vivo examinations of mice to patients that brings together the nanolab, optical imaging, and PET.

Optical imaging provides a molecular imaging link from cells to mice because of its successful and growing use for in vitro cell culturesand in vivo mouse settings. In the mouse, optical imaging is joined with microPET scanners for mice to build assays and knowledge from the level of imaging gene expression and DNA replication to signal transduction and metabolism.

Molecular imaging and molecular therapeutics

At present molecular imaging and molecular therapeutics have come together to develop molecular probes that are analogs of each other but have common disease targets. In imaging with PET, the probe is used in extremely low mass amounts (tracers with resulting tissue concentrations of ~ femtomoles/g tissue) to image and measure the concentration and function of the target without mass effects on the target. In the case of the drug, the molecule is given in sufficient amounts to therapeutically alter or block the function of the target.

The molecular imaging probe can be used diagnostically or to provide the means to image and measure the pharmaco kinetics of the drug in the living mouse and patient, first at tracer levels and then to titrate the drug to selected occupancy on the target. In addition, other PET probes can be used as surrogate markers to examine the drug's effectiveness to modify or terminate a biological process such as metabolism, gene expression, transmitter synthesis, and cell proliferation. Since PET is a quantitative imaging technique, the concentration of the labeled drug analog can be measured throughout all the organ systems of the body over time. Such studies can be repeated at various pharmacologic doses to assess how the pharmaco kinetics throughout the body are altered by mass levels of the drug with a reference to the percent occupancy on the therapeutic target. Such studies can be performed in mice and then in patients.

Today, an increasing number of pharmaceutical companies have incorporated PET into their drug discovery process to be able to watch and measure their drugs and their effectiveness in vivo from mouse to patient. Optical imaging and MRI are also being employed to examine various structure-function relationships to aid their drug discovery process.

PET has become the lead imaging technology to illustrate the general principles and value of molecular imaging of the biology of disease in patients. This is illustrated by the fact that in 20 different cancers in the diagnosis, staging, detecting recurrent disease, and assessing therapeutic responses, that on average, PET is from nine percent to 43% more accurate than conventional imaging, depending on the specific clinical question.

In addition, the use of PET changes the way these patients are treated in 15% to 50% of the cases, across all these cancers and all stages of disease. As a second example of the value of molecular imaging in the brain, PET provides a 93% accuracy in the diagnosis of Alzheimer's disease 3.4 years before the conventional diagnosis can reach with lower accuracy the diagnosis of probable Alzheimer's. MRI and CT scans of these patients are normal or show non-specific changes.

Further, PET has been shown to detect Alzheimer's disease about five years before symptoms and Huntington's disease about seven years before symptoms, while in both cases the MRI and CT studies and all other tests are normal. This represents the value provided from molecular imaging of the biology of disease, independent of the specific molecular imaging technology.

Molecular Biomimetics

Traditionally, biomimeticists, inspired by biological structures and their functions, focused on emulating or duplicating biosystems using mostly synthetic components and following traditional approaches. With the recent developments of molecular and nanoscale engineering in physical sciences, and advances in molecular biology, biomimetics is now entering the molecular scale. By combining nature's molecular tools with synthetic nanoscale constructs, molecular biomimetics is emerging as a hybrid methodology. Materials have uniquely functional properties at nanometre-scale dimensions that, if harnessed effectively, could lead to novel engineering systems with highly useful characteristics.

Mechanical properties of nanostructured composites, electronic properties of low-dimensional semiconductors, magnetic properties of single-domained particles, and solution properties of colloidal suspensions, are all attractive and interesting, and correlate directly to the nanometre-scale structures that characterise these systems. The realisation of the full potential of nanotechnological systems, however, has so far been limited due to the difficulties in their synthesis and subsequent assembly into useful functional structures and devices. Despite all the promise of science and technology at the nanoscale, the control of nanostructures and ordered assemblies of materials in two- and three-dimensions still remains largely elusive.

Biomaterials, on the other hand, are highly organised from the molecular to the nano- and macroscales, often in a hierarchical manner, with intricate nano-architectures that ultimately make up a myriad of different functional soft and hard tissues (Fig. 10). Under genetic control, biological tissues are synthesised in aqueous environments under mild physiological conditions using biomacromolecules, primarily proteins but also carbohydrates and lipids. Proteins both collect and transport raw materials, and consistently and uniformly self- and co-assemble subunits into short- and long-range-ordered nuclei and substrates. Whether in controlling tissue formation, biological functions or physical performance, proteins are an indispensable part of biological structures and systems.

Engineering materials are synthesised using a combination of approaches, for example,melting and solidification processes, followed by thermomechanical treatments, or solution/vacuum deposition and growth processes. In many cases, however, the final product is dictated by the kinetics and thermodynamics of the system and often achieved through 'heat-and-beat' approaches. By contrast, in biological systems, evolutionary selection processes result in specific molecular recognition.

In molecular biomimetics, a marriage of the physical and biological fields, hybrid materials could potentially be assembled from the molecular level using the recognition properties of proteins under the premise that inorganic surface-specific polypeptides could be used as binding agents to control the organisation and specific functions of materials.

Molecular biomimetics simultaneously offers three solutions to the development of heterofunctional nanostructures. The first is that protein templates are designed at the molecular level through genetics. This ensures complete control over the molecular structure of the protein template (that is, DNA-based technology).

The second is that surface specific proteins can be used as linkers to bind synthetic entities, including nanoparticles, functional polymers, or other nanostructures onto molecular templates (molecular and nanoscale recognition). The third solution harnesses the ability of biological molecules to self- and co-assemble into ordered nanostructures. This ensures a robust assembly process for achieving complex nano-, and possibly hierarchical structures, similar to those found in nature (self-assembly). The current knowledge of protein-folding predictions and surface-binding chemistries does not provide sufficiently detailed information to perform rational design of proteins.

To circumvent this problem, massive libraries of randomly generated peptides can be screened for binding activity to inorganic surfaces using phage and cell-surface display techniques. It may ultimately be possible to construct a 'molecular erector' set, in which different types of proteins, each designed to bind to a specific inorganic surface, could assemble into intricate, hybrid structures composed of inorganics and proteins. This would be a significant leap towards realising molecularly designed, genetically engineered technological materials. There are several possible ways of obtaining polypeptide sequences with specific affinity to inorganics.

A number of proteins may fortuitously bind to inorganics, although they are rarely tested for this purpose. Inorganic-binding peptides may be designed using a theoretical molecular approach similar to that used for pharmaceutical drugs. This is currently impractical because it is time consuming and expensive.

Another possibility would be to extract biomineralising proteins from hard tissues followed by their isolation, purification and cloning. Several such proteins have been used as nucleators, growth modifiers, or enzymes in the synthesis of certain inorganics. One of the major limitations of this approach is that a given hard tissue usually contains many proteins, not just one, all differently active in biomineralisation and each distributed spatially and temporally in complex ways.

Furthermore, tissue-extracted proteins may only be used for the regeneration of the inorganics that they are originally associated with, and would be of limited practical use. The preferred route, therefore, is to use combinatorial biology techniques. Here, a large random library of peptides with the same number of amino acids, but of different sequences, is used to mine specific sequences that strongly bind to a chosen inorganic surface. Since their inception, well-established in vivo combinatorial biology protocols (for example, phage display (PD) and cell-surface display (CSD)) have been used to identify biological ligands and to map the epitope (molecular recognition site) of antibodies.

Libraries have also been screened for various biological activities, such as catalytic properties or altered affinity and specificity to target molecules in many applications including the design of new drugs, enzymes, antibodies, DNA-binding proteins and diagnostic agents. The power of display technologies relies on the fact that an a priori knowledge of the desired amino acid sequence is not necessary, as it can simply be selected and enriched if a large enough population of random sequences is available.

In vitro methods, such as ribosomal and messenger RNA display technologies, have been developed for increased library size compared to those of in vivo systems.

Combinatorial biology protocols can be followed in molecular biomimetics to select polypeptide sequences that preferentially bind to the surfaces of inorganic compounds chosen for their unique physical properties in nano- and biotechnology.

Libraries are generated by inserting randomised oligonucleotides within certain genes encoded on phage genomes or on bacterial plasmids. This leads to the incorporation of a random polypeptide sequence within a protein residing on the surface of the organism.

The eventual result is that each phage or cell produces and displays a different, but random peptide. At this stage, a heterogeneous mixture of recombinant cells or phages are contacted with the inorganic substrate. Several washing cycles of the phages or the cells eliminate non-binders by disrupting weak interactions with the substrate. Bound phages or cells are next eluted from the surfaces. In PD, the eluted phages are amplified by reinfecting the host. Similarly in CSD, cells are allowed to grow. This step completes a round of biopanning. Generally, three to five cycles of biopanning are repeated to enrich for tight binders.

Finally, individual clones are sequenced to obtain the amino acid sequence of the polypeptides binding to the target substrate material. Outer membrane proteins, lipoproteins, fimbria and flagellar proteins have all been used for heterologous surface display on bacteria. In PD, most of the research has been performed using filamentous phages such as M13 or the closely related fd and f1. Random peptide libraries have been displayed on bacteriophages T7, T4 and λ, but these systems are not yet used on a routine basis. PD and CSD need to be investigated and optimised in the selection of inorganic-surface-binding polypeptides. In general, cell surfaces are more complex than the coat of bacteriophages, but a single host is required. By contrast, PD requires bacteriophage and its host bacterium, and reinfection is necessary for the amplification of selected variants.

Eluting bound phages from an inorganic surface might be problematic leading to a loss of good binders. This may be overcome by reamplifying unreleased phages from the substrate despite the low yields. Material instability in the screening buffers and nonspecific binding of phages or bacteria to inorganic surfaces could also be a problem. These issues can be remedied by a careful choice of buffer combinations. It should be noted that even if a material appears to be unaffected in a particular screening buffer, its surface might be chemically modified, resulting in the recovery of peptides that bind to a surface or morphology different from the one that was originally intended. Growth competition or poor expression of a peptide due to rare codons, misfolding, degradation or inefficient export, may also bias the screen.

Thus, parallel use of multiple screening techniques may allow greater flexibility in working with unstable materials and maximising the number of useful screens. In the quest for inorganic-binding polypeptides, new methodologies are likely to be needed. For example, the use of in vitro systems and a combination of rational and random approaches could prove useful for the identification of very rare sequences, and to increase the diversity and affinity of sequences isolated in previous selections. A genetically engineered polypeptide for inorganics (GEPI) defines a sequence of amino acids that specifically and selectively binds to an inorganic surface.

The surface could be well defined, such as a single crystal or a nanostructure. It might also be rough, or totally non-descriptive, such as a powder. Many early studies used powder samples, including the seminal work of Brown. In recent research, Mehmet Sarikaya et. al has focused on using materials that can be synthesised in aqueous environments under physiological conditions (biocompatible) and that exhibit fairly stable surface structures and compositions. These include noble metals (Pt and Pd) as well as oxide semiconductors (Cu_2O and ZnO) that were biopanned using either PD or flagellar display. In the PD panning, a disulphide-constrained M13 peptide library, seven amino acids long, was used.

The purpose was to determine whether there were any similarities in metal-binding domains between the short Pt- and Pd-binding sequences and the 14-aa Au binding sequences selected by CSD and/or the 12-aa Ag-binding sequences selected by PD. Others focused on PD-based sequences with interesting size-selective binding capabilities to semiconductors (GaAs and ZnS), metal-oxide-binding motifs (SiO_2, ZnO, and zeolites), and binders to ionic crystals ($CaCO_3$, Cr_2O_3, and Fe_2O_3/Fe_3O_4). The specificity of a protein for a surface may originate from both chemical (for example, hydrogen bonding, polarity and charge effects) and structural (size and morphology) recognition mechanisms.

Some conclusions may be drawn from the available set of inorganic-binding sequences. For example, goldbinding sequences isolated by CSD could be moved from an extracellular loop of maltoporin to the Nterminus of alkaline phosphotase with retention of gold-binding activity, suggesting portability and independence of the surrounding protein framework. Although many proteins bind to Au at low salt concentrations, the gold-binding sequences were selected for binding at high salt concentrations.

As a result, they exhibit substantially improved binding compared with native Escherchia coli alkaline phosphotase even in the presence of a detergent. Their initial assembly studies focused on the 14-amino-acidlong Au-binding peptide, GBP1 (MHGKTQATSGTIQS). To increase binding activity, tandem repeats of the sequence were generated by genetic engineering, and it was found that at least three repeats were required for high-affinity binding. Similar tetrapeptide repeats (SEKL and GASL) were observed in the sequences identified that control the morphology of gold crystals. The Ag-, Pt-, and Pd-binders were all selected using M13 PD libraries. For Ag binders, a 12-aa library was used a constrained heptamer library to identify the smallest sequences capable of binding Pt and Pd.

Inspection of the sequences of the noble-metal binders suggests that serine and threonine are important for binding. These amino acids have similar structures and contain aliphatic hydroxyl groups in their side chains. Participation in hydrogen bonding by nitrogen atoms was also a common feature of noble-metal binders. Interestingly, most of the sequences isolated to date have not contained cysteine, and only a few of them contained histidines, two residues known to bind to transition metal ions. Aromaticity was rarely observed, and only when it was coupled with a hydroxyl or amine functional group.

Overall, noblemetal-binding sequences appear to predominantly consist of hydrophobic and hydroxyl-containing polar amino acids. For both metal oxides and zeolites, basic amino acids (arginine and lysine) and hydroxyl-containing residues were common, especially in ZnO, zeolite and, to a lesser extent, in SiO_2. Of the ionic crystals, Cr_2O_3 and Fe_2O_3 binders have similar characteristics, such as being basic and charged. Unlike biological $CaCO_3$-binding proteins where asparagines and glutamine dominante, PD selected $CaCO_3$-binders contained mostly uncharged or basic amino acids, with small differences possibly originating from different mineral forms, aragonite and calcite.

Finally, sequences binding to semiconductors GaAs and ZnS contain polar amino acids composed of mostly uncharged ones. Overall, both metal oxide and ionic crystal binders exhibit strong basic characteristics and high positive charges, whereas non-oxide semiconductor binders are close to the neutral range, and metal binders are slightly basic.

Physical specificity of peptide binding

Ideally, selection of sequences should be performed using an inorganic material of specific morphology, size, crystallography or surface stereochemistry. In practice, however, powders of various sizes and morphologies have been used for selection. The sequence space should be largest for powders, as peptides can attach to surfaces with various morphological features. On the other hand, because powders are non-descriptive, the selected polypeptides may exhibit little or no homology and solve' the binding problem through different strategies.

Binders selected for a given size, morphology, crystallography or stereochemistry may share a higher degree of homology. For example, a GEPI binding to a material of a certain size may also bind to a smaller particle of the same material, but less strongly. Similarly, a GEPI binding strongly to a specific crystallographic surface may bind with an altered affinity to another surface of the same material.

Finally, a GEPI strongly binding to a material of composition A may bind less strongly to a material B with a different composition but having similar structure (for example, perovskites). Therefore, if one seeks highly specific binders, the physical and chemical characteristics of the material must be known. An alternative approach is that, once a relatively large number of binders have been identified by panning on powders, a subset specific for morphology, size or surface could be identified on well-defined materials.

The researchers performed structure-modelling studies to predict the shape of the 3-repeat Au-binding peptide GBP1 in solution. This work was carried out in the hope that a match between amino acids of GBP1 and the spacing of the inorganic atomic lattice would shed light on the mechanism of binding. Simulation results indicate that the repeats form an antiparallel β-sheet, and that their close contacts between peptide and Au(111) surfaces mainly involve the polar side chains of serine and threonine, which places a periodic structure of OH^- groups into a regular lattice. In the same study, GBP1 does not bind to Au(112) as tightly, because of the migration of water molecule through the atomic grooves of the crystallographic surface, which decouples the polypeptide from the surface.

Nanoassembly and Inorganic-Binding Polypeptides

Nanometre-sized particles and nanostructured inorganics could be fundamental building blocks for future technological materials and devices. Numerous challenges must be addressed before they are successfully implemented into working systems. These include synthesising nanostructures with uniform size and shape, controlling their mineralogy, surface structures and chemistry, and predicting their spatial distribution.

The molecular biomimetics approach holds great promise in overcoming some of these difficulties. Because inorganic surface-binding polypeptides are selected to specifically bind to a material based on its physical or chemical characteristics, they may find applications in controlling materials morphology and uniformity, and could be used to generate heterostructures combining different inorganics and molecules that would normally phase-separate.

The availability of amino acid sequences binding to inorganics offers a fresh perspective towards future studies in self-assembling nanostructured components with distinct functionalities. One could select a GEPI from the available sequences and insert it within the framework of another protein exhibiting properties (for example, DNA-binding) and use the resulting designer protein or the DNA as a molecular substrate.Alternatively, a GEPI could be chemically linked to a synthetic polymer with functional properties (for example, conductive or light-sensitive) to create multifunctional hybrid polymeric units. Whether fused to biological or synthetic macromolecules, the role of the GEPI would be to endow them with another functionality: specific inorganic-binding.

10

Nanomanipulation

The Atomic Forice Microscopy (AFM) is a conceptually simple apparatus. A micrometer-scale cantilever with a sharp tip (diameter ~ 10-50 nm) is scanned over a sample at distances on the order of a few nm. Interatomic forces between the tip and the sample are sensed by the cantilever, whose deflection is measured (usually) by a laser and a photodetector. In contact mode operation, the tip is in the repulsive region of the curve, and the force is kept constant during the scan by a feedback circuit that monitors the photodetector signal.

A tip in contact mode exerts a relatively large normal force on the sample, and also a substantial lateral force. As a result, fragile samples are damaged, and tips tend to wear out rapidly. In addition, the deflection signal is low-pass and the process is subject to low-frequency noise. The preferred mode of operation often is Dynamic Force Microscopy (DFM), which uses a vibrating cantilever and avoids the force and noise problems of contact mode. There are two versions of DFM. In noncontact mode, the tip oscillates above the sample in the attractive force regime, whereas in intermitent contact mode, the tip contacts the sample for a short time interval ("taps") during each cycle of the oscillation.

DFM Operation

First let us consider non-contact mode. An oscillating cantilever can be approximated by a point mass m attached to a spring of stiffness k, moving in a medium with coefficient of friction c, and subject to a non-linear force $F(z)$, which depends on the tip-sample separation. For small amplitudes, we can expand the force in Taylor series, neglect higher order terms, and linearise the equations of motion about the equilibrium. The resulting equation of motion is

$$m\, d^2z/dt^2 + c\, dz/dt + (k - dF/dz)\, z = 0.$$

This shows that, to a first approximation, the non-linear force has an effect equivalent to a change in the spring constant (or stiffness) of the cantilever. It follows that the resonance frequency depends on z:

$$\omega_0^2 = (k - dF/dz)/m.$$

For large values of z the interaction force $F = 0$, and the response of the cantilever to a forced excitation of frequency f_{drive} is characterised by the thick resonance curve shown in Figure 1. In the figure $f_{res} = \omega_0/2\pi$ is the resonance frequency in Hz. A DFM user controls the instrument by selecting three parameters:

Figure 1. DFM operation

— the drive frequency, which typically is chosen close to resonance;

— the free amplitude, i.e., the amplitude of vibration that corresponds to zero *F*, or large *z*;

— the setpoint, or desired amplitude of vibration A_{set}.

The AFM electronics extract the amplitude of cantilever vibration A, and a feedback circuit moves the piezo motors to ensure that $A = A_{set}$. In the figure, the feedback must adjust z so that the resonance curve shifts to the left until the amplitude that corresponds to the drive frequency equals the setpoint. In essence, the feedback must search for a suitable value of the stiffness dF/dz. Therefore, scanning at a given amplitude setpoint is equivalent to keeping a constant stiffness, or force gradient. This simple theory is adequate for non contact operation with small amplitudes. For intermitent contact mode the situation is more complicated, because the amplitudes are relatively large. Numerical simulation is necessary to deal with the non-linear force. Research on intermitent mode AFM is still under way, and is beyond the scope of this paper.

Raw image

The raw image produced by the AFM is an array of values $V_z(V_x, V_y)$, where the *V* denote voltages applied to the piezo drives responsible for motion in the x, y and z directions. In the ideal situation, in which the tip is a dimensionless point and the piezos are perfectly linear, the image faithfully reproduces the surface z(x, y). Here x, y, z are piezo displacements.

Recall that in DFM imaging the sample height does not necessarily equal the z piezo displacement. Therefore, even with ideal piezos, the so-called topographic image does not represent the true height of the sample. If the sample is relatively homogeneous and therefore the force-separation curve is approximately constant across the sample, there is an approximate one-to-one relationship between tipsample separation and force gradient in stable operation. The topographic image is then qualitatively correct but the z scale may be distorted. Non-linearity arises because of the force-separation curves, even for perfect piezos. For now, one can compute average, or approximate conversion factors from Volts to nm by measuring known samples. For example, x and y calibrations can be done using a crystaline surface whose lattice constant is known. For z calibration, samples with atomic steps are appropriate.

Colloidal particles with known diameters (measured with an SEM, for example) are also convenient for z calibration. Note that z calibration in DFM will not give the true piezo conversion factor because of the influence of the force-separation curve. Contact mode will provide better results in this regard. The only truly reliable way of measuring x, y, z is by using feedback. This is the approach taken in machine tools and robots in the macroscopic world. Position feedback is used in some AFMs for large scans and features.

Some commercial instruments offer 100 μm scanners with feedbackcontrolled x, y positioning. Note, however, that a typical 256x256 pixel image with a scan size of 100 μm has a resolution or pixel size of ~ 400 nm, which is quite large. For the work done in the lab, scan sizes are usually < 1 μm and accuracies ~ 1 nm are required. Unfortunately, sensors and feedback circuits cannot normally offer such accuracies. Hence, commercial instruments are operated open loop for small scan sizes.

DFM as a Manipulator

Tip Positioning

Let us now look at the AFM operating in DFM as a manipulator, rather than as a sensor. Ignoring the high frequency vibration, the tip in its DC or average position can be considered a mobile robot with 3 degrees of freedom, x, y, z. The simplest robotic command one can think of is MoveTo(x, y, z). For small scan sizes, the x, y motion will be open loop and subject to the uncertainties discussed below. But in z we can use feedback, with the cantilever as a sensor. However, we cannot command directly a z value; instead we must select suitable values for the DFM parameters.

The crucial issue is the relationship between A_{set} and z, for fixed A_{free} and f_{drive}. This can be determined experimentally by the following procedure, which is based on the fact that the tip vibration is quenched when the DC position of the tip approaches a surface. This has been demonstrated experimentally and predicted by non-linear simulations using the oscillator mode. First measure the height of a spherical nanoparticle by using standard non-contact AFM with a given Aset. Then turn off the feedback and move towards the center of the particle.

Monitor the cantilever vibration amplitude to ensure that it goes to zero, and measure the maximum DC deflection of the cantilever, which will occur at the highest point of the particle. Then z = H - D as shown in Figure 3. The operating parameters must be chosen so that the particle does not move, and the amplitude decreases to zero. This approach only works for values of Aset below the particle's height. Note that the height H is measured in z piezo Volts and the cantilever deflection D, often called the "A - B signal", in photodetector Volts.

To obtain the z displacement in nm we need to convert the piezo *V* into nm, as explained in the previous section, and we also need a conversion factor between photodiode voltage and cantilever deflection. This latter can be estimated by the following techniques. The standard method for calibrating the photodiode is to push the tip against a hard surface and compare the z displacement of the piezo with the cantilever deflection measured as the output of the photodiode. They should be equal. Unfortunately, this procedure invariably ruins the sharp tips that we need to use for successful nanomanipulation. An alternative and gentler approach consists of executing a line scan over the centers of two nanoparticles of known but different heights. As shown in Figure 4, we can write $z = H_2 - cV_2 = H_1 - cV_1$ and therefore the conversion factor c can be calculated as $c = (H_2 - H_1)/(V_2 - V_1)$.

Pushing

Nanoscale objects such as nanoparticles can be pushed mechanically by the tip of an AFM. There are several protocols for manipulation by pushing, all of which share the following aspects. First image the sample to determine where is the desired particle. Then move against the particle, but change the operating parameters so that a force higher than that used for imaging is applied. In the lab we usually push by imaging in DFM and then moving with the feedback off along a line that goes through the center of the particle. We observe that the amplitude goes to zero, the DC cantilever deflection becomes non-zero, and the particle moves, if the deflection is above a certain threshold, which depends on the cantilever and various other characteristics of the setup.

Sample preparation

Imaging and manipulation with an AFM depend on the relative magnitudes of the forces between tip, objects and substrate. For example, if the attractive forces between objects and substrate are small, imaging is impossible because the objects move unpredictably when the tip interacts with them; if the forces are large, the objects do not move. Sample preparation techniques must therefore ensure that forces are in a suitable range. This is done by careful selection of the substrate surface and coatings (for the substrate and sometimes the objects), and of deposition procedures. Typically the objects are in solution and a drop is deposited on the substrate. The Au particles usually have a Cl coating which renders them negative. If we deposited them directly on mica, which also is negative when freshly cleaved, they would not adhere sufficiently for imaging. An additional layer of poly-L-lysine, which is positive and serves to anchor the Cl-cappped particles.

Other useful anchoring layers are composed of silanes such as APTS or APTES, which also provide positive charges for attachment. In some cases, use covalent bonding rather than the electrostatic interactions just described.

Spatial Uncertainty

There are many sources of spatial uncertainty in AFM manipulation:

Tip Effects: When the tip moves in contact with a sample it traverses a contact manifold in configuration space. Therefore, we obtain the image of the c-space obstacle that corresponds to the sample rather than the image of the sample itself.

Drift : The major cause of spatial uncertainty in the lab is thermal drift between the tip and the sample. We work at room temperature, in ambient air and without careful temperature and humidity control. A typical value for drift velocity is 0.05 nm/s. This implies that for an image with 256x256 pixels obtained in a 1 Hz scan an object will drift by ~ 12.5 nm, which is approximately the size of the particles we usually manipulate. If we ignored the drift, the manipulation would fail very often.

Creep: A large voltage step will produce a rapid displacement of the tip followed by a slow creeping motion, which can last several minutes. The four images are taken at 12 sec intervals, at 20 Hz, with a scan size of 200 nm and resolution 64x64. Over a 40 sec interval creep values can reach 50 nm for a 1000 nm offset.

Hysteresis: The extension of a piezo depends on the history of the voltages applied to it. For example, scanning right-to-left or left-to-right produces different results. The differences can be large. For example, for a 500 nm scan one can find a displacement of ~ 15 nm, which is comparable to the particle sizes.

Other Nonlinearities: Even ignoring hysteresis the piezo's response is not linear with the voltage. Therefore the V/nm conversion factor is not constant and must be calculated for different conditions. In additon, the tube scanners used in most AFMs move approximately in a circle and not in a straight line. Interactive nanomanipulation can rely on imaging to sense a particle's position immediately before it is moved, and therefore can finesse some of these problems. However, automatic manipulation must address them.

Approaches to Linking and Embedding

Patterns of unlinked nanoparticles can be useful for certain applications such as high-density data storage and single-electron electronics. However, many applications require nanostructures of specific shapes. These can be approximated by groups of suitably positioned and linked nanoparticles. There are two approaches to linking. The first uses covalent bonding to a linker. For example, Au particles can be connected with di-thiols. The di-thiols self-assemble to the gold and serve as chemical glue. There are two variants of this approach: (i) first deposit the particles, position them and then immerse the sample in the di-thiols; or (ii) deposit the particles, apply the thiols and then manipulate.

The second approach to linking also uses selfassembly: additional material is selectively deposited on the particles but not on the remainder of the sample. For example, we have shown that a pattern of Au nanoparticles can be used as a template for the electroless deposition of additional Au. Gold wires of arbitrary geometry can be built in this manner. For certain applications we may need to ensure that nanocomponents are fixed on the substrate. This can also be done by selective self-assembly. Now we need a material that will assemble to the substrate but not the particles, and thus will embed the particles in a thin layer. We have demonstrated particle embedding in a silicon oxide layer by first depositing a monolayer of a silane and then oxidizing it. We have used embedding of particles in successive layers for a new rapid prototyping technique at the nanoscale.

Nanowires

Nanowires have two quantum confined directions, while still leaving one unconfined direction for electrical conduction. This allows nanowires to be used in applications where electrical conduction, rather than tunnelling transport, is required. Because of their unique density of electronic states, nanowires in the limit of small diameters are expected to exhibit significantly different optical, electrical and magnetic properties from their bulk 3D crystalline counterparts.

The increased surface area, very high density of electronic states and joint density of states near the energies of their van Hove singularities, enhanced exciton binding energy, diameter-dependent bandgap, and increased surface scattering for electrons and phonons are just some of the ways in which nanowires differ from their corresponding bulk materials. Yet the sizes of nanowires are typically large enough (> 1nm in the quantum confined direction) to have local crystal structures closely related to their parent materials, thereby allowing theoretical predictions about their properties to be made on the basis of an extensive literature relevant to their bulk properties.

Not only do nanowires exhibit many properties that are similar to, and others that are distinctly different from, those of their bulk counterparts, nanowires have the advantage from an applications standpoint that some of the materials parameters that are critical for certain properties can be independently controlled in nanowires, but not in their bulk counterparts, such as, for example, their thermal conductivity. Also certain properties can be enhanced non-linearly in small diameter nanowires, by exploiting the singular aspects of the 1D electronic density of states. Furthermore, nanowires have been shown to provide a promising framework for applying the bottom-up approach for the design of nanostructures for nanoscience investigations and for potential nanotechnology applications. Driven by:

1) these new research and development opportunities,
2) the smaller and smaller length scales now being used in the semiconductor, opto-electronics and magnetics industries, and
3) the dramatic development of the biotechnology industry where the action is also at the nanoscale, the nanowire research field has developed with exceptional speed in the last few years.

Synthetic Approaches

The most common synthetic approaches that have successfully afforded high quality nanowires of a large variety of materials.

Template-assisted synthesis

The template-assisted synthesis of nanowires is a conceptually simple and intuitive way to fabricate nanostructures. These templates contain very small cylindrical pores or voids within the host material, and the empty spaces are filled with the chosen material, which adopts the pore morphology, to form nanowires. In template-assisted synthesis of nanostructures, the chemical stability and mechanical properties of the template, as well as the diameter, uniformity and density of the pores are important characteristics to consider.

Templates frequently used for nanowire synthesis include anodic alumina (Al_2O_3), nano-channel glass, ion track-etched polymers and mica films. Porous anodic alumina templates are produced by anodizing pure Al films in various acids.

The self-organisation of the pore structure in an anodic alumina template involves two coupled processes: pore formation with uniform diameters and pore ordering. The pores form with uniform diameters because of a delicate balance between electric-field-enhanced diffusion which determines the growth rate of the alumina, and dissolution of the alumina into the acidic electrolyte.

The pores are believed to self-order because of mechanical stress at the aluminum-alumina interface due to expansion during the anodisation. This stress produces a repulsive force between the pores, causing them to arrange in a hexagonal lattice. Depending on the anodisation conditions, the pore diameter can be systematically varied from < 10nm up to 200nm with a pore density in the range of 10^9–10^{11} pores/cm^2. It has been shown by many groups that the pore size distribution and the pore ordering of the anodic alumina templates can be significantly improved by a two-step anodisation technique, where the aluminum oxide layer is dissolved after the first anodisation in an acidic solution followed by a second anodisation under the same conditions.

Another type of porous template that is commonly used for nanowire synthesis is the template type fabricated by chemically etching particle tracks originating from ion bombardment, such as track-etched polycarbonate membranes, and also mica films. There are other porous materials that can be used as host templates for nanowire growth, as discussed by.

Nano-channel glass (NCG), for example, contains a regular hexagonal array of capillaries similar to the pore structure in anodic alumina with a packing density as high as 3×10^{10} pores/cm^2. Porous Vycor glass that contains an interconnected network of pores less than 10nm was also employed for the early study of nanostructures. Mesoporous molecular sieves, termed MCM-41, possess hexagonally-packed pores with very small channel diameters which can be varied between 2nm and 10 nm.

Conducting organic filaments have been fabricated in the nanochannels of MCM-41. Recently, the DNA molecule has also been used as a template for growing nanometer-sized wires. Diblock copolymers, which consist of two different polymer chains with different properties, have also been utilised as templates for nanowire growth. When two components are immiscible in each other, phase segregation occurs, and depending on their volume ratio, spheres, cylinders and lamellae may self-assemble. To form self-assembled arrays of nanopores, copolymers composed of polystyrene and polymethylmethacrylate [P(S-b-MMA)] were used. By application of an electric field while the copolymer was heated above the glass transition temperature of the two constituent polymers, the self-assembled cylinders of PMMA could be aligned with their main axis perpendicular to the film. Selective removal of the PMMA component afforded the preparation of 14-nm-diameter ordered pore arrays with a packing density of 1:9 $\times 10^{11}$ cm^{-3}.

Pressure injection technique

The pressure injection technique is often employed for fabricating highly crystalline nanowires from a low-melting point material or when using porous templates with robust mechanical strength. In the high-pressure injection method, the nanowires are formed by pressure injecting the desired material in liquid form into the evacuated pores of the template.

Due to the heating and the pressurisation processes, the templates used for the pressure injection method must be chemically stable and be able to maintain their structural integrity at high temperatures and at high pressures. Anodic aluminum oxide films and nano-channel glass are two typical materials used as templates in conjunction with the pressure injection filling technique.

Metal nanowires (Bi, In, Sn, and Al) and semiconductor nanowires (Se, Te, GaSb, and $Bi_2Te_{3)}$ have been fabricated in anodic aluminum oxide templates using this method. The pressure P required to overcome the surface tension for the liquid material to fill the pores with a diameter d_w is determined by the Washburn equation:

$$d_w = -4\gamma\cos\ \theta/P \qquad (1)$$

where γ is the surface tension of the liquid, and μ is the contact angle between the liquid and the template. To reduce the required pressure and to maximise the filling factor, some surfactants are used to decrease the surface tension and the contact angle.

For example, it is found that the introduction of Cu in the Bi melt can facilitate the filling of the anodic alumina pores with liquid Bi and increase the number of nanowires that are prepared. However, some of the surfactants might cause contamination problems and therefore should be avoided. Nanowires produced by the pressure injection technique usually possess high crystallinity and a preferred crystal orientation along the wire axis.

Electrochemical deposition technique

The electrochemical deposition technique has attracted increasing attention as a promising alternative for fabricating nanowires. Traditionally, electrochemistry has been used to grow thin films on conducting surfaces. Since electrochemical growth is usually controllable in the direction normal to the substrate surface, this method can be readily extended to fabricate 1D or 0D nanostructures, if the deposition is confined within the pores of an appropriate template.

In the electrochemical methods, a thin conducting metal film is first coated on one side of the porous membrane to serve as the cathode for electroplating. The length of the deposited nanowires can be controlled by varying the duration of the electroplating process. This method has been used to synthesise a wide variety of nanowires e.g., metals Bi; Co; Fe; Cu; Ni; Ag; Au; conducting polymers; superconductors; semiconductors; and even superlattice nanowires with A/B constituents have been synthesised electrochemically.

In the electrochemical deposition process, the chosen template has to be chemically stable in the electrolyte during the electrolysis process. Cracks and defects in the templates are detrimental to the nanowire growth, since the deposition processes primarily occur in the more accessible cracks, leaving most of the nanopores unfilled.

Particle track-etched mica films or polymer membranes are typical templates used in the simple dc electrolysis. To use anodic aluminum oxide films in the dc electrochemical deposition, the insulating barrier layer which separates the pores from the bottom aluminum substrate has to be removed, and a metal film is then evaporated onto the back of the template membrane. Compound nanowire arrays, such as Bi_2Te_3, have been fabricated in alumina templates with a high filling factor using the dc electrochemical deposition.

It is also possible to employ an ac electrodeposition method in anodic alumina templates without the removal of the barrier layer, by utilising the rectifying properties of the oxide barrier. In ac electrochemical deposition, although the applied voltage is sinusoidal and symmetric, the current is greater during the cathodic half-cycles, making deposition dominant over the etching, which occurs in the subsequent anodic half-cycles.

Since no rectification occurs at defect sites, the deposition and etching rates are equal, and no material is deposited. Hence, the difficulties associated with cracks are avoided. In this fashion, metals, such as Co and Fe, and semiconductors, such as CdS, have been deposited into the pores of anodic aluminum oxide templates without removing the barrier layer. In contrast to nanowires synthesised by the pressure injection method, nanowires fabricated by the electrochemical process are usually polycrystalline, with no preferred crystal orientations.

Polycrystalline CdS nanowires, fabricated by an ac electrodeposition method in anodic alumina templates, possibly have a preferred wire growth orientation along the c-axis. In addition, Xu et al. have prepared a number of single-crystal II-VI semiconductor nanowires, including CdS, CdSe and CdTe, by dc electrochemical deposition in anodic alumina templates with a non-aqueous electrolyte. Furthermore, single-crystal Pb nanowires can be formed by pulse electrodeposition under over-potential conditions, but no specific crystal orientation along the wire axis was observed.

The use of pulse currents is believed to be advantageous for the growth of crystalline wires because the metal ions in the solution can be regenerated between the electrical pulses and, therefore, uniform deposition conditions can be produced for each deposition pulse. Similarly, single crystal Ag nanowires were fabricated by pulsed electro-deposition.

One advantage of the electrochemical deposition technique is the possibility of fabricating multi-layered structures within nanowires. By varying the cathodic potentials in the electrolyte which contains two different kinds of ions, different metal layers can be controllably deposited. In this fashion, Co/Cu multi-layered nanowires have been synthesised.

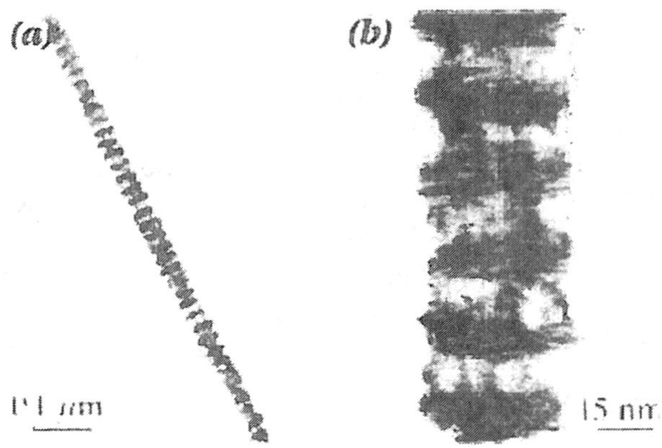

Figure 2. (a) TEM image of a single Co(10 nm)/Cu(10 nm) multilayered nanowire. (b) A selected region of the sample at high magnification.

Figure 2 shows TEM images of a single Co/Cu nanowire of about 40nm in diameter. The light bands represent Co-rich regions and the dark bands represent Cu-rich layers. This electrodeposition method provides a low-cost approach to prepare multi-layered 1D nanostructures.

Vapour deposition of nanowires

Vapour deposition of nanowires includes physical vapour deposition (PVD), chemical vapour deposition (CVD), and metallorganic chemical vapour deposition (MOCVD). Like electrochemical deposition, vapour deposition is usually capable of preparing smaller-diameter (~ 20 nm) nanowires than pressure injection methods, since it does not rely on the high pressure and the surface tension involved to insert the material into the pores. In the physical vapour deposition technique, the material to be filled is first heated to produce a vapour, which is then introduced through the pores of the template and cooled to solidify.

Using an especially designed experimental setup, nearly single-crystal Bi nanowires in anodic aluminum templates with pore diameters as small as 7nm have been synthesised, and these Bi nanowires were found to possess a preferred crystal growth orientation along the wire axis, similar to the Bi nanowires prepared by pressure injection. Compound materials that result from two reacting gases have also be prepared by the chemical vapour deposition (CVD) technique. Single-crystal GaN nanowires have been synthesised in anodic alumina templates through a gas reaction of Ga_2O vapour with a flowing ammonia atmosphere.

A different liquid/gas phase approach has been used to prepare polycrystalline GaAs and InAs nanowires in a nanochannel glass array. In this method, the nanochannels are filled with one liquid precursor (e.g., Me_3Ga or Et_3In) via a capillary effect and the nanowires are formed within the template by reactions between the liquid precursor and the other gas reactant (e.g., AsH_3).

Nanotube synthesis and templates

Recently, carbon nanotubes, an important class of 1D nanostructures, have been fabricated within the pores of anodic alumina templates using a chemical vapour deposition technique to form highly ordered two-dimensional carbon nanotube arrays. A small amount of metal catalyst (e.g., Co) is first electrochemically deposited on the bottom of the pores. The templates are then placed in a furnace and heated to ~ 700–800°C with a flowing gas consisting of a mixture of N_2 and acetylene (C_2H_2) or ethylene (C_2H_4). The hydrocarbon molecules are pyrolysed to form carbon nanotubes in the pores of the template with the help of the metal catalysts. Well-aligned nanotube arrays have stimulated much interest because of their great potential in various applications, such as cold-cathode flat panel displays.

Of particular interest is the use of zeolite templates with very narrow pores (< 1nm diameter) that permit the growth of carbon nanotubes with diameters of 0.42 nm, having only 10 carbon atoms around the circumference. The hollow cores of carbon nanotubes have also been used to synthesize a variety of nanowires of very small diameter. These very small diameter nanowires have been extensively studied by high resolution TEM, but have not yet been characterised to the same degree regarding their physical properties.

VLS Method

Some of the recent successfully synthesised semiconductor nanowires are based on the so-called vapour-liquid-solid (VLS) mechanism of anisotropic crystal growth. This mechanism was first proposed for the growth of single crystal silicon whiskers 100 nm to hundreds of microns in diameter. The proposed growth mechanism involves the absorption of source material from the gas phase into a liquid droplet of catalyst (a molten particle of gold on a silicon substrate in the original work. Upon supersaturation of the liquid alloy, a nucleation event generates a solid precipitate of the source material. This seed serves as a preferred site for further deposition of material at the interface of the liquid droplet, promoting the elongation of the seed into a nanowire or a whisker, and suppressing further nucleation events on the same catalyst.

Since the liquid droplet catalyses the incorporation of material from the gas source to the growing crystal, the deposit grows anisotropically as a whisker whose diameter is dictated by the diameter of the liquid alloy droplet. The nanowires thus obtained are of high purity, except for the end containing the solidified catalyst as an alloy particle.

Real-time observations of the alloying, nucleation, and elongation steps in the growth of germanium nanowires from gold nanoclusters by the VLS method were recorded by in-situ TEM. Reduction of the average wire diameter to the nanometer scale requires the generation of nanosized catalyst droplets. However, due to the balance between the liquid-vapour surface free energy and the free energy of condensation, the size of a liquid droplet, in equilibrium with its vapour, is usually limited to the micrometer range.

This obstacle was overcome in recent years by several new methodologies:

1) Advances in the synthesis of metal nanoclusters have made monodispersed nanoparticles commercially available. These can be dispersed on a solid substrate in high dilution so that when the temperature is raised above the melting point, the liquid clusters do not aggregate.

2) Alternatively, metal islands of nanoscale sizes can self-form when a strained thin layer is grown or heat treated on a non-epitaxial substrate.

3) Laser-assisted catalytic VLS growth is a method used to generate nanowires under non-equilibrium conditions. By laser ablation of a target containing both the catalyst and the source materials, a plasma is generated from which catalyst nanoclusters nucleate as the plasma cools down. Single crystal nanowires grow as long as the particle remains liquid.

4) Interestingly, by optimisation of the material properties of the catalyst-nanowire system, conditions can be achieved for which nanocrystals nucleate in a liquid catalyst pool supersaturated with the nanowire material, migrate to the surface due to a large surface tension, and continue growing as nanowires perpendicular to the liquid surface. In this case, supersaturated nanodroplets are sustained on the outer

end of the nanowire due to the low solubility of the nanowire material in the liquid.

A wide variety of elemental, binary and compound semiconductor nanowires has been synthesised via the VLS method, and relatively good control over the nanowire diameter and diameter distribution has been achieved. Researchers are currently focusing attention on the controlled variation of the materials properties along the nanowire axis. GaAs/GaP modulated nanowires have been synthesised by alternately ablating targets of the corresponding materials in the presence of gold nanoparticles. *p*-Si/n-Si nanowires were grown by chemical vapour deposition from alternating gaseous mixtures containing the appropriate dopant. $Si/Si_{1-x}\,Ge_x$ nanowires were grown by combining silicon from a gaseous source with germanium from a periodically ablated target.

Finally, using an ultra-high vacuum chamber and molecular beams, InAs/InP nanowires with atomically sharp interfaces were obtained. These compositionally-modulated nanowires are expected to exhibit exciting electronic, photonic, and thermoelectric properties. Interestingly silicon and germanium nanowires grown by the VLS method consist of a crystalline core coated by a relatively thick amorphous oxide layer (2-3 nm).

These layers are too thick to be the result of ambient oxidation, and it has been shown that these oxides play an important role in the nanowire growth process. Silicon oxides were found to serve as a special and highly selective catalyst, that significantly enhances the yield of Si nanowires, without the need for metal catalyst particles. A similar yield enhancement was also found in the synthesis of Ge nanowires from the laser ablation of Ge powder mixed with GeO_2.

The Si and Ge nanowires produced from these metal-free targets generally grow along the crystal direction, and have the benefit that no catalyst clusters are found on either ends of the nanowires. Based on these observations and other TEM studies, an oxide-enhanced nanowire growth mechanism different from the classical VLS mechanism was proposed, where no metal catalyst is required during the laser ablation-assisted synthesis. It is postulated that the nanowire growth is dependent on the presence of SiO (or GeO) vapour, which decomposes in the nanowire tip region into both Si (or Ge), which is incorporated into the crystalline phase, and SiO_2 (or GeO_2), which contributes to the outer coating. The initial nucleation events generate oxide-coated spherical nanocrystals.

The crystal faces have the fastest growth rate, and therefore the nanocrystals soon begin elongating along this direction to form one-dimensional structures. The Si_mO or Ge_mO ($m > 1$) layer on the nanowire tips may be in or at temperatures near their molten states, catalysing the incorporation of gas molecules in a directional fashion. Besides nanowires with smooth walls, a second morphology of chains of non-oriented nanocrystals linked by oxide necks is frequently observed.

In addition, it was found by STM studies that about 1% of the wires consist of a regular array of two alternating segments, 10nm and 5nm in length, respectively. The segments, whose junctions form an angle of 30°, are probably a result of alternating growth along different crystallographic orientations.

There are several other general procedures available for the synthesis of a variety of nanowires. The bottom-up approaches, which afford many kinds of nanowires in large numbers, and do not require highly sophisticated equipment, and exclude cases for which the nanowires are not self sustained. A solution-phase synthesis of nanowires with controllable diameters has been demonstrated, without the use of templates, catalysts, or surfactants. Instead, Gates et al. make use of the anisotropy of the crystal structure of trigonal selenium and tellurium, which can be viewed as rows of 1D helical atomic chains. Their approach is based on the mass transfer of atoms during an aging step from a high free-energy solid phase (e.g., amorphous selenium) to form a seed (e.g., trigonal selenium nanocrystal) which grows preferentially along one crystallographic axis. The lateral dimension of the seed, that dictates the diameter of the nanowire, can be controlled by the temperature of the nucleation step.

Furthermore, Se/Te alloy nanowires were synthesised by this method, and Ag_2Se compound nanowires were obtained by treating selenium nanowires with $AgNO_3$ More often, however, the use of surfactants is necessary to promote the anisotropic 1D growth of nanocrystals. Solution phase synthetic routes have been optimised to produce monodispersed quantum dots, i.e., zero-dimensional isotropic nanocrystals. Surfactants are necessary in this case to stabilise the interfaces of the nanoparticles and retard oxidation and aggregation processes. Heath and LeGoues synthesised germanium nanowires by reducing a mixture of $GeCl_4$ and phenyl-$GeCl_3$ at high temperature and high pressure. The phenyl ligand was essential for the formation of high aspect ratio nanowires.

In growing CdSe nanorods, a mixture of two surfactants was used, whose concentration ratio influenced the structure of the nanocrystal. It is believed that different surfactants have different affinities, and different absorption rates, for the different crystal faces of CdSe, thereby regulating the growth rate of these faces.

A coordinating alkyl-diamine solvent was used to grow polycrystalline PbSe nanowires at low temperatures. Here, the surfactant-induced directional growth is believed to occur, due to the formation of organometallic complexes in which the bidentate ligand assumes the equatorial positions, thus hindering the ions from approaching each other in this plane. Additionally, the alkyl-amine molecules coat the external surface of the wire, preventing lateral growth. The aspect ratio of the wires increased as the temperature was lowered in the range 10 < T < 117°C.

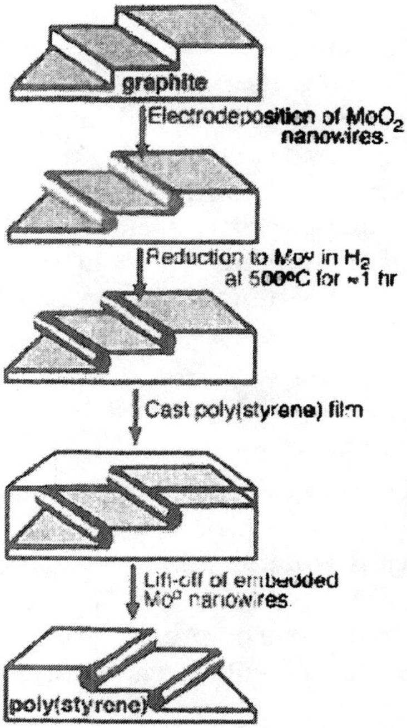

Figure 3. Schematic of the electrodeposition step edge decoration of HOPG (highly oriented pyrolytic graphite) for the synthesis of molybdenum nanowires

Ethylenediamine was used to grow CdS nanowires and tetrapods by a solvo-thermal recrystallisation process starting with CdS nanocrystals or amorphous particles. While the coordinating solvent was crucial for the nanowire growth, its role in the shape and phase control was not clarified. Stress-induced crystalline bismuth nanowires have been grown from sputtered films of layers of Bi and CrN. The nanowires presumably grow from defects and cleavage fractures in the film, and are up to several millimetre in lengths with diameters ranging from 30 to 200nm. While the exploration of this technique has only begun, stress-induced unidirectional growth should be applicable to a variety of composite films.

While these nanowires cannot be removed from the substrate, they can be reduced to metallic molybdenum nanowires, which can then be released as free-standing nanowires. The cross-section of artificially prepared superlattice structures has also been used for site-selective electrodeposition of parallel and closely spaced nanowires. Nanowires prepared on the above mentioned sub-strates would have semicircular, rectangular, or other unconventional cross sectional shapes.

Hierarchical arrangement and superstructures

Ordering nanowires into useful structures is another challenge that needs to be addressed in order to harvest the full potential of nanowires for applications. The nanowires having a non-trivial structure, and then proceed to describe methods to create assemblies of nanowires of a predetermined structure. The preparation of nanowires with a graded composition or with a superlattice structure along their main axis was demonstrated by controlling the gas-phase chemistry as a function of time during the growth of the nanowires by the VLS method.

Control of the composition along the axial dimension was also demonstrated by a template-assisted method, for example by the consecutive electrochemical deposition of different metals in the pores of an alumina template. Alternatively, the composition can be varied along the radial dimension of the nanowire, for example, by first growing a nanowire by the VLS method and then switching the synthesis conditions to grow a different material on the surface of the nanowire by CVD. This technique was demonstrated for the synthesis of Si/Ge and Ge/Si coaxial (or core-shell) nanowires, and it was shown that by a thermal annealing process, the outer shell can be formed epitaxially on the inner core.

A different approach was adopted by Wang et al. who generated a mixture of coaxial and biaxial SiC-SiOx nanowires by the catalyst-free high-temperature reaction of amorphous silica and a carbon/graphite mixture. A different category of non-trivial nanowires is that of nanowires having a non-linear structure, resulting from multiple one-dimensional growth steps. In this process, a tetrahedral quantum-dot core is first grown, and then the conditions are modified to induce a one-dimensional growth of a nanowire from each one of the facets of the tetrahedron.

A similar process produced high-symmetry In_2O_3/ZnO hierarchical nanostructures. From a mixture of heat-treated In_2O_3, ZnO, and graphite powders, faceted In_2O_3 nanowires were first obtained, on which oriented shorter ZnO nanowires were crystallised. Brush-like structures were obtained as a mixture of 11 structures of different symmetries.

Control of the position of a nanowire in the growth process is important for preparing devices or test structures containing nanowires, especially when involving a large array of nanowires. The first method involves the orientation of the nanowires by the liquid flow direction and by the interaction of the nanowires with the side walls of the channel. The second method involves the alignment of nanowires at a liquid-gas or liquid-liquid interface by the application of compressive forces on the interface.

The third technique is based on dielectrophoretic forces that pull polarizable nanowires toward regions of high field strength. The nanowires align between two isolated electrodes which are capacitatively coupled to a pair of buried electrodes biased with an AC voltage. Once a nanowire shorts the electrodes, the electric field is eliminated, preventing more nanowires from depositing. The above techniques have been successfully used to prepare electronic circuitry and optical devices out of nanowires.

Alternatively, alignment and positioning of the nanowires can be specified and controlled during their growth by proper design of the synthesis method. For example, ZnO nanowires prepared by the VLS method were grown into an array in which both their position on the substrate and their growth direction and orientation were controlled. The nanowire growth region was defined by patterning the gold film, which serves as a catalyst for the ZnO nanowire growth, employing soft-lithography, e-beam lithography, or photolithography.

The orientation of the nanowires was achieved by selecting a substrate with a lattice structure matching that of the nanowire material to facilitate the epitaxial growth. These conditions result in an array of nanowire posts at predetermined positions, all vertically aligned with the same crystal growth orientation.

A similar structure could be obtained by the template-mediated electrochemical synthesis of nanowires, particularly if anodic alumina with its parallel and ordered channels is used. The control over the location of the nucleation of nanowires in the electrochemical deposition is determined by the pore positions, which can be precisely controlled by imprint lithography, and by growing the template on a patterned conductive substrate that serves as a back-electrode, different materials can be deposited in the pores at different regions of the template.

Physical Properties of Nanowires

The discovery and investigation of nanostructures were spurred on by advances in various characterisation and microscopy techniques that enable materials characterisation to take place at smaller and smaller length scales, reaching length scales down to individual atoms.

For applications, characterisation of the nanowire structural properties is especially important so that a reproducible relationship between their desired functionality and their geometrical and structural characteristics can be established. Due to the enhanced surface to volume ratio in nanowires, their properties may depend sensitively on their surface condition and geometrical configuration.

Even nanowires made of the same material may possess dissimilar properties due to differences in their crystal phase, crystalline size, surface conditions, and aspect ratios, which depend on the synthesis methods and conditions used in their preparation. Structural and geometric factors play an important role in determining the various attributes of nanowires, such as their electrical, optical and magnetic properties.

Therefore, various novel tools have been developed and employed to obtain this important structural information at the nanoscale. At the micron scale, optical techniques are extensively used for imaging structural features. Since the sizes of nanowires are usually comparable to or, in most cases, much smaller than the wavelength of visible light, traditional optical microscopy techniques are usually limited in characterising the morphology and surface features of nanowires.

Therefore, electron microscopy techniques play a more dominant role at the nanoscale. Since electrons interact more strongly than photons, electron microscopy is particularly sensitive relative to x-rays for the analysis of tiny samples.

Scanning tunnelling probes

Several scanning probe techniques, such as scanning

tunnelling microscopy (STM), electric field gradient microscopy (EFM), magnetic field microscopy (MFM), and scanning thermal microscopy (SThM), combined with atomic force microscopy (AFM), have been employed to study the structural, electronic, magnetic, and thermal properties of nanowires. Magnetic field microscopy (MFM) has been employed to study magnetic polarisation of magnetic nanowires embedded in an insulating template, such as an anodic alumina template.

X-ray analysis

Other characterisation techniques that are commonly used to study the crystal structure and chemical composition of nanowires include x-ray diffraction and x-ray energy dispersion analysis (EDAX). The peak positions in the x-ray diffraction pattern can be used to determined the chemical composition and the crystaı phase structure of the nanowires.

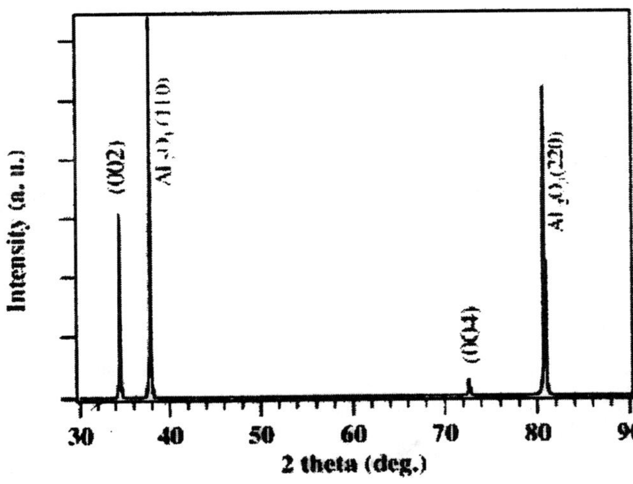

Figure 4. X-ray diffraction pattern of aligned ZnO nanowires grown on a sapphire substrate

As another example of an XRD pattern for an array of aligned nanowires, Fig. 4 shows the x-ray diffraction pattern of the ZnO nanowires. Only diffraction peaks are observed for these aligned ZnO nanowires, indicating that their preferred growth direction is (001) along the wire axis. A similar preferred growth orientation was also observed for Bi nanowires produced by high pressure injection, while the vapour phase and low pressure injection filling techniques give preferred alignment along lower symmetry axes. EDAX has been used to determine the chemical composition, stoichiometry of compound nanowires or the impurity content in the nanowires. However, the results from EDAX analysis should be interpreted carefully to avoid systematic errors.

Transport Properties of Nanowires

The study of electrical transport properties of nanowires is important for nanowire characterisation, electronic device applications, and the investigation of unusual transport phenomena arising from one-dimensional quantum effects. Important factors that determine the transport properties of nanowires include the wire diameter, which is important for both classical and quantum size effects, material composition, surface conditions, crystal quality, and the crystallographic orientation along the wire axis for materials with anisotropic materials parameters, such as the effective mass tensor, the Fermi surface, or the carrier mobility. Electronic transport phenomena in low-dimensional systems can be roughly divided into two categories: ballistic transport and diffusive transport.

Ballistic transport phenomena occur when the electrons can travel across the nanowire without any scattering. In this case, the conduction is mainly determined by the contacts between the nanowire and the external circuit, and the conductance is quantised into an integral number of universal conductance units $G_0 = 2_e^2 = h$. Ballistic transport phenomena are usually observed in very short quantum wires, such as those produced by using mechanically controlled break junctions (MCBJ) where the electron mean free path is much longer than the wire length and the conduction is a pure quantum phenomenon. Another requirement to observe ballistic transport is that the thermal energy obey the relation kBT << $\varepsilon_j - \varepsilon_{j-1}$, where $\varepsilon_j - \varepsilon_{j-1}$ is the energy separation between sub-band levels j and $j-1$.

On the other hand, for nanowires with lengths much larger than the carrier mean free path, the electrons (or holes) undergo numerous scattering events when they travel along the wire. In this case, the transport is in the diffusive regime, and the conduction is dominated by carrier scattering within the wires, due to phonons (lattice vibrations), boundary scattering, lattice and other structural defects, and impurity atoms.

Quantised conductance in metallic nanowires

The ballistic transport of 1D systems has been extensively studied since the discovery of quantised conductance in 1D systems in 1988. The phenomena of conductance quantisation occurs when the diameter of the nanowire is comparable to the electron Fermi wavelength, which is on the order of 0.5nm for most metals. Most conductance experiments up to the present were performed by bringing together and separating two metal electrodes. As the two metal electrodes are slowly separated, a nano-contact is formed before it breaks completely, and conductance in integral multiple values of G_0 is observed through these nano-contacts.

The conductance quantisation behaviour is found to be independent of the contact material, and has been observed in various metals, such as Au, Ag, Na, Cu, and Hg. For semimetals such as Bi, conductance quantisation has also been observed for an electrode separation of as long as 100nm at 4K because of the long Fermi wavelength

(~ 26 nm), indicating that the conductance quantisation may be due to the existence of well-defined quantum states localised at a constriction instead of resulting from the atom rearrangement as the electrodes separate. Since conductance quantisation is only observed in breaking contacts, or for very narrow or for very short nanowires, carrier scattering in most nanowires of practical interest (possessing lengths of several microns), occurs in the diffusive transport regime.

I-V Characterisation

The electronic transport behaviour of nanowires may be categorised based on the relative magnitude of three length scales: carrier mean free path *l*W, the de Broglie wavelength of electrons λ_e, and the wire diameter d_W. For wire diameters much larger than the carrier mean free path ($d_W >> l_W$), the nanowires exhibit transport properties similar to bulk materials, which are independent of the wire diameter, since the scattering due to the wire boundary is negligible compared to other scattering mechanisms.

For wire diameters comparable or smaller than the carrier mean free path ($d_W \sim l_W$ or $d_W < l_W$), but still much larger than the de Broglie wavelength of the electrons (d_W >>, λ_e), the transport in nanowires is in the classical finite size regime, where the band structure of the nanowire is still similar to that of bulk, while the scattering events at the wire boundary alter their transport behaviour. For wire diameters comparable to the electronic wavelength dW » ,e, the electronic density of states is altered dramatically and quantum sub-bands are formed due to the quantum confinement effect at the wire boundary. In this regime, the transport properties are further influenced by the change in the band structure.

Therefore, transport properties for nanowires in the classical finite size and quantum size regimes, are highly diameter-dependent.

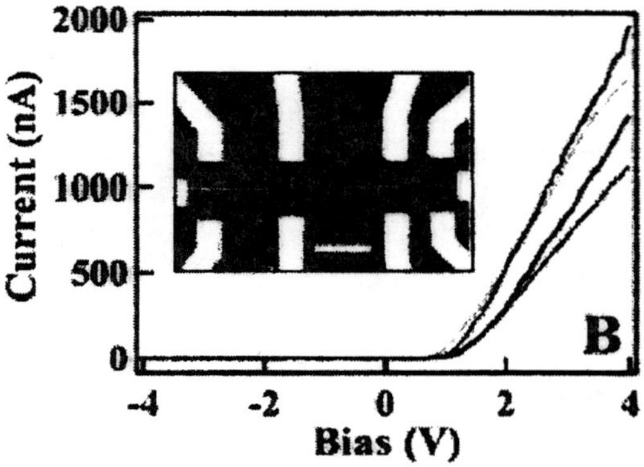

Figure 5. I-V behaviour for a 4(p) by 1(n) crossed p-Si/n-GaN junction array shown schematically in the inset

Researchers have investigated the transport properties of various semiconducting nano-wires and have demonstrated their potential for diverse electronic devices, such as for *p-n* diodes, field effect transistors, and memory cells and switches. Interestingly, the physical principles for describing bulk semiconductor devices also hold for devices based on these semiconducting nanowires with wire diameters of tens of nanometers.

Because of the enhanced surface to volume ratio of nanowires, their transport behaviour may be modified by changing their surface conditions. For example, researchers have found that by coating *n*-InP nanowires with a layer of redox molecules, such as cobalt phthalocyanine, the conductance of the InP nanowires may change by orders of magnitude by altering the charge state of the redox molecules to provide bistable nanoscale switches. The resistance (or conductance) of some nanowires (e.g., Pd nanowires) is also very sensitive to the presence of certain gases (e.g., H_2), and this property may be utilised for sensor applications to provide improved sensitivity compared to conventional sensors based on bulk material. Although it remains unclear how the size effect may influence the transport properties and device performance of semiconducting nanowires, many of the larger diameter semiconducting nanowires are expected to be described by classical physics, since their quantisation energies $\hbar^2=(2m_e d^2_W)$ are usually smaller than the thermal energy kBT.

By comparing the quantisation energy with the thermal energy, the critical wire diameter below which quantum confinement effects become significant is estimated to be 1nm for Si nanowires at room temperature, which is much smaller than the size of many of the semiconducting nanowires that have been investigated so far. By using material systems with much smaller effective carrier masses me (such as bismuth), the critical diameter for which such quantum effects can be observed is increased, thereby facilitating the study of quantum confinement effects.

It is for this reason that the bismuth nanowire system has been studied so extensively. Furthermore, since the crystal structure and lattice constants of bismuth nanowires are the same as for 3D crystalline bismuth, it is possible to carry out detailed model calculations to guide and to interpret transport and optical experiments on bismuth nanowires. For these reasons bismuth can be considered as a model system for studying 1D effects in nanowires.

Temperature-dependent resistance measurements

Although nanowires with electronic properties similar to their bulk counterparts are promising for constructing nano-devices based on well-established knowledge of their bulk counter-parts, it is expected that quantum size effects in nanowires will likely be utilised to generate new phenomena absent in bulk materials, and thus, provide enhanced performance and novel functionality for certain applications. The very small electron effective mass

rise to a different transport behaviour. Localisation effects are also expected to be more pronounced as the dimensionality and sample size are reduced. Localisation effects on the transport properties of nanowire systems have been studied on Bi nanowires and, more recently, on Zn nanowires.

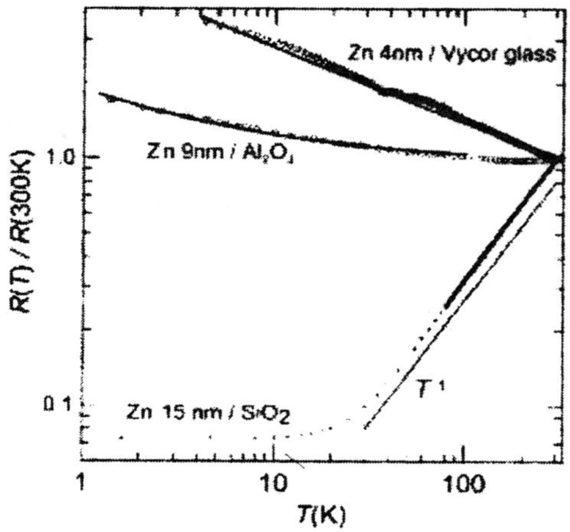

Figure 7. Temperature dependence of the resistance of Zn nanowires synthesised by vapour deposition in various porous material templates

Figure 7 shows the measured $R(T) = R(300\ K)$ of Zn nanowires fabricated by vapour deposition in porous silica or alumina. While 15nm Zn nanowires exhibit an $R(T)$ behaviour with a T^1 dependence as expected for a metallic wire, the $R(T)$ of 9nm and 4nm Zn nanowires exhibits a temperature dependence of $T^{-1/2}$ at low temperature, consistent with 1D localisation theory. Thus, due to this localisation effect, the use of nanowires with very small diameters for transport applications may be limited.

Bibliography

Bawa, R. "Nanotechnology Patenting in the U.S.," *Nanotechnology Law and Business,* 1 (1) 2004.

Cassell, J. Li, Q.Ye, A. H. T. Ng, R. Stevens, J. Han, and M. Meyyappan, "Bottom-up approach for carbon nanotube interconnects," *Appl. Phys. Lett.*, vol. 82, pp. 2491–2493, Apr. 2003.

Delzeit, L., C. V. Nguyen, B. Chen, R. Stevens, A. Cassell, J. Han, and M. Meyyappan, "Multiwalled carbon nanotubes by chemical vapor deposition using multilayered metal catalysts," *J. Phys. Chem. B*, vol. 106, 2002.

Feynman, 1. R.P. "There's Plenty of Room at the Bottom," *Engineering and Science.* Caltech, 1960.

Hornbogen, E. "Precipitation Hardening—The Oldest Nanotechnology," *Lightweight Alloys for Aerospace Application,* ed. K. Jata et al. Warrendale, PA: TMS, 2001.

Huang, Z. P., J. W. Xu, Z. F. Ren, J. H. Wang, M. P. Siegal, and P. N. Provencio, "Growth of highly oriented carbon nanotubes by plasma-enhanced hot filament chemical vapor deposition," *Appl. Phys. Lett.*, vol. Dec. 1998.

Iijima, S. "Helical microtubules of graphitic carbon," *Nature*, vol. 354, 1991.

Jones, R. "The Future of Nanotechnology" August 2004.

Kittelson, D. B., "Engines and Nanoparticles: A Review". *Journal of Aerosol Science* 1998.

Murr L.E. et al., "Carbon Nanotubes and Other Fullerene-Related Nanocrystals in the Environment: A TEM Study," *JOM*, 56 (6) 2004.

Peters A. Wichmann H. E.; Tuch T.; Heinrich J. and Heyder J. "Respiratory Effects are Associated with the Number of Ultrafine Particles", *American Journal of Respiratory and Critical Care Medicine*, Vol.155, Issue 4, 1376-1383. 1997.

Reynolds J.G. and B.R Hart, "Nanomaterials and Their Application to Defense and Homeland Security," *JOM*, 56 (1) 2004.

Rittner, M.N. "Nanomaterials in Nanoelectronics: Who's Who and What's Next," *JOM*, 56 (6) 2004.

Roncone, K. "Nanotechnology: What Next- Generation Warriors Will Wear," *JOM*, 56 (1) 2004.

Sioutas, Li, N., C., Froines, J.R., Cho, A., Misra, C and Nel, A. "Ultrafine Particulate Pollutants Induce Oxidative Stress and Mitochondrial Damage" *Environmental Health Perspectives*, 2003.

Stevens, J. Li, R., L. Delzeit, H. T. Ng, A. Cassell, J. Han, and M. Meyyappan, "Electronic properties of multiwalled carbon nanotubes in an embedded vertical array," *Appl. Phys. Lett.*, vol. 81, pp. 910–912, July 2002.

Stix, G. "Little Big Science," *Scientifi c American.com* September 16, 2001

Suryanarayana, C. "The Structure and Properties of Nanocrystalline Materials: Issues and Concerns," *JOM*, 54 (9) 2002.

Taniguchi, N. "On the Basic Concept of 'NanoTechnology," *Proc. Intl. Conf. Prod. Eng. Tokyo, Part II* Tokyo: Japan Society of Precision Engineering, 1974.

Woo, K.S., Chen, D.R., Pui, D.Y.H., and McMurry, P.H. "Measurement of Atlanta Aerosol Size Distributions: Observation of Ultrafine Particles Events", *Aerosol Science and Technology* 34. 75-87. 2001.

Index